Martyrdom
and the Politics of Religion

Martyrdom
and the Politics of Religion

Progressive Catholicism in El Salvador's Civil War

Anna L. Peterson

State University of New York Press

Cover photograph by Adam Kufeld, from *El Salvador*, published by W. W. Norton. Used with permission.

Published by
State University of New York Press, Albany

For information, address State University of New York Press,
State University Plaza, Albany, NY 12246

Production by Cynthia Tenace Lassonde
Marketing by Theresa Abad Swierzowski

Library of Congress Cataloging-in-Publication Data

Peterson, Anna Lisa, 1963–
    Martyrdom and the politics of religion / Anna L. Peterson.
        p.   cm.
    Includes bibliographical references and index.
    ISBN 0-7914-3181-9 (alk. paper). — ISBN 0-7914-3182-7 (pbk. :
alk. paper)
        1. Catholic Church—El Salvador—History—20th century.
    2. Martyrdom.   3. El Salvador—Politics and government—1979–1992.
    4. El Salvador—Church history—20th century.   I. Title.
    BX1446.2.P47   1997
    282'.7284'09047—dc20   96-367
                                                                        CIP

10 9 8 7 6 5 4 3 2 1

For Francisca and her brothers
and in memory of Niña Paquita

Copyright Permissions

No me siento solo en la noche,
en la oscuridad de la tierra.
Soy pueblo, pueblo innumerable.
Tengo en mi voz la fuerza pura
para atravesar el silencio
y germinar en las tinieblas.
Muerte, martirio, sombra, hielo,
cubren de pronto la semilla.
Y parece enterrado el pueblo.
Pero el maíz vuelve a la tierra.
Atravesaron el silencio
sus impecables manos rojas.
Desde la muerte renacemos.

Pablo Neruda
Canto General

Contents

Acknowledgements

Anyone who undertakes a project this size accrues many debts, and it is a pleasure to acknowledge mine. I am obliged first and most of all to the Salvadorans who shared their experiences and commitments with me and to the pastoral workers who helped me visit communities throughout El Salvador. Because of continuing political uncertainty in El Salvador, most of them asked to remain anonymous. Without their courage and generosity, this project would have been unthinkable, and I extend to them my very deep gratitude and affection.

Some names can and should be mentioned. Jon Cortina, Steve Privett, Jon Sobrino, and the people of Jesuit Refugee Services in San Salvador offered support in many ways. The Pastoral Center of the Universidad Centroamericana was a congenial host in spite of extremely difficult circumstances. The Archdiocese of San Salvador kindly made archival materials available to me and offered many other types of assistance. I am grateful also to the Salvadorans who spoke with me in Nicaragua, Mexico, and the United States and to the people who helped me in those countries. In Nicaragua, I thank especially Juan Hernández Pico, the Instituto Histórico Centroamericano, and the Coordinación de Comunidades; in Mexico, *mil gracias* to the Centro de Reflexión Teológica, CEBES, the Hermanas Filipenses, and David Ungerleider. Thanks are due as well to Nicaraguan friends, especially the family of Julio Sequeira, who have served as examples of commitment and courage in the face of terrible odds.

I owe a great deal to various institutions in the United States. The University of Chicago and the Divinity School supported me materially and intellectually throughout graduate school. I am grateful as well for a Tinker Foundation grant administered by the University of Chicago Latin American Studies Center for preliminary research in 1988 and for a Regular Training Grant from the Organization of American States for fieldwork in 1990. St. Norbert College helped me conduct follow-up research with a faculty development grant in the summer of 1992, and the Division of Sponsored Research of the University of Florida offered similar support for archival work in the summer of 1994. I am grateful more generally to my colleagues in the Department of Religion and the Center for Latin American Studies at the University of Florida, who have provided a supportive setting for writing and revising.

Many individuals have helped at various points in this process. Early on, John Wiser and Mark C. Taylor, two extraordinary teachers, set standards for intellectual rigor that I am still trying to meet. Particularly in the earlier phases of research and writing, Robin Lovin, Anne Carr, and John Coatsworth offered encouragement and constructive criticism for which I am truly thankful. Jean Comaroff's insights about research methods and the relations between religion and politics have been invaluable. John Coleman and Hal Sanks have been wonderful teachers, colleagues, and friends. I am grateful to Lana Dalberg for sharing her extensive knowledge of El Salvador and much more. Thanks also to Peter Burns, Aldo Lauria, and Michael Shifter, who read early drafts, and to Michael Burdick, Eric Selbin, David Stoll, and Philip Williams, who in various ways helped me sharpen later revisions. Very special thanks are due to Kay Read and Kristen Bole, who carefully read the whole thing, and to Manuel Vásquez, whose patient and critical readings of various drafts helped immeasurably. I also appreciate the thoughtful and constructive suggestions of two anonymous reviewers for the State University of New York Press and the assistance and encouragement of Christine Worden of SUNY Press.

Finally, for their support and friendship I give thanks to Jane Appling, Kristen Bole, Don Braxton, Steve Butler, Felícita Carranza and her family, Gustavo del Chucho Bravo, Jane Fischberg, Judith Peterson, Kay Read, Dan Robinson, Sam Schuchat, Kevin Snape, Manuel Vásquez, Francisca Velásquez and her family, and all the other unnamed but much-appreciated friends and relatives who helped make the whole process bearable.

Abbreviations

ARENA. Alianza Republicana Nacionalista; Nationalist Republican Alliance.

BPR. Bloque Popular Revolucionario; Popular Revolutionary Bloc.

CEB. Comunidad eclesial de base; base (grassroots) ecclesial (or Christian) community.

CEBES. Base Ecclesial Communities of El Salvador; Comunidades Eclesiales de Base de El Salvador.

CELAM. Conferencia Episcopal Latinoamericana; Latin American Episcopal Conference.

CONIP. The National Committee of the Popular Church; Comité Nacional de la Iglesia Popular.

CRIPDES. Comité Cristiano Pro-Desplazados de El Salvador; Christian Committe for the Displaced of El Salvador.

CRM. Coordinadora Revolucionaria of the Masses; Revolutionary Coordinator of the Masses (a precursor of the FDR).

FAPU. Frente de Acción Popular Unificada; Unified Popular Action Front.

FDR. Frente Democrático Revolucionario; Democratic Revolutionary Front.

FECCAS. Federación de Campesinos Cristianos; Federation of Christian Peasants.

FMLN. Frente Farabundo Martí para la Liberación Nacional; Farabundo Martí Front for National Liberation. Until 1994, the FMLN included the following five groups:

> **ERP.** Ejército Revolucionario del Pueblo; Revolutionary Army of the People. (Known since 1993 as the "Expresión Renovadora del Pueblo," Expression of the People's Renewal.")
>
> **FAL.** Fuerzas Armadas de la Liberación; Armed Forces of Liberation.
>
> **RN.** Resistencia Nacional; National Resistance.
>
> **FPL.** Fuerzas Populares de Liberación; Popular Liberation Forces.
>
> **PRTC.** Partido Revolucionario de Trabajadores Centroamericanos; Central American Revolutionary Workers Party.

FTC. Federación de Trabajadores del Campo; Federation of Farmworkers (the union of the UTC and FECCAS).

FUNPROCOOP. Fundación Promotora de Cooperativas; Foundation for the Promotion of Cooperatives.

ORDEN ("Order"). Organización Democrática Nacional; National Democratic Organization.

PCN. Partido de Conciliación Nacional; Party of National Conciliation.

PDC. Partido Demócrata Cristiano; Christian Democratic Party.

UCA. Universidad Centroamericana "José Simeón Cañas"; Central American University "José Siméon Cañas."

UES. Universidad de El Salvador; University of El Salvador (also called "La Nacional," the National).

UGB. Unión Guerrera Blanca; White Warriors' Union (also called the *Mano Blanca*, or White Hand).

UNO. Unión Nacional de la Oposición; National Opposition Union.

UTC. Unión de Trabajadores del Campo; Union of Farmworkers.

Glossary of Spanish and Salvadoran Terms

Barrio. Urban neighborhood, usually poor or working-class.

Campesino. Peasant or farmworker.

Cantón. A hamlet or very small village.

Cofradía. Confraternity, brotherhood, sodality; a lay-run, usually traditional Catholic group that organizes religious celebrations in a village or neighborhood.

Colonia. Urban residential area or neighborhood.

Comunidad eclesial de base. Grassroots (or base) Christian community; a small group of neighbors who meet regularly to read the Bible and discuss their own experiences in the light of religious values.

Conciencia (adj. *consciente*). Literally conscience or consciousness; in Latin America, a critical awareness of sociopolitical realities and a commitment to change injustices in these realities.

Conscientización. Popularized by Brazilian educator Paulo Freire. An educational process in which learners develop conciencia.

Cursillo. A short course, usually lasting from a weekend to a month, in which laypeople learn about religious and social themes.

Delegado de la palabra. Literally, "delegate of the word"; a Catholic lay preacher, qualified to lead religious services ("Celebrations of the Word") but not to perform the sacramental functions of the priesthood.

Iglesia popular. Literally, popular church, used in some parts of Latin America, including El Salvador as an umbrella term for progressive Catholic groups, ideas, practices, and movements.

Misa. Mass (Catholic).

Monseñor. Monsignor; popularly used as a term of respect and affection for Catholic leaders, especially bishops. In El Salvador, used especially to refer to Archbishop Romero.

Pueblo (adj. *popular*). The people, especially the poor.

Reflexión. Reflection, used especially in grassroots Christian communities to refer to collective reflection and discussion of the Bible and religious and political issues.

Vía Crucis. The ways or stations of the cross, walked every Friday evening during Lent.

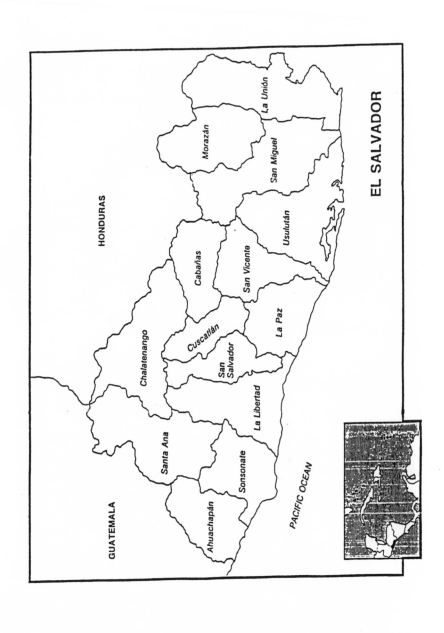

Methodology and Sources

The Subject/Object of Study

This study concerns not a particular geographic community (like a traditional ethnography), but a particular sector, which I call "progressive Catholics" or "the popular church." Strictly speaking, the popular church (*iglesia popular*)[1] is a distinctively Latin American variant of the progressive currents in Catholicism more generally. Chapter 3 outlines the history and characteristics of this group.

The popular church in El Salvador includes elite or official institutional actors as well as grassroots or lay actors, and the various levels exert continual, mutual influence on each other. This book focuses on the worldviews of the popular sector within progressive Catholicism, i.e., the laypeople who constitute its "base." These worldviews developed in interaction with representatives of both the institutional church and other social actors, including secular political organizations and other religious groups. It is important to bear this mutual shaping in mind, and not to reify the *iglesia popular* as an isolated or "pure" example of the religious sentiment or class consciousness of the Salvadoran poor. At the same time, however, laypeople's religious ideas do not simply come from above. It is, in fact, a central claim of this book that ordinary people can and do create complex systems of belief, not separated from social conditions or from other (often more powerful) actors, but with substantial autonomy, creativity, and self-awareness nonetheless.

The "ordinary people" on whom this book focuses include poor and working-class Salvadorans, from urban and rural areas, who have been influenced by the ideas and practices of progressive Catholicism. While many people's contact with this kind of religiosity comes through participation in grassroots Christian communities (*comunidades eclesiales de base* or CEBs) or courses (*cursillos*) offered at pastoral centers, progressive

Catholic thought and practice have also influenced a wide range of people involved in secular political organizations and, even more generally, in neighborhoods and villages with high levels of participation in progressive religious and/or political groups. Again, it is important to recall that these popular groups did not emerge in a vacuum; they worked with, influenced, and were influenced by more elite levels of the church and also other institutions. Priests and nuns played a particularly important role in shaping popular worldviews. At the same time, as most pastoral agents themselves readily admit, laypeople affected pastoral workers' religious and political views, sometimes quite radically.

I focus on the *iglesia popular* for a variety of reasons. While its members are not representative of all Salvadorans, neither are they totally atypical. Although the progressive church represents a numerical minority of Salvadoran Catholics, it has had a substantial impact on religion and politics in El Salvador, particularly among the working classes and poor.[2] This impact stems from progressive Catholicism's ability to make popular religious conceptions, symbols, values, and practices relevant to contemporary events, insofar as it criticizes the established order, envisions an alternative order, and motivates action in terms that make sense and appeal to a significant sector of Salvadoran society.

I have concentrated on the popular church not only for its social impact but most importantly because I am interested in the ways that religious people make sense of and respond to political events in "boundary" or extreme situations. I want to explore the centrality of religion to popular consciousness and political action, the distinctive ways that religion provides ordinary people with resources for creative interpretations of and action in history. Progressive Catholicism in El Salvador provides an excellent focus for this type of study of religion and politics at the grassroots.

Research Sites

I do not claim to have documented all or typical Salvadorans; this is a qualitative, not quantitative, study. While using an ethnographic approach, I did strive for representativity within my target sector. Thus, in fieldwork I sought a good sampling of progressive Catholics, primarily via a wide range of interviews. Perhaps the best way to view these interviews and other sources is as a series of concentric circles.[3] The core consists of extended interviews with seventy-two Salvadoran laypeople, of which I conducted fifty-five in El Salvador in 1988 and 1990 and the remainder in Nicaragua, California, and Mexico between 1986 and 1990. I filled in gaps via follow-up interviews with CEB members, pastoral workers, and members of popular organizations on several return visits to El Salvador between 1990 and 1994.

In El Salvador, I concentrated on urban and rural areas with strong religiously grounded activism. My procedure for selecting research sites was a mixture of science and luck. On an initial visit, I asked a number of priests and nuns for names of likely communities. Based on their suggestions, on discussions with pastoral workers in these areas, and on secondary sources, I chose several urban and rural communities as "target" sites. The repression and chaos that followed the guerrilla offensive of November 1989, however, made it difficult to enter and to speak with people in certain neighborhoods in San Salvador and almost impossible to travel to rural zones of conflict. Thus, when I returned to El Salvador in early 1990, I modified my plan and decided to strive for a combination of in-depth knowledge of one community and familiarity with a variety of others. My method for achieving this was to conduct nearly half of the in-country interviews in a single parish, which I have called "San Pablo," and the rest in other neighborhoods of the city as well as in rural areas.

San Pablo, a working-class community on the northern edge of San Salvador, was the site of very active pastoral work in the 1970s. It suffered as much repression against religious activists as any place in the city, and by the early 1980s, after a priest and hundreds of laypeople had been murdered, the grassroots Christian community shrank to a tiny core. Since the mid-1980s, committed laypeople, along with foreign and Salvadoran pastoral agents, have worked to rebuild the local church; today laypeople in the parish participate in a wide range of pastoral and social projects, including literacy campaigns and health clinics as well as Bible studies and catechism classes.

I also interviewed people in other neighborhoods in the capital city and in towns and villages in the departments (provinces) of San Salvador, Chalatenango, Morazán, Cabañas, San Vicente, La Libertad, and La Paz. Spending time in these areas helped expose me to a wide variety of pastoral styles and experiences, and interviews in different places helped confirm and expand ideas suggested in conversations in the main research site. Despite differences between rural and urban residents in both religious attitudes and political experiences, they generally expressed remarkably consistent interpretations of martyrdom. This consensus confirmed my decision to study progressive popular Catholicism as a distinctive and coherent sector within Catholicism nationally. This coherence is aided considerably by El Salvador's small size, which facilitates communication among pastoral agents in different parts of the country, permits laypeople from different areas to exchange experiences in retreats and meetings, and strengthens the ability of pastoral groups to provide materials, training, and advice to projects throughout the national territory. El Salvador is also relatively homogeneous in terms of culture and ethnicity, at least in comparison with other countries in Latin America.

My research was complicated by the difficulty, especially in early 1990, of travelling to the countryside. The main obstacle was the Salvadoran government's requirement that foreigners travelling to "conflicted" areas obtain a *salvo conducto* (safe-conduct pass) from the military high command. This task, difficult throughout the 1980s, proved nearly impossible in the months following the November 1989 offensive. The mass expulsions of foreign pastoral agents, especially lay workers, in late 1989 also reduced the possibilities for visiting rural parishes. Thus, I was not able to conduct as many interviews in rural areas as I would have liked. I tried to compensate for this deficiency, at least in part, by interviewing rural Salvadoran refugees in Mexico, Nicaragua, and the United States. Conversations with refugees are important not only because of the difficulty of working inside El Salvador during the war, but also because such a large percentage (between a quarter and a third) of Salvadorans were displaced by the war. Because many refugees have experienced intense repression in their places of origin, in addition to the trials of leaving their homes, they often have particularly vivid and insightful interpretations of political violence.[4]

Another "circle" of resources consists of conversations with Salvadoran and foreign pastoral agents, who offered insights into popular interpretations of martyrdom and resurrection as well as information about pastoral work and church history in El Salvador. Here I relied on interviews conducted in El Salvador, Mexico, Nicaragua, and the United States with Salvadoran and foreign sisters and priests who work or have worked in El Salvador. I also interviewed a number of participants in secular and religiously based social movements.

In addition to interviews, I attended numerous base community meetings, Bible studies, masses, *vía crucis* (stations of the cross) processions, and other rituals in parishes in San Salvador and a variety of rural areas. My observations of these events form yet another "ring" of resources upon which this study draws. The interviews also served as a check on the relevance of themes that emerged in written sources.

Other Resources

While I relied primarily on field research for both details and generalizations, I also drew from a variety of other sources. In addition to interviews with laypeople and pastoral agents, I spoke with a number of theologians and social scientists in El Salvador, Nicaragua, Mexico, and the United States who helped to clarify themes and point me to other resources. Jon Sobrino, Carlos Bravo, and the late Ignacio Martín-Baró were especially helpful.

I also used a variety of written materials. Probably the most important of these are the *misas populares* (popular masses) and other songs written to accompany the mass. The *misas* and other songs are very popular; they both reflect and inculcate widely accepted theological and political assumptions. I have relied on the songs I heard most often in popular Catholic rituals in El Salvador. Salvadoran base communities most often use the *Misa Popular Salvadoreña*, the Salvadoran Popular Mass, written between 1978 and 1980 by CEB members in San Salvador. Almost as popular is the *Misa Campesina Nicaragüense*, the Nicaraguan Peasant Mass, written in 1975 by Carlos Mejía Godoy, a professional musician and Sandinista activist. Salvadorans also sing parts of the Nicaraguan Popular Mass, written by members of CEBs in eastern Managua in 1968, and songs from different parts of Latin America. In most cases, I have used the versions of these songs available in *El pueblo canta*, a songbook published by the Archdiocese of San Salvador.

Popular rituals in El Salvador also utilize booklets with *vía crucis* reflections, *novenario* pamphlets, catechism guides, and study guides to various books of the Bible and to sacraments. These documents are usually written by priests and nuns working in the archdiocese or other pastoral institutions, although some are produced by CEB members or by laypeople and clergy together. I have concentrated on materials that are widely used in base communities and churches throughout El Salvador.

Other written primary sources include published and unpublished oral histories, interviews, and testimonial literature, as well as commentaries and analyses written by various political and religious groups in El

Salvador. In addition, research in the archives of the Archdiocese of San Salvador provided valuable documentation of developments and conflicts within the church during the 1970s and '80s.

Pseudonyms

Of all the Salvadoran laypeople interviewed for this study, only two (Mirtala López and Guadalupe Mejía) did not request anonymity. I have given pseudonyms to all other laypeople and most of the pastoral agents I interviewed in El Salvador. For clarity's sake, I have given laypeople a pseudonymous first name only; to pastoral workers I have given pseudonymous first and last names. When pseudonyms are used, I have so noted in the bibliography.

I have also used pseudonyms for several research sites. I have called the three neighborhoods in San Salvador where I conducted most of my research San Pablo, San Juan, and San Lucas. I have given the pseudonyms San Felipe and Santa María to two villages in Chalatenango. Otherwise, I have used actual place names.

References

For the sake of fluidity and brevity, I have not used endnotes to cite interviews I conducted, but rather have identified the speaker by name in the text. Two exceptions are quotations from people I interviewed more than once and from people who have written articles or books to which I also refer. In such cases, I use endnotes to avoid confusion about the source of the quotation. I have also incorporated references to Bible studies, masses, and other rituals or meetings into the text by noting the place name and date of the event.

Translations and Acronyms

All English translations of interviews and texts originally in Spanish are my own. Where a word is used in an unusual or ambiguous way, I have supplied the Spanish term in brackets after my translation. Following standard usage, I use Spanish acronyms for Salvadoran groups, such as "FMLN" for the Farabundo Martí National Liberation Front (Frente Farabundo Martí para la Liberación Nacional). While I have tried to use initials only immediately following a reference to the entire name, the widespread use of acronyms in Central America is contagious, and I apologize in advance to any readers who may spend half a chapter wondering what "FECCAS" or "CEBES" means. To remedy any potential confusion, I have given full Spanish names and English translations for most acronyms in the glossary.

Endnotes

1. Progressive Catholics in El Salvador often employ the term *iglesia popular*, a usage I will follow. In parts of Latin America, including Nicaragua, however, progressive Catholics avoid this term, because it suggests that progressive Catholics are trying to form a separate or "parallel" church. Most Catholic activists in El Salvador, Nicaragua, and elsewhere, however, insist that they wish not to separate from the church but to reform it.

2. In El Salvador and elsewhere, progressive Catholicism has probably thrived most not among the "poorest of the poor," but rather among the lower working classes, at least in urban areas. Some commentaries have referred to this fact, often as a criticism of progressive Catholic pastoral work (and often in comparison to Pentecostalism). See, for example, a review essay by John Burdick, "The Progressive Church in Latin America: Giving Voice or Listening to Voices," *Latin American Research Review* 29, no. 2 (1994): 184–197.

3. I am grateful to Jean Comaroff for suggesting the image of concentric circles.

4. See Harold J. Recinos, "The Politics of Salvadoran Refugee Popular Religion" (Ph.D. Dissertation, American University, Washington, DC, 1993) for a detailed discussion of Salvadoran refugees' religious ideas and values, including their interpretations of martyrdom.

1

Introduction

Although we're Christians and we follow Jesus, we're not going to
stay inside the church asking God for peace. We have to do something ourselves. God illuminates us, but we have to do something . . .
Even if we're not on our knees asking God for help, God will help.
But we have to do something too. Since Christ gave his life, we have
to do the same.

Mirtala López

Over the course of the 1970s, El Salvador slid, or rather crashed,
into a political crisis that shared much in common with circumstances
elsewhere in South and Central America. Like most of the region, El
Salvador suffered extreme economic and political inequities, which economic crises, natural disasters, and military dictatorships only worsened.
Also like other Latin Americans, many Salvadorans participated in
social movements that challenged the status quo. Throughout Latin
America, a number of these movements received sponsorship or at least
inspiration from the Catholic Church, which had begun a process of
massive self-reflection and reform following the Second Vatican Council
(1962–1965) and the meeting of the Latin American Bishops'
Conference (CELAM) at Medellín, Colombia, in 1968.

The political, economic, and religious upheaval common to much of
Latin America in the 1970s seemed in El Salvador to be magnified in
intensity. In a violent and poor region, El Salvador was more violent and
poorer than almost anywhere. Responses to violence and poverty in El
Salvador also took more intense forms than in most countries. While
left-leaning opposition movements mobilized throughout Latin
America, El Salvador was one of a handful of countries with a leftist
opposition that was genuinely revolutionary, genuinely popular, and gen-

uinely threatening to the status quo. El Salvador's political opposition and eventually its guerrilla army were surpassed in strength and success only by the Sandinistas in Nicaragua.

Throughout the changes and crises of this period, Catholicism played a crucial role. The Salvadoran church, especially the Archdiocese of San Salvador, had initiated pastoral reforms even prior to Vatican II, and after the Medellín conference numerous new groups, meetings, methods, and projects expanded the process of innovation in the Salvadoran Catholic Church. These reforms, stressing greater participation by laypeople and increased attention to social problems, again reflected changes that were occurring, in varying degrees, in many parts of Latin America. In a number of places, including El Salvador, numerous pastoral workers and even some bishops supported projects and movements that sought social change. In many cases, these efforts brought Catholics into conflict with political, economic, and/or military elites. In El Salvador, again, these conflicts were more explosive and more costly than almost anywhere else in Latin America. By the start of 1981, the country had plunged into a civil war that lasted eleven years and eventually claimed the lives of approximately 80,000 people, including an archbishop and twenty-two Catholic priests and nuns, as well as a seminary student and a Lutheran minister.

Scholars examining the tragic history of El Salvador during the 1970s and 1980s have often remarked upon the central role of the Catholic Church in the conflict. Students of religion and politics in Latin America, in fact, frequently point to El Salvador as an extreme case of the political "radicalization" experienced in Catholic institutions throughout the region.[1] Very few scholars, however, have investigated the sources and evolution of Catholic militancy in El Salvador or, more importantly, the precise nature of "radical" religious beliefs and practices.

In El Salvador, as elsewhere, believers draw on their religious traditions to make sense of their own experiences and to help them continue negotiating those experiences. Religious people often do this via the articulation and diffusion of narratives that put their lives in terms of sacred history, organized around the themes that most resonate in their context. These themes vary, as experiences and historical factors shape the ways people understand and respond to particular topics. Thus, in Brazil, for example, discussion may center on the Exodus (understood as the *caminhada*), while during the revolutionary period in Nicaragua, progressive Catholics seemed to turn especially to the idea of the reign of

God. In El Salvador during the late 1970s and 1980s, I believe, progressive Catholics found the concept of martyrdom most relevant.[2] These diverse cases share a common process by which people construct a theology and ethos, or a "practical religion," appropriating from the symbolic capital of Latin Catholicism those elements (stories, images, values) that resonate most in their particular situations.[3] This can be seen as a particular case of the task of religion more generally to make sense of diverse and often challenging experiences and events and to help suggest and legitimize appropriate responses. In these circumstances, as in many times and places, religion helps render graspable and thus, perhaps, more bearable a world that is often confusing and painful.

If belief systems develop, at least in part, to make sense of the historical and structural conditions of believers' lives, then the particular conditions in which the ideas emerge ought also to be taken into account. In the present case, attention must focus on certain conditions characterizing Salvadoran society in the 1970s and 1980s: extreme economic inequity, lack of political and social openness, and systematic violence against individuals and groups challenging the established order. In and through these circumstances, particular styles of religious community and discourse and distinctive systems of thought developed. An understanding of this context ought to ground any examination of the content of this practical religion and also any suggestions about the ways such an examination can deepen understandings of the multiple relations between religion and politics, in Latin America and beyond.

I. Religion and Politics

Concern for the ways religion and especially religious ideas operate at the grassroots has not played a particularly large role in scholarship on religion and politics. While some anthropologists have focused on the political implications of the ideas and especially the practices of particular religious communities, most social scientists have looked at religious and political institutions, the ideas and practices of elites (religious and political), and documents produced by these elites. Scholars in the history of religion and theology have, in turn, often concentrated on texts rather than on living religious communities. While attention to texts, institutions, and elites is certainly necessary, because those are influential and sometimes determining forces, this type of approach cannot explain relations between religion and politics.

Scholarship on religion and politics in Latin America and other parts of the "Third World" has also been marred by a tendency to explain religiously motivated political movements as "primitive," "fanatical," or "nativistic." These terms, like certain uses of the term *millenarian*, suggest that religio-political movements in the southern hemisphere (or among native or minority people in the north) are not to be taken seriously; they are seen, rather, as utopian, radical, outside the margins of both rational discourse and political efficacy.[4] This perspective tends to view religious belief as incompatible with a reasoned and realistic understanding of and response to political conditions. Because they do not take religiously grounded belief systems and movements seriously as political ideologies or movements, such approaches cannot illuminate many recent (and older) social movements, including not only dramatic uprisings but also quieter forms of oppositional consciousness and mobilization.

Recent scholarly trends have begun to correct some of the weaknesses of earlier work. A number of political scientists and sociologists, for example, have begun to attend to grassroots religious practices and groups and to the impact of religiosity at the personal level. Many of these new approaches no longer confine "religion and politics" to the institutional dynamics of church and state but assume, to varying degrees, that everyday experiences influence the ways religion shapes people's political ideas and behavior. This perspective also helps make it possible to investigate the logic and efficacy of religiously motivated political movements without recourse to notions such as "fanaticism." I hope to build on the insights of scholars who explore the subtle links between religion and politics, particularly in grassroots religious communities and practices. With these scholars, I believe that the indirect, even hidden influences of religion upon politics, especially changes in individual identity and new forms of associational life, may, in the long run, be more profound than the explicit machinations of church and state. I hope that this study helps to illuminate these various dimensions and underscores the complex connections among them.

In this book, I try to take into account both institutional dynamics and grassroots practices as essential dimensions of the relationship between religion and politics, in El Salvador as elsewhere. However, I concentrate on a third dimension, rarely addressed by social scientists. This involves the ways ordinary people (i.e., neither church officials nor professional theologians) formulate their conceptions of God, Christ, the kingdom, salvation, and sin, and their consequences for believers' political commitments and actions. These ideas are not irrational or simple (or "untheological," as Hobsbawm calls the labour sects in nineteenth-century Britain).[5] In fact, I argue, religiously based political action generally involves a great deal of reasoned reflection, as well as passionate conviction, on the part of participants.

While theological ideas are important, they cannot by themselves explain religious and political change or the interplay between the two. Ideas, as Daniel Levine reminds us, "never come in the abstract; they appear to particular people in specific historical and social circumstances."[6] Further, ideas never come without a history. Even the most innovative philosophy or theology stands on the shoulders of those preceding it. In the case of Salvadoran Catholic thought, biblical stories, church tradition, and post-Vatican II Latin American theology, along with Salvadoran political history and culture, provide a foundation for contemporary progressive Christianity. What is important in this light is not "ideas for their own sake," but the ways that believers elaborate ideas, by building on their traditions and responding to particular historical circumstances, and employ these ideas to make sense of and act in this situation.

While ideas should not be abstracted from social context, then, neither is it possible to understand how religious ideas affect believers' lives, including their political actions, without knowing what the ideas themselves are. This apparently self-evident truth has not always been apparent to scholars of religion and politics, who at least in research on Latin America often leave the presentation and analysis of religious ideas to theologians.[7] An integral understanding of religion's cultural and political impact at the grassroots as well as in more elite spheres should attend to the substance of theology, in addition to factors such as the religious community's structure, leadership style, and social setting. The interplay among these various factors, rather than any single factor in isolation, shapes believers' political ideas and beliefs.

Another way to frame this discussion is in terms of a dialectical relationship between what I call "internal" and "external" explanations. H. Richard Niebuhr also makes this distinction between internal and external descriptions, which he says "point to the same ultimate realities" but are "seen in different aspects and apprehended in different contexts." The difference between the two types of description revolves not around accuracy, but rather around perspective: "In one case the events of history are seen from the outside, in the other from the inside."[8] In my definition, the content of belief constitutes the "internal" dimension, that is, the understanding of people within a religious community. This includes, for example, the ways that believers understand political events in biblical or theological terms. When, as often occurs, scholars neglect this dimension, or address it only in passing, they impoverish their comprehension of the ways religion shapes politics and vice-versa. Greater attention to this internal dimension is necessary, not only to unearth local variants of theological doctrine but more importantly to gain the insights of believers "on the ground" regarding the ways religious symbols, stories, and values shed light (a slanted light, but light nonetheless) on the local unfolding of history.

By themselves, of course, internal theological explanations do not constitute a sufficient explanation of the relations between religion and politics. Religious insiders themselves usually recognize the need for both types of explanation, in fact, and point to historical and political factors as well as religious convictions. In scholarly contexts, internal analyses should be related dialectically (in constant, mutually transformative interplay) to "external" approaches to the reasons and ways particular forms of religiosity emerge and affect political behavior and events. External analysis should take into account such issues as the religious community's organizational structure; the origins, character, and role of religious leaders; the style of pastoral work; the form of associational life; and the group's range of activities. In addition, scholarly analysis should explore the particular religious group's linkages to larger institutions and historical forces, as well as the political and economic circumstances of believers' lives.

The dynamic relationship between internal and external dimensions of analysis parallels, in some ways, the dialectic between political (and economic, social, and cultural) factors and religious ideas and values. While material and secular circumstances influence the selection of religious themes by particular groups, religious ideas and values also help shape those circumstances. This dialectical relationship results in what David Laitin calls "practical religion—the realm where theology and social and economic conditions meet."[9] Following Weber, Laitin argues that this is not a directly causal relationship but one of "elective affinity," strongly affected but never fully determined by material-structural factors. While acknowledging that theological ideas emerge in the midst of and are shaped by a specific social setting, Laitin argues also that "ideas and values . . . take on a life of their own and affect future understanding of new social settings."[10] Thus, religious ideas maintain a relative autonomy (but never a complete separation) from material conditions, and the influence of one on the other is always mutual and fluid, never static or unidimensional.

This book presents a relatively autonomous system of ideas, developed for the most part (although certainly not in isolation or spontaneously) by people living in and responding to extraordinary historical events. It departs from most scholarship on religion in Latin America in two senses: first, by looking not at elites but at ordinary, usually poor people; and second, by focusing on religious ideas rather than institutions and practices. The actual ideas of laypeople have received little attention in work on religion in Latin America. Although many Latin American (and other) theologians claim to be speaking for "the people," only a few work closely enough with ordinary believers to know in much detail what "the people" actually believe. Certainly, this distance from "the people" does not invalidate their work. Most of these theologians are intellectually sophisticated as well as politically and religiously committed, and their writings make tremendous contributions to Christian theology and political analysis. Still, for all the talk about the theology "born of the people," we have yet to see much theology or ethics in the specific terms, or even the basic framework, used by ordinary believers.[11] I hope this book can make a start towards filling this gap by detailing a sophisticated, complex, and compelling popular belief system.

The word *popular* requires some clarification, for it has multiple and often contested meanings. I use it in two different senses. When I speak of a "popular political movement," I use the term as a translation of the Spanish term *popular*, meaning of the people and especially of poor people. While not entirely transparent, this term is relatively straightforward.[12] I also use the term in speaking of popular religion (or dimensions thereof). Popular religion is the subject of a complicated debate in various academic disciplines. These debates concern, among other issues, the relative orthodoxy of local lay practices and beliefs; the distinctions between "official" (or "elite") and "popular" (or "folk") culture; the extent to which popular religion is influenced by "official" religion; differences between urban and rural religiosity; the class dimensions of popular culture; and the sources of and influences on popular ideas and practices. Many authors reject the term because of the negative connotations often linked to it. Others prefer to use a more specific phrase, such as "popular Catholicism."[13] While recognizing the importance of many of these debates, I will use here a relatively simple working definition of popular religion, or more specifically of the sector of popular Catholicism linked to progressive currents in Catholicism in Latin America during the 1970s and 1980s. First, this religion is *popular* in the same sense as Latin American social movements, insofar as it involves mainly working-class and poor people. This class dimension is important in El Salvador, since the vast majority of Salvadorans are poor, and thus most "common" religious practices and ideas are tied to the culture, history, concerns, and daily lives of the poor.[14]

Second, this popular Catholicism is not opposed to official Catholicism, although it is quite definitely distinct from it. Official Catholicism, or its keepers (church leaders and pastoral agents), has tended to be concerned mainly with the fulfillment of certain guidelines (i.e., sacraments, moral rules), the maintenance of the church as an institution, and the protection of correct beliefs and values. What I call popular Catholicism, however, consists of the ideas, practices, and values of laypeople who may not come into frequent contact with church officials. They usually operate within traditions and certain broad guidelines set by the official church, but their practices and beliefs do not always conform closely to church orthodoxy.[15] Further, popular Catholic groups, regardless of their ideology or theology, often retain and even insist on a great deal of independence, especially in relation to ritual practices, images, and values tied to everyday experiences.

Further, popular religiosity is not limited to explicitly or conventionally "religious" issues or events. Religion can be defined as beliefs and actions that refer to and look for validation in a dimension or beings beyond the purely natural, or what Peter Worsley calls "a dimension beyond the empirical-technical realm of action."[16] However, religious ideas and actions are also linked to practical concerns and actions. Often, no sharp lines divide religion from other aspects of people's lives, especially in the minds and behavior of believers. Religious values and explanations enter into everyday activities and practical concerns about health, family, livelihood, community, and politics, as well as into efforts to explain and respond to more extraordinary occurrences. Religion seems to play an especially important role in responses to threats (social or natural). In these cases, rites, images, and convictions about human relations to the divine are often central to people's efforts to maintain or recover well-being.[17] This does not mean that "spiritual" or "otherworldly" dimensions are not important,[18] but these are most often embedded in people's thinking and practice concerning practical matters.

Finally, I am concerned with a particular sector of popular Catholicism, or of Catholic laypeople. I look at the history, beliefs, and practices of Salvadorans linked, more or less closely, to the progressive currents that began developing in El Salvador and in Latin America in the late 1960s. Progressive Catholicism, which I will outline later on, includes institutional and academic sectors as well as popular groups. I focus mainly on the "popular" (i.e., lay and poor) dimension of this progressive wing.

Many studies of popular religion, and of popular Catholicism in particular, focus on rituals, processions, and other types of practices rather than on ideas. Scholars often seem to assume that "popular" religiosity is not as theoretically complex or interesting as more "elite" religions. More simply, many writers seem to think that while understanding official Catholicism (or Buddhism, etc.) requires a knowledge of doctrine, we can know all there is to know about popular religion(s) by observing simply what people do during religious celebrations. I believe that, at least in the setting studied here, ordinary believers understand their religion in terms of ideas and values as much as practices. Their religion is not just what they do, but also, and sometimes most of all, what they believe. We cannot understand popular religiosity without listening to and taking seriously these beliefs.

I should emphasize here the hopefully self-evident point that the presentation of a popular theology is not an argument that it is necessarily either orthodox or original. Nor is the presentation of other people's theology an exercise in constructive theology. I outline progressive Catholic beliefs in El Salvador as a case study in both the history of Latin American Catholicism and a particular way of approaching the relations between religion and politics. In examining what people believe, in other words, I am interested in why, how, and to what effect they believe it, rather than its truth value or orthodoxy. I cannot explore the why and how, however, without detailing the content of the beliefs themselves.

II. The Structure of the Book

This book examines progressive Catholicism in El Salvador with two goals in mind. First and most specifically, I seek to present the religious worldview of a particular sector of Salvadoran society—specifically, the reinterpretation of the classic Christian category of martyrdom by progressive Catholics. I have made a special effort to document as carefully as I can the views of the actors themselves, in their own words when possible. Here a clarification may be appropriate. As previously noted, I am not writing my own theology but rather presenting the theology developed by progressive Salvadoran Catholics. Because I am interested in the links between people's ideas and their actions, however, I have approached the worldview of the popular church with what hermeneutic philosophy calls "charity of interpretation." In other words, I take seriously what my informants say and not just what I see them do. I believe this is important not only in this particular case but more generally in understanding the role of religion, especially religious ideas and values, in political action. Taking people's words seriously, of course, does not require accepting everything informants say as true, good, or unshaped by outside forces.

This documentation and analysis of the theology of martyrdom articulated by progressive Salvadoran Catholics occupies the four central chapters of the book. In these chapters, I describe this theology, which is really a theological ethics, largely in terms of a narrative, grounding a complex and coherent belief system, which places contemporary events in the light of sacred history. More specifically, this theology understands political killings as re-enactments of the passion of Jesus and the deaths of later martyrs, with essentially the same causes and consequences. Progressive Catholics in El Salvador built this narrative not only in formal and informal discussions, but also in and through religious rituals, as outlined in chapter 4. The popular understandings thus constructed bring together a number of specific issues, such as the definition of martyrdom itself (chapter 5); the reasons for and inevitability of persecution (chapter 6); and the benefits persecution brings (chapter 7). These theological concepts are sometimes novel, and other times they largely restate traditional Christian ideas. The issue at stake here, of course, is not their originality or value as theology, but their import to the believers. As background for contemporary understandings, I discuss several relevant aspects of early Christian understandings of martyrdom later in this chapter.

My second task, after presenting a theology of martyrdom as the practical religion of progressive Salvadoran Catholics, is to explore the ways their experiences shed light on the links between religion and politics. As outlined in chapter 3, Catholicism in El Salvador reflects and builds on general changes that occurred as churches throughout Latin

America implemented Vatican II and Medellín reforms. These changes in theology, pastoral method, and stance towards "the world" significantly altered the relations between religion and politics in many parts of Latin America, most prominently in Nicaragua, Brazil, and Chile, as well as El Salvador. As noted earlier, scholars often identify El Salvador, along with Nicaragua, as occupying the "radical" extreme on a continuum of contemporary Latin American Catholicism. This perception suggests that the Salvadoran experience can illuminate the range and consequences of possible responses to the Vatican II reforms in contemporary Catholicism, globally as well as in Latin America. For various reasons, however, including the difficulty of conducting research in El Salvador during most of the 1980s, the Salvadoran church has received little serious scholarly attention. With this study, I hope to broaden our understandings of what Vatican II, Medellín, liberation theology, base communities, and other reforms in Latin American Catholicism meant "on the ground."

I also discuss the relations between religion and politics at a more general level of analysis. I am interested, in particular, in the ways religious belief systems affect sociopolitical praxis at the grassroots level, i.e., how religion enables people to make sense of the world and act in it. In exploring religion's political dimensions, I bypass the argument about whether or not religion must always serve as a conservative social force. A number of recent studies have demonstrated that religion can, in certain circumstances, support political resistance.[19] Rather than enter into the debate over "whether," then, I will accept the evidence and turn to the question of "how." I will answer, in brief, that religion strengthens (or can strengthen) resistance not only as one (especially valued or protected) social institution among many, but in distinctively religious ways, particularly through theological conceptions and values organized into coherent narratives linking sacred and secular history. Underlying this argument is an assumption that ordinary people, and not just professional theologians, construct, adapt, and seek to live by theological and ethical systems. I believe that taking these "popular theologies" seriously will strengthen our understandings of the ways that religion shapes political action in particular conditions. It is the interplay of particular ideas and material circumstances that, at different historical moments, makes such action possible. I hope this book both exemplifies and makes a case for this way of studying religion and politics.

III. Martyrdom

They love all men and are persecuted by all men . . . They are put to death and they gain life.

                    Anonymous, "Epistle to Diognetius"

For thousands of years, diverse groups of Jews and Christians, in efforts to understand their own experiences of persecution, have been constructing the foundations of contemporary "martyrologies." Persecution was, of course, a reality for Jews at various points prior to (as well as since) the emergence of Christianity, and early Jewish interpretations of repression helped shape Christian responses to martyrdom. For early Christians, life in the Roman Empire was characterized by "diffuse persecution," outbreaks of repression in different regions, alternating with periods of toleration, from around the burning of Rome (64 C.E.) until Constantine's edict of toleration in 313.[20] Early Christians' experiences of persecution, which they interpreted in light of both Jewish tradition and Jesus' own death, helped give the category of martyrdom a central role in defining Christianity's collective identity and illuminating its theological message.

Christianity's assumption that believers must suffer for their convictions and that this suffering leads to redemption and/or victory springs from the Jewish tradition. The Gospel notion of Jesus as the "ransom for many," for example, expresses a fundamental Jewish belief that God will deliver the chosen people because of the martyrs' sacrifices, seen, for example, in the suffering of the heroes of the Maccabean revolt (c. 176–63 B.C.E.) to atone for Israel's sins.

Despite clear links to Jewish tradition, what sets Christian conceptions of martyrdom apart is the fact that this suffering follows a model set by the object of faith. Christianity, as Mexican theologian Carlos Bravo notes, differs from other world religions, certainly from Judaism, in worshipping a god who dies in apparent defeat of a divine mission.[21] This theme emerges clearly in the New Testament writings, most of which were produced during the period of persecution. In the Gospel of John, Jesus tells the disciples to expect difficult times. "If the world hates you, know that it has hated me before it hated you . . . a servant is not greater than his master. If they persecuted me, they will persecute you" (Jn

15:18, 20). A number of the first disciples suffered persecution and death for their faith. Their sacrifices served as atonement, as signs of the last days, as witness to the true faith, and, not least, as imitation of the model of self-sacrifice set by Christ himself. For believers, Christianity became the religion of the cross, and bearing the cross became the mark of Christ's disciples.

From its beginnings, then, Christian martyrdom included dual elements of witness to and imitation of Christ. The early Christian martyrs repeated Jesus' passion and death as "an innocent victim who dies for the faith at the hands of a tyrant who is opposed to the faith." Also like Jesus, early martyrs strove to withstand trial and even torture without recanting (and, in the end, to forgive their enemies). Thus, Stephen, the first "canonized" Christian martyr, was recognized as a saint "by way of analogy with the story of Jesus' passion and death . . . To be a saint, then, was to die not only *for* Christ, but also *like* him."[22] Later, as the Christian community's distance from Jesus' death increased, the aspect of witness to Christ, rather than direct imitation of him, took precedence, but the idea of martyrdom as an *imitatio Christi* never entirely disappeared.

Perhaps the most distinctive theological feature of popular understandings of martyrdom in Latin America is the renewed emphasis on sacrifice for a cause as *imitatio Christi*. While faith in and witness to Christ remain important, certainly, Salvadoran and other Central American believers have emphasized the ways that their experiences re-enact Jesus' passion, with the same goals and constituent elements. Like the earliest Christians, many Salvadorans in the 1970s and 1980s believed that the martyrs of their communities gave their lives not only in witness to Christ but in his image.

The central religious value given to sacrifice, as both witness and *imitatio Christi*, made persecution inevitable and even desirable for early Christians. "All who desire to live a godly life in Christ Jesus can expect to be persecuted," asserts the second letter of Timothy (3:12); the writer goes on to suggest that, in fact, believers can attain the kingdom of God only through affliction. During the second and third centuries C.E., believers came to understand persecution not as a threat to avoid, but as a sign of the new age, to be accepted with stoicism and even joy. In this view, the new covenant must be sealed in the blood of the innocent, beginning with Christ's crucifixion and continuing in the sufferings of his followers.[23]

As persecution came to occupy a central practical and theological space for early Christians, they celebrated the sufferings of their contemporaries just as they commemorated the passion of Christ in the eucharist. According to the story of Polycarp's martyrdom, the faithful commemorated the anniversary of his death "both as a memorial for those who have already fought the contest and for the training and preparation of those who will do so one day."[24] Martyrs provided a focus and a point of unity for early Christian communities. In gatherings and rituals,

> the witness of sisters and brothers in captivity for the faith, or martyred, was always recalled and celebrated as fidelity to the example of Christ. The martyrs were honored not as dead, but as living, united with the celebrants as permanent intercessors before the throne of God.[25]

The notion that martyrs were "not dead, but living" highlights the paradox at the heart of Christianity. Early Christians believed that they, like their martyred founder, could achieve victory over death only through death. Thus, a Christian named Julius, told by the emperor Maximus to sacrifice to Roman gods to live, responded, "If I choose life, I choose death; if I die, I live forever."[26] Because of their conviction that they would share in Jesus' resurrection only through unhesitating witness, many accepted persecution and martyrdom as a route to eternal life. They not only followed the route taken by Jesus himself, but even brought him into their own history. For early Christians, as Herbert Workman notes,

> When martyrs are delivered up to death, it is Christ who is made manifest in them. And what looks like defeat is exactly the opposite: brute force is incapable of subduing those who have made this radical option . . . The one who vanquishes death is the ultimate ruler of the world. Over such a one, the powers of evil can no longer prevail.[27]

This paradox formed the core of the Christian theology of martyrdom that developed, in varying circumstances, over the first three centuries after Jesus' death.

The Politics of Martyrdom in Early Christianity

Martyrdom inverts the usual logic that equates rightness with historical success, ultimate victory with temporal survival. The martyrs insist with their lives that certain principles transcend life itself. Thus, martyr-dom raises crucial theological and ethical questions: To what does a believer owe ultimate loyalty? What works does faith demand? What are the consequences of meeting those demands? Martyrdom is never just a religious issue, however. Because it has to do with repression and power, it also asks essentially political questions: What is the relationship between faith and political action? Between religious and secular authority? Martyrs dramatize the limits that faith imposes upon allegiance to civil power and provide a model for believers' correct response to a political situation.

This model is an absolute one. In early Christianity, as in other times and places, the public message of martyrdom was that true commitment to God makes compromise impossible, even when the only alternative is death. In this light, renouncing the faith meant degradation and medioc-rity. Certainly, this pressure to take risks for a cause can be manipulated, even instilled, by sometimes unscrupulous leaders. However, the drive to martyrdom is not only imposed from above. For many early Christians, a strongly felt personal relation to Jesus lay beneath their willingness to take risks. "For eighty-six years I have served Him, and He has done me no wrong, and how can I blaspheme my King who has saved me?" asked Polycarp.[28] In this radical fidelity, martyrs believed they imitated both Jesus' sacrificial faithfulness to God and Yahweh's covenant with Israel. As God was radically true to God's word, so believers must not betray theirs. The early church generalized this absolute commitment: "The liv-ing of the radicality of the gospel was a demand upon all, without distinc-tion. All were expected to be ready to give a living account of their hope, to confess the faith when interrogated."[29]

The requirement for a radical attachment to Christ made Christ-ianity unable to coexist with other religious or secular powers. In the Roman era, this caused conflicts and persecution, since Roman citizen-ship required obeisance to Roman gods as well as to the emperor. Christianity's insistence that believers have no master except the one God motivated accusations that Christians were hostile to the Roman state. Although early Christians often saw themselves in opposition to "the world," and not necessarily to the authorities or the Roman Empire in particular, many Romans viewed Christian behavior in political terms, and not as a religious response to a belief in the approaching apocalypse. Christians' claim of a "heavenly citizenship under a deity who transcended the Roman gods and the Caesars" threatened the Roman political order as well as the religious status quo.[30]

Early martyrs sought, above all, to clarify the "double citizenship" of Christians in the empire. Like the monks who withdrew from the world, martyrs specified the point at which allegiance to Caesar began to clash with the greater pull of loyalty to Christ. Martyrs usually endorsed loyalty to the empire up to that point but maintained the priority of faith, providing exemplary responses to the dilemmas of how to respond to "the world" and bringing "into sharp focus the line of demarcation that separated the followers of Christ from the pagan world."[31]

Christianity also created a political threat to the empire because it drew people from all spheres, even women and slaves. Christianity's egalitarianism and its insistence that the state had no absolute claim on one's loyalty appealed to people dissatisfied with Rome's rule, especially in northern Africa, where rural conditions were poor and the new church provided refuge that traditional religions could not. By the 270s C.E., Christian monks were leading popular opposition to Rome, thus strengthening the link between religious persecution and political mobilization. In Egypt in the late third and early fourth centuries, Christian martyrs became a symbol of national resistance against Rome and helped convince north African Christians that the empire had lost its power to the moral and social strength of the resisters.

The experiences of Christians in the Roman Empire demonstrated several ways martyrdom can prove helpful for resistance struggles. One of the most important political lessons of early Christian history, in fact, was that repression intended to destroy a movement can instead reinforce it. In many cases, persecution did not halt but rather strengthened recruitment and evangelization by early Christians. "As the killing went on, so more turned to Christ," according to historian W. H. C. Frend. "Persecution even quickened the pace of conversion," as public trials and executions made the new faith more visible and more compelling. Paradoxically, as the Donatist Petilian wrote in the late fourth century, "Christianity makes progress by the deaths of its followers."[32]

This progress occurred, in part, through the public relations value of martyrdom for the victims. "Martyrdom is a dramatic strategy that cannot lose," claims Olga Klapp (with some exaggeration); "the resister, being passive, is extremely hard to see as a villain, while the opponent, whether he [sic] wins or not, can hardly avoid being cast as an aggressor by an open-minded audience."[33] While the public "spin" on martyrdom is probably less predetermined than Klapp suggests, in certain conditions martyrdom can badly damage the attackers' image and moral legitimacy, as, according to many historians, it did in the Roman Empire.

Martyrs' sacrifices also strengthened early Christian communities by providing examples of extraordinary faith, which often intensified ordinary devotion and encouraged believers to reject compromise. In his Letters, Cyprian wrote to believers in prison: "We are still in the world, still drawn up in line of battle; we fight daily for our lives . . . You have been made an example to the rest of the brethren for whose lives your life and reactions ought to be a stimulation."[34] (Conversely, of course, martyrs could not sustain their motivation without a supportive community of fellow believers.)

The Politics of Martyrdom

This discussion of the ways that martyrdom contributed to early Christianity requires a few caveats, which also apply to the contemporary case that follows. What believers—in Rome or elsewhere—understand as the fortification of their position often appears to outsiders (and scholars) as radicalization and social polarization. In sociological terms, popular responses to repression often entail an "ascendancy of the resolute,"[35] intensifying the conviction of average members and bolstering the influence of more determined participants. In addition to radicalizing the victims' side, violence can often harden positions among the attackers, to whom ritualized "acceptance" of persecution demonstrates not authenticity but irrationality and extremism. The stiffening of both these positions, in turn, can alienate those outside the conflict.

In early Christianity and other cases, the radicalizing tendencies of martyrdom may well emerge from genuinely popular (although generally not "spontaneous") responses to persecution. Ordinary people, in other words, often perceive violence against themselves or another social group in black-and-white terms, regardless of public or elite interpretations of this violence. This "extremism" is not necessarily irrational. It often represents one of the few possible responses to an extreme situation, in which the patterns and goals of mainstream (instrumental) rationality may not be useful or appropriate.

Radicalization can also stem from the manipulation of images of martyrdom by political and religious leaders seeking to intensify positions on either side of a struggle. This manipulation may involve the idealization of dead heroes, sometimes in support of causes that they themselves did not support, or at minimum for exaggerated versions of their own ideals. Dead heroes can also be used by different groups in different ways. The fate of Nicaraguan journalist Pedro Joaquín Chamorro, assassinated in 1978, illuminates this process through his passage from banner of the Sandinista Front for National Liberation (*Frente Sandinista para la Liberación Nacional*, or FSLN), whose ideology was, in fact, to the left of his own, to the emblem of conservative-centrist forces running against the Sandinistas in the 1990 elections (won by Chamorro's widow, in no small part because she was his widow). In this and count-less other cases, differing and sometimes opposing forces compete as the "true" heirs of a fallen hero. One side eventually wins the contest, often not because of the accuracy of its portrayal of the martyr's vision but because it presents the version that most appeals to its base of support.

Sometimes these elite understandings or public portrayals of perse-cution do not coincide with the ways ordinary people understand the fallen hero, the killing, and/or the issues at stake. In such cases, the lead-ers may well fail to rally support in the name of their martyr, whose "cult" sooner or later fades. A persistent and well-organized public rela-tions campaign, of course, might eventually resonate with people who were initially indifferent, or at least create the appearance of a cult of personality even in the absence of much popular support.

In many ways, then, martyrdom enters into politics and is used or misused for more or less admirable causes. Early Christianity seems to pre-sent a case in which, for the most part, genuine (although never unani-mous) popular sentiment honored and kept alive the memory of believers killed for their refusal to compromise their faith. Similarly "authentic" popular cults of martyrdom have arisen in many times and places since (and before) that time, as, of course, have countless cases of elite manipu-lation, disingenuous propaganda, and distortions of other "sacrificial" deaths. While acknowledging the diverse forms taken by cults of martyrs, I focus here on a relatively "authentic" case. By this, I mean that ordinary Salvadorans revered and sustained the memory of persons killed for a cause that both the fallen and the survivors for the most part supported. This popular cult of martyrdom represented not only a tribute to the dead but an ethical and existential code for the living.

Martyrdom in Contemporary Latin America

Early Christians articulated a theology and ethics of martyrdom to make sense of persecution that, while occasionally intense, probably claimed, over two-and-a-half centuries, no more than a few thousand lives throughout the Roman Empire. Contemporary repression in Latin America, while not focused on a single religious group, has occurred on a much larger scale.[36] In El Salvador, political violence touched virtually every citizen and prompted searches for new ways to understand and respond to such massive suffering.

Religion played a central role in this effort, both because Salvadoran culture is highly religious and because many of the victims were practicing Christians, whose religious faith motivated the commitments and actions that led to their deaths. These commitments cannot be dismissed as manipulation by radical leaders, religious or political. Nor can popular interpretations of these deaths be seen as only the results of an elite-constructed ideology. Deeply embedded Catholic and biblical themes, as well as pre-Hispanic indigenous traditions, provided resources on which many ordinary Salvadorans drew to construct relatively autonomous worldviews, political attitudes, and rationales for action regarding a number of topics. The political repression of the 1970s and 1980s proved no exception.

At this tremendously cruel point in their history, Salvadorans sought to glean from the events of their lives not only meaning but also a reason to keep struggling towards a less tragic future. For many, a re-interpretation of martyrdom, focusing on the story of Christ's passion, helped make political killings more comprehensible by placing them in the light of God's perceived plan for humankind. This interpretation also prescribed a particular course of action—political resistance—in response. I hope this study of the religious worldview of progressive Salvadoran Catholics, placed in their historical and material context, can suggest both the value of looking carefully at popular belief systems in studying religion and politics, and, more simply, the compelling power of an ethos that ordinary people have constructed and, in the face of enormous obstacles, sought to live by.

Endnotes

1. See, for example, Daniel Levine's use of El Salvador as an example of the "radical" type of popular Catholic organization, in *Popular Voices in Latin American Catholicism* (Princeton, NJ: Princeton University Press, 1992), 48.

2. Recinos also sees martyrdom as the dominant "root metaphor" in Salvadoran popular Catholicism. See "The Politics of Salvadoran Refugee Popular Religion," 42.

3. For a historical perspective on this phenomenon, see Orlando Espín, "Trinitarian Monotheism and the Birth of Popular Catholicism," *Missiology: An International Review* 20, no. 2 (April 1992): 177–204.

4. Even writers sympathetic to these movements, such as E. J. Hobsbawm and Peter Worsley, tend to question the "rationality" of millenarian or other religiously based political movements. See Hobsbawm, *Primitive Rebels: Studies in Archaic Forms of Social Movements in the 19th and 20th Centuries* (New York: W. W. Norton, 1959) and Worsley, *The Trumpet Shall Sound: A Study of "Cargo" Cults in Melanesia* (New York: Schocken Books, 1968).

5. Hobsbawm, *Primitive Rebels*, 132.

6. Levine, *Popular Voices*, 180.

7. Weber's classic study of the Protestant ethic serves as a rare example of sociological analysis of the political role of religion that takes the content of religious belief seriously. Weber focused on theology, of course, partly because he did not conduct field work. Contemporary studies of religion and politics can correct this weakness and still retain Weber's emphasis on the relevance of ideas. See Max Weber, *The Protestant Ethic and the Spirit of Capitalism* (New York: Charles Scribner's Sons, 1958).

8. H. Richard Niebuhr, *The Meaning of Revelation* (New York: MacMillan, 1941), 45.

9. David Laitin, "Religion, Political Culture, and the Weberian Tradition," *World Politics* 30, no. 4 (July 1978): 589.

10. Ibid., 586.

11. Ernesto Cardenal, *The Gospel in Solentiname* (Maryknoll, NY: Orbis, 1978–1982), four volumes of conversations at a Nicaraguan base community, represents the major exception. Although it includes no analysis, and Cardenal's voice often dominates discussions, the volumes provide invaluable documentation of a progressive grassroots theology emerging from a particular historical situation (Nicaragua in the 1970s).

12. See Kenneth Aman and Cristián Parker, eds., *Popular Culture in Chile: Resistance and Survival* (Boulder, CO: Westview Press, 1991), pp. 2–9, for a discussion of the meaning of the Spanish term *popular*.

13. William Christian argues for the term "local" religion; *Local Religion in Sixteenth Century Spain* (Princeton, NJ: Princeton University Press, 1981), 178. Michael Carroll prefers to speak of popular Catholicism; *Madonnas that Maim: Popular Catholicism in Italy Since the Fifteenth Century* (Baltimore and London: Johns Hopkins University Press, 1992). For other helpful discussions of popular

religion, see Thomas Kselman, ed., *Belief in History: Innovative Approaches to American and European Religion* (Notre Dame, IN: University of Notre Dame Press, 1991).

14. Class constitutes the defining feature in a number of recent definitions of popular religion. See Lynn Stephen and James Dow, "Introduction: Popular Religion in Mexico and Central America," in *Class, Politics, and Popular Religion in Mexico and Central America*, eds. L. Stephen and J. Dow (Washington, DC: American Anthropological Association, 1990), p. 7; and Michael Candelaria, *Popular Religion and Liberation: The Dilemma of Liberation Theology* (Albany: State University of New York Press, 1990), 196.

15. Here I depart from Carroll's definition of popular Catholicism as developing within the "allowable limits" set by official Catholicism; *Madonnas that Maim*, 8.

16. Worsley, *The Trumpet Shall Sound*, xxxv.

17. On the practical dimension of popular religion, see Dow and Stephen, "Introduction," 8, and John Ingham, *Mary, Michael, and Lucifer: Folk Catholicism in Central Mexico* (Austin: University of Texas Press, 1986), 1. On popular religion as a response to threats, see Carroll, *Madonnas that Maim*, 138 and Christian, *Local Religion*, 20.

18. Here I disagree with William Rowe and Vivian Schelling, who argue that spiritual values are not at all important to popular religion. *Memory and Modernity: Popular Culture in Latin America* (London and New York: Verso, 1991), 70.

19. See, among others, Jean Comaroff, *Body of Power, Spirit of Resistance: The Culture and History of a South African People* (Chicago: University of Chicago Press, 1985); Reynaldo Ileto, *Pasyon and Revolution: Popular Movements in the Philippines, 1840–1910* (Manila: Ateneo de Manila Press, 1979); and Michael Taussig, *The Devil and Commodity Fetishism in Latin America* (Chapel Hill: University of North Carolina Press, 1981).

20. Ivo Lesbaupin, *Blessed Are the Persecuted: Christians in the Roman Empire, AD 64–313* (Maryknoll, NY: Orbis, 1987), 8.

21. Carlos Bravo, Centro de Reflexión Teológica, Mexico City, interview by author, 30 May 1990.

22. Kenneth Woodward, *Making Saints: How the Catholic Church Determines Who Becomes a Saint, Who Doesn't, and Why* (New York: Simon and Schuster, 1990), 129, 53. Emphasis in original.

23. For a full discussion of martyrdom in early Christianity, see Arthur J. Droge and James D. Tabor, *A Noble Death: Suicide and Martyrdom Among*

Christians and Jews in Antiquity (San Francisco: Harper Collins, 1992), esp. chap. 4–7.

24. William Clebsch, *Christianity in European History* (New York: Oxford University Press, 1979), 49.

25. Lesbaupin, *Blessed Are the Persecuted*, 18.

26. Herbert B. Workman, *Persecution in the Early Church* (Oxford: Oxford University Press, 1980), 31.

27. Ibid., 87.

28. Quoted in ibid., 29.

29. Lesbaupin, *Blessed Are the Persecuted*, 48.

30. Workman, *Persecution*, 35; see also Clebsch, *Christianity*, 20.

31. Clebsch, *Christianity*, 36. See also Winston A. Van Horne, "St. Augustine: Death and Political Resistance," *Journal of Religious Thought* 38, no. 2 (Fall–Winter 1981): 43.

32. W. H. C. Frend, *Martyrdom and Persecution in the Early Church* (London: Basil Blackwell, 1965), 520–521, 555–556.

33. Olga Klapp, *Symbolic Leaders: Public Dramas and Public Men* (Chicago: Aldine, 1974), 86, quoted in Anita Weiner and Eugene Weiner, *The Martyr's Conviction* (Atlanta: Scholar's Press, 1990), 42.

34. Quoted in Lesbaupin, *Blessed Are the Persecuted*, 53.

35. Weiner and Weiner, *The Martyr's Conviction*, 63.

36. On the centrality of martyrdom in theological and other works on Latin American Christianity since the late 1970s, see the following: Centro Pastoral de la Universidad Centroamericana, "Tiempo de pasión en El Salvador: quince estaciones en el Vía Crucis salvadoreño, *Christus* (Mexico City) 55, no. 632 (Feb. 1990), 5–27; "Conmemorando a nuestros mártires," *Mártires de El Salvador* (Managua), no. 61 (Jan.–Feb. 1990), 7–9; Enrique Dussel, "The People of El Salvador," *Concilium* 169 (Sept. 1983): 61–68; Roberto García Ramírez, "El Martirio en la Iglesia Latino-Americana," *Nuevo Mundo: Revista de Teología Latinoamericana* (Buenos Aires) 30 (1985): 43–70; Juan Hernández Pico, "Martyrdom in Latin America Today: Stumbling-block, Folly, and Power of God," *Concilium* 163 (March 1983): 37–42; Michael James Higgins, "Marytrs and Virgins: Popular Religion in Mexico and Nicaragua," in *Class, Politics, and Popular Religion in Mexico and Central America*, eds. Lynn Stephen and James Dow (Washington, DC: American Anthropological Association, 1990);

Instituto Histórico Centroamericano, *La sangre por el pueblo: Memoria de martirio en América Latina* (Bilbao, Spain: Descleé de Brouwer, 1983); Martin Lange and Reinhold Iblacker, eds., *Witnesses of Hope: The Persecution of Christians in Latin America* (Maryknoll, NY: Orbis, 1981); José Marins et al., eds., *Memoria peligrosa: heroés y mártires en la iglesia latinoamericana* (Mexico City: Centro de Reflexión Teológica, 1989); and Manuel Useros and María López Vigil, *La vida por el pueblo: cristianos de comunidades populares en América Latina* (Madrid: Editorial Popular, 1981).

2

El Salvador

In its minimal geography fit the most contradictory realities of death and joy, of repression and freedom.

Pedro Casaldáliga

The smallest and most densely populated republic in Latin America, El Salvador (the savior) is also one of the poorest. Average per capita gross national product was slightly over one thousand U.S. dollars in 1991, and combined under- and unemployment hovers around seventy percent. Conditions are worst in the countryside, where seventy percent of the population lives in absolute poverty, i.e., they cannot afford the food necessary to fulfill minimum requirements. Nearly half of El Salvador's five and a half million people have no regular source of potable water, only thirty-seven percent have access to medical care, and illiteracy is around twenty-eight percent. The results of this situation are predictable: half the country's children are malnourished, fifty-six of every thousand infants die in their first year, and life expectancy is about sixty-three years. These conditions are based in the chronic land shortage (fewer than one-third of the country's 8,620 square miles are arable), and especially in the highly unequal distribution of land and income that has prevailed since the Spanish conquest in the sixteenth century. In a society in which most families have traditionally depended on agriculture for their livelihood, one percent of the population controls seventy-one percent of the farmland, and over ninety-six percent of the rural population has twelve acres or less. Half of the national income goes to only eight percent of the population.[1]

The roots of this inequity and of the current political crisis can be found in colonial Salvadoran history, when Spanish policies first established sharp economic divisions and the concentration of land and wealth in the hands of a few. Prior to the Spanish conquest of Mesoamerica, most of what is now El Salvador was populated by Pipil people, Nahua (or Nahuatl) speakers related ethnically and linguistically to the Mexica (Aztecs) of central Mexico, rather than to the Maya who predominate in the rest of Central America and southern Mexico. The Pipil population was concentrated in what is now the province of Cuscatlán, where their agricultural production centered on maize, beans, and squash. They had well-developed systems of regional and interregional exchange, including the sale of crops such as cotton. The Pipils' religious organization, ritual, and beliefs were also similar to those of the Mexica, with a pantheon of divinities, elaborate temples, a complex religious calendar, and a hierarchical priesthood. The Pipil, like the Mexica, practiced human and animal sacrifices, which they believed helped sustain the gods and ensure the survival of their society and of the cosmos.[2]

The Spanish "pacified" the Pipil and other indigenous groups in Mesoamerica in the mid-sixteenth century. As they had in Mexico, the conquerors proceeded to institute a "mercantile, military, individual capitalism."[3] The colonial economy initially relied on the forced labor of indigenous people and later was maintained through a debt peonage system that established the semifeudal social structure that persists in El Salvador today. The Spanish priests who followed the conquerors forced the native people to convert to Catholicism and sought to destroy indigenous religious symbols, rituals, and temples, thus consolidating the colonizers' psychological, physical, and economic control. The missionaries and other Spaniards found ritualized human sacrifice particularly abhorrent and banned all manifestations of this central dimension of Pipil religion. Despite the Spaniards' systematic and sometimes violent efforts to eradicate "idolatry," however, many elements of popular religious beliefs and practices remained and contributed to the construction of distinctive forms of "popular" and "syncretic" Catholicism in colonial and postcolonial El Salvador.

Throughout the colonial period and even after independence in 1821, indigenous communities lost land used for subsistence farming to large plantations producing cash crops, first indigo and then, in the second half of the nineteenth century, coffee. After the 1870s, coffee production became the dominant agro-export activity. Coffee took over the most fertile and accessible farmlands, in areas where the population was densest, thus threatening "the traditional rights of the communities [in these areas] to the land."[4] Government decrees abolishing Indian communal lands and ejidal lands in 1881 and 1882 opened the way for coffee producers eager to increase their land holdings. As coffee production rose, the indigenous population suffered increasing displacement, joining the growing pool of landless and land-poor peasants forced to work in the coffee harvest. The loss of subsistence farmland created an itinerant population, which served to fill seasonal labor needs on large estates and strengthened the monocultural economy. By the early twentieth century, a landed oligarchy, primarily coffee growers (cafetaleros) was firmly in place, as was the landless and near-landless population that it sometimes employs. This oligarchy has continued to dominate Salvadoran political and economic life throughout this century, although a new urban-based elite (involved in manufacturing and capital investment) has also emerged in recent years.

The concentration of land and wealth in the hands of a few and the "feudal" system of labor have spurred various uprisings throughout colonial and postcolonial history, particularly during periods of economic crisis, which struck hardest at the poor. In 1833, twelve years after independence from Spain, indigenous people attacked Spanish installments in various parts of the country to protest government repression and the tribute demanded by local authorities. When the rebellion failed, the military killed indigenous leader Anastasio Aquino and displayed his head in a cage. That incident was followed in the 1880s and 1890s by a series of protests against the transformation of farmland to coffee plantations. These uprisings prompted a build-up of arms and security forces by both private landowners and the government, precursors of contemporary military and paramilitary squads. To repress popular protest, the government imposed a state of siege and imprisoned, tortured, and executed opponents of the regime. The events of the nineteenth century helped establish instruments and mechanisms of repression that continue to function today. In addition to witnessing the beginning of modern means of repression, however, the nineteenth century also provided enduring models of resistance.

In the first part of the twentieth century, two Salvadoran leaders both symbolized and helped fix the pattern of repression and rebellion that characterizes modern Salvadoran history. The first was Agustín Farabundo Martí, a communist and leader of the Regional Federation of Salvadoran Workers in the late 1920s, who fought for a time alongside Augusto César Sandino, the Nicaraguan guerrilla leader. The second man, General Maximiliano Hernández Martínez, claimed power in a military coup d'etat in December 1931, initiating a repressive regime that lasted until 1944. Hernández Martínez helped form the military into a self-conscious caste; prohibited the entry of blacks, Arabs, Hindus, and Chinese; supported fascists in Europe; and dabbled in the occult. His fame stems most, however, from his role in *la matanza*, the massacre of 1932.

La Matanza

We were all born half-dead in 1932.

Roque Dalton, *Miguel Marmol*

The events of 1932, like many other conflicts in Salvadoran history, emerged from economic problems originating in the dependence on coffee and the shortage of land. A downturn in the international coffee market in the late 1920s, aggravating economic weaknesses due to the world depression, provoked a serious economic crisis in El Salvador. On December 2, 1931, in the midst of economic and political turmoil, army officers overthrew reformist President Arturo Araujo, who had been elected earlier that year. The military named Hernández Martínez, who had been Araujo's vice-president, president of the provisional government. In January, around five thousand people, mainly indigenous (with some leadership from the Communist Party), revolted, primarily in the western provinces of Sonsonate and Ahuachapán. The rebels killed at most one hundred people, civilians and soldiers, according to the definitive study of the insurrection.[5] The government and the oligarchy responded by killing not only the insurrection's participants and leaders, including Farabundo Martí, but also huge numbers of people with no links to the rebellion. Most scholars accept figures between 10,000 and 30,000 deaths, or up to two percent of the national population at the time.[6]

After the massacre, fear of repression drove most indigenous people to abandon native dress and the Nahua language and to adopt the customs of *mestizos* or *ladinos*, people of mixed indigenous and European blood. Largely in response to the *matanza*, El Salvador today lacks a large distinctly indigenous population and culture, although some small communities survive in the far western part of the country. In this aspect and many others, the massacre changed the face of the country. Since 1932, asserts Miguel Mármol, one of the few surviving participants in the uprising, El Salvador has been "another country," "the work of that barbarity."[7] The uprising and the massacre of 1932 remain central reference points for twentieth-century Salvadoran history and especially for the cycles of militant rebellion and massive repression that have marked El Salvador since.

Repression and Protest

Hernández Martínez ruled El Salvador until another military coup unseated him in April 1944. The interim president, General Andrés Menéndez, tried to implement moderate reforms and a transition to democratic rule. Lack of support from the military and oligarchy sabotaged his efforts, and Menéndez was forced to resign before the end of the year. Elite resistance to even mild reforms continued in subsequent decades and led to the failure of a number of moderate political proposals and groups. In this and other ways, the seeds of the political crisis of the 1980s emerged from the failure of reforms in 1944 (and 1932) and, more deeply, from the inability of both reform and reaction to resolve basic problems of political and economic organization.[8]

Following the coup of 1944, a series of military regimes ensured that unequal socioeconomic structures remained in place for the next forty years, with little organized opposition to the ruling alliance of landowning elites and military officers. In 1960, moderate Catholics formed the Christian Democratic Party (PDC), which adopted a moderate critical position and by the 1960s had achieved substantial popular support. It could not achieve political power in the closed system maintained by the ruling conservative party and its military allies, however. More left-leaning groups, such as the Salvadoran Communist Party, were even more politically marginalized and frequently repressed.

In the post–World War II period, the introduction of new export crops exacerbated the concentration of land ownership in the hands of a tiny minority. Coffee has remained the country's leading export throughout the twentieth century, but by 1970 cotton and sugar accounted for close to thirty percent of total extra-regional exports.[9] Cotton and beef cattle production was concentrated in the Pacific lowlands, which had become the last refuge for peasants displaced by coffee production in the highlands. Some peasants squatted on hacienda lands while others

worked as *colonos* (sharecroppers). With the expansion of cotton production, however, sharecropping decreased, as landowners rented to the
new class of cotton entrepreneurs. Consequently, a growing number of
peasants no longer had access to land.[10] These crops "generated neither a
permanent nor a seasonal labor demand sufficient to provide the peasant
economy with some form of generalized balance for the loss of land," as
James Dunkerley notes. In response, many peasants chose to migrate to
urban areas or to cross into Honduras in search of land.[11] On the eve of
the Soccer War in 1969, some 300,000 Salvadorans had migrated to
Honduras. The expulsion of 130,000 Salvadorans by the Honduran government in the aftermath of the war only added to the building land
pressures. Between 1961 and 1975, the landless population grew from
11.8 to 40.9 percent of rural families.[12] Salvadoran government and economic elites, with support from the United States and the Central
American Common Market, began industrialization during the 1960s
and 1970s, but this process failed to provide sufficient work for the growing influx of migrants to urban areas. Much of the finance for new industries came from abroad and was biased toward capital-intensive
maquila-type industries, which created a relatively small number of
jobs.[13]

The economic crises of the 1960s and 1970s deepened the chronic
poverty of the majority, making income distribution even less equal and
leaving ninety percent of rural households without the minimum
income necessary for basic nutrition. Increased concentration of land
and wealth, combined with a birth rate of three percent a year, intensified "land hunger."[14] While large coffee and cattle estates made comfortable profits, many small farmers faced starvation, bankruptcy, or
emigration to cities or Honduras. By the late 1960s, some elites feared
that another uprising would erupt if government policies did not address
the desperate poverty of the majority. Supported by the U.S. government through the Alliance for Progress, the Salvadoran government
proposed small-scale agrarian reforms to appease the growing landless
and near landless population. The Salvadoran oligarchy (widely known
as the "fourteen families," although it, in fact, includes some 200 families) opposed all types of land reform, however, and very little land actually reached small farmers.

In the midst of economic crisis, the 1972 presidential election
became a turning point in popular opposition to the regime. An opposition coalition, the National Opposition Union (UNO), ran José

Napoleón Duarte, a Christian Democrat and formerly a popular mayor of San Salvador, for president against Arturo Molina of the Party of National Conciliation (PCN). When vote totals were doctored to achieve a PCN victory, the UNO called a general strike, which led to an attempted coup, arrests and killings of many opposition leaders, and the closing of the national University of El Salvador (UES). Although repression scattered the opposition and Molina was inaugurated, a new cycle of protest and repression began. The pattern recurred in 1977, when a blatantly doctored vote count showed PCN candidate General Carlos Humberto Romero beating the UNO candidate by a three-to-one margin. Again protest followed fraud, only to be met with repression. For many opposition activists, the 1972 and 1977 elections marked "the end of electoral approaches to change in our country."[15]

Hope for another route to change flared briefly October 15, 1979, when young army officers promising reforms and an end to repression overthrew General Romero. A number of respected liberal intellectuals, including members of the left wing of the Christian Democrat Party, participated in the new government. Opposition leaders withheld judgment in the junta's early days, viewing the coup as the last chance for peaceful change. This hope died, however, as attacks on popular organizations increased. The new levels of violence prompted Minister of Education Salvador Samayoa and four other government officials to resign December 29, 1979. Samayoa's announcement shortly thereafter that he had joined a guerrilla group seemed to symbolize liberal disillusionment with the possibility of peaceful change.

Resignations of other Christian Democrats followed, and by mid-1980, with few civilians left in the government, military leaders desperately sought a way to regain credibility. They found it in José Napoleón Duarte, who still wanted the presidency that had been stolen from him in 1972 and who, perhaps, believed he would wield real power over the military officers in the ruling junta. Duarte was inaugurated November 21, 1980, as the first civilian (although still not elected) president of El Salvador since the 1931 coup. The kidnapping and murder of five prominent opposition leaders less than a week after Duarte's inauguration suggested, however, that the military would continue to pursue its own solutions to the country's political crisis.

While the machinery of central government remained out of reach of the opposition, political organizing intensified at the grassroots. Spurred by continued corruption and economic injustices and, in some cases, inspired by movements in Cuba, Chile, and elsewhere in Latin America, a number of militant popular organizations emerged during the late 1960s and early 1970s to challenge the traditional division of power and resources. In parts of the countryside, peasants organized to demand fairer wages, land distribution, and living conditions. Both the main peasant groups, FECCAS (the Christian Peasants' Federation) and the UTC (Union of Farmworkers), were led by active Catholics. In many, probably most, cases, the leaders as well as the rank-and-file activists of peasant federations first developed leadership and organizational skills, as well as their ideas about social justice and the value of collective action, in base Christian communities, *cursillos*, *encuentros*, and other Catholic educational and pastoral programs.

In rural areas in particular, such projects provided the only sites where poor people could get to know each other, discover and discuss common grievances and goals, and arrive at plans for action to address their concerns. Thus, from the early 1970s on, especially in the archdiocese of San Salvador (including Chalatenango province), in the "paracentral" region (mainly San Vicente province), and in the coastal and eastern parts of the country (especially Usulután, Cabañas, and Morazán provinces), progressive Catholic projects were the primary gathering site and source of both material and ideological resources for the growing political opposition.[16]

The relation of Catholic projects and opposition politics proved problematic for church leaders and pastoral agents in many areas. In some cases, priests and nuns actively encouraged their parishioners to participate in peasant federations or other opposition organizations. In Suchitoto, for example, parish priest José Inocencio Alas was instrumental in the 1974 formation of FAPU (Front of Unified Popular Action), a left-leaning coalition of opposition groups. In Aguilares, where a team of Jesuits coordinated pastoral work, many laypeople developed close links to peasant organizations in the area. In other cases, however, pastoral workers were ambivalent, frightened, or even hostile toward the involvement of lay Catholics in social movements. Belgian priest Rogelio Ponceele, who worked in the Zacamil neighborhood of San Salvador, recalls that he and his fellow pastoral agents felt great hesitation when some of their parishioners first moved towards opposition political groups.[17]

The intense mobilization in the mid-1970s created ambivalence and divisions among different church sectors, as in the general population.

During this period, a core of Catholic activists emerged, mostly laypeople but some nuns and priests, committed to popular political organizations, such as FAPU and FECCAS. Around this core were many other
Catholics who felt varying degrees of sympathy for popular movements.
The repression of the late 1980s drove many in this group to move
closer to the political left, while others fled the country or sought, not
always successfully, to maintain a "neutral" stance in the face of intense
polarization.

Within a few years, the two main peasant groups, the UTC and
FECCAS, united; in 1975 this coalition (renamed the FTC, or
Federation of Farmworkers) joined other popular organizations to form
the Popular Revolutionary Bloc (BPR). The BPR and similar groups,
such as FAPU, hoped to forge a common agenda and strengthen the
opposition's bargaining position vis-à-vis the government. A number of
BPR leaders, again, emerged from grassroots Catholic projects in rural
areas, including Juan Chacón, son of the murdered peasant leader and
catechist Felipe de Jesús Chacón.

By the late 1970s, leaders of the BPR, FAPU, and other popular
organizations became convinced of the need for an umbrella organization with a clearly revolutionary political platform to push for major
political changes. In January 1980, these organizations joined forces as
the Revolutionary Coordinator of the Masses (CRM). Four months
later, the CRM, joined by most remaining opposition groups and former
Christian Democrat leaders Guillermo Ungo, Román Mayorga, and
Rubén Zamora, became the Democratic Revolutionary Front (FDR).
The formation of the FDR, which established a broad popular front
bringing diverse constituencies together around a revolutionary political
agenda, marked a crucial step for the popular opposition movement. The
FDR suffered a great political and moral setback on November 27, 1980,
when its president, Enrique Alvárez, and four other leaders, including
Juan Chacón, were kidnapped from the Jesuit high school in San
Salvador and found murdered a few days later.

The FDR leaders, like most opposition activists killed in the late
1970s and early 1980s, were victims of "death squads" (escuadrones de la
muerte), heavily armed groups that usually consisted of soldiers, police,
and/or National Guardsmen in civilian clothes, along with some civilians. Some death squads included members of ORDEN, a paramilitary
group founded by National Guard leaders in the late 1960s to organize
peasants into anticommunist brigades. One of the best-known death

squads was the White Warriors' Union (Unión Guerrera Blanca, or UGB), whose custom of leaving a white handprint on the door of its victims gave the group its nickname the "white hand" (*mano blanca*). Another death squad took the name of General Maximiliano Hernández Martínez, a hero to the right for his role in the 1932 massacre. Death squads typically kidnapped their victims from their homes, cars, or workplaces; tortured and killed them; and then left the corpses at "body dumps," such as the famous Puerta del Diablo east of San Salvador, or locations chosen to instill fear (for example, in front of a church deemed too sympathetic to the left). While many victims were labor leaders or peasant activists, a large number were apolitical, killed for a family connection to activists or merely because they happened to be in a particular neighborhood when the squads were looking for victims. Residents of the San Pablo parish in San Salvador often recall, for example, the killings of a young couple, parents of twin infants, whom a death squad murdered even though the family had no ties to any political groups.

The randomness of many killings demonstrated that death squads did not exist simply to eliminate opposition to the government and oligarchy. While this was certainly one goal, achieved with chilling efficiency, the squads also sought to intimidate potential activists and to divide the opposition. Especially in poor areas, people never knew whether a neighbor, coworker, or even a relative might "point a finger" (*poner el dedo*), accusing them of "subversive" ideas or activities. Paramilitary activities helped create a "culture of fear," common to rightist regimes throughout Latin America, that kept a great deal of activism clandestine and unstable.

In the late 1970s and early 1980s political violence in El Salvador was characterized not only by the work of death squads and other killings that targeted individuals but also by massacres, primarily but not only in rural areas. In many cases, army units or paramilitary groups killed dozens or even hundreds of people at a time. Some of the best known of these include the December 1980 massacre at the village of El Mozote, where around a thousand civilians were murdered[18] and, especially during 1980 and 1981, numerous attacks on people trying to flee their villages in northern El Salvador, such as the massacres at the Rio Lempa and the Rio Sumpul.[19]

The severe repression of 1977–1981, which made open protest and participation in electoral politics impossible, encouraged the growth of armed revolutionary groups. The two largest opposition armies were the

Popular Forces of Liberation (FPL), formed in 1970 by dissident members of the Salvadoran Communist Party, and the Revolutionary Army of the People (ERP), formed in 1971. Between 1975 and 1980, three other guerrilla armies emerged: the Party of Revolutionary Central American Workers (PRTC), the Armed Forces of Liberation (FAL), which was linked to the Salvadoran Communist Party; and the National Resistance (RN), which was formed by ERP members alienated by the group's 1975 killing of one of its best-known members, poet Roque Dalton.

Most of the guerrilla groups advocated some sort of socialism, although their economic platforms ranged from the eclectic proposals of the FPL to the more Soviet-style approach of the Communist Party/FAL. The groups' strategies for guerrilla war also differed in significant ways, from advocacy of a prolonged, broadly based popular struggle to more "vanguardist" or "foquista" strategies, such as those developed by Fidel Castro and Ernesto "Che" Guevara in Cuba. Most of the political-military organizations had links to other Latin American leftist groups. After the 1979 Sandinista victory in Nicaragua, ties between Salvadoran revolutionary groups and the FSLN were especially important, and many Salvadoran organizations maintained offices in Managua.

One important feature of many Salvadoran revolutionaries, in common with the Sandinista leadership, was their sympathy or at least tolerance for Christian groups and activists. These alliances were manifested in a variety of ways, including the participation of many Catholic lay activists and some pastoral agents in mass organizations and even guerrilla groups as well as expressions of support for the left by religiously identified groups. In 1981, for example, a number of Christian organizations, including the Archdiocesan Caritas office, the Conference of Men and Women Religious of El Salvador, the Federation of Centers of Catholic Education, the Archdiocesan Pastoral Council, Fe y Alegría (a Catholic educational program), the church-based Foundation of Promoters of Cooperatives (FUNPROCOOP), Christian Life Communities, the Baptist Assembly, and the Christian Student Movement, issued a statement of support for the popular opposition movement.[20]

Most of the Christians who supported the political opposition were Catholic (as, of course, were the vast majority of Salvadorans), but a number of Protestant groups, including the Baptist Assembly previously mentioned and Salvadoran Lutherans and Episcopalians, also aided or participated in opposition movements or at least provided services to victims of government abuses. The participation of Christians in the revolutionary left in El Salvador, as in Nicaragua, marks a shift from the situation in Cuba, where the revolutionary leadership, influenced by orthodox Marxist-Leninist doctrine, generally viewed Christians as by definition counterrevolutionary. (This situation has changed somewhat in recent years, and Fidel Castro has expressed admiration for the Christian left in Central America and elsewhere.)

Throughout the 1970s, Salvadoran guerrilla groups were small, divided, and ineffectual, concentrating on small-scale sabotage and on fund-raising operations such as kidnappings and robberies. In the mid-1970s, some groups also suffered from factional conflicts that damaged their effectiveness and morale. These conflicts led to the emergence of the RN as a split-off from the ERP. By the late 1970s, however, the groups as a whole had developed significant political and military strength. In November 1980, the four largest armies formed the Farabundo Martí National Liberation Front (FMLN), named for the leader of the 1932 uprising. The fifth group joined in December 1980. By the early 1980s, the FMLN established a formal alliance with the FDR, and the groups became known as the FMLN-FDR. As the revolutionary opposition's political wing, the FDR established offices throughout the United States, western Europe, and Latin America and received formal recognition from the French and Mexican governments, demonstrating the Salvadoran left's desire and ability to build links with a wide range of governments and nongovernmental organizations. The U.S. government continued to consider the FMLN-FDR an illegitimate, "terrorist" organization with close links to revolutionary governments in Cuba and Nicaragua and with financial backing from the Soviet Union. This perception justified the provision of millions of dollars of U.S. military aid to the Salvadoran government throughout the 1980s, even in the face of widely documented human rights abuses, including the killings of U.S. citizens in El Salvador.

As the revolutionary opposition was consolidating its forces, the military and the right-wing intensified repression against popular political and religious movements. By March 1980, when Archbishop Romero was assassinated saying mass, death squads and the army murdered five to eight hundred people for political reasons each month. This repression, the militancy of the popular opposition, and the apparent absence of peaceful alternatives led the newly united guerrilla forces to launch a "final offensive" in January 1981 with the hope of sparking a general insurrection and achieving a definitive military victory. Although the offensive failed to bring the FMLN to power, it did mark the beginning of a permanent civil war, especially in the countryside. The civil war divided the country not only ideologically but also geographically, with three kinds of territory: government-dominated areas, mainly the large cities; conflicted areas, where the FMLN and government armies battled for control; and "liberated zones," areas of guerrilla control, comprising perhaps a quarter of the national territory, primarily in the northern mountains and along the coast in the departments of Morazán, Chalatenango, Cabañas, and Usulután.

Counter-Insurgency and Stalemate

By most measures, the Salvadoran government should have defeated the guerrillas shortly after the war began. The armed forces grew rapidly (peaking in 1990 at 56,000 men), and the Salvadoran government received over four billion dollars in U.S. aid between 1980 and 1990. With this aid and substantial U.S. training and "advice," the Salvadoran military unleashed a brutal counterinsurgency war, centering on the rural areas of greatest FMLN strength. Despite a return to formal civilian rule in 1984 with a presidential election won by Duarte, this time a candidate for the PDC, the government played a weak role during most of the 1980s, as the armed forces and their U.S. sponsors determined the course not only of the military war but of equally crucial political battles as well. (During the November 1989 FMLN offensive, for example, the U.S. embassy in San Salvador issued press releases for the Salvadoran government.) Repression against opposition leaders continued, and by the mid-1980s the popular movement had lost much of its original leadership to death squads or exile. While political murders never ended, in the mid- and late 1980s aerial bombs and mortar attacks replaced death squads as the leading killer of Salvadoran civilians, who always received more of the army's wrath than did the guerrillas.

Civilian support for the FMLN was concentrated in rural areas, especially in the northern departments of Chalatenango and Cabañas, San Vicente in the "para-central" region, Usulután on the coast, and Morazán in the east. The FMLN also had a strong base in the area around the Guazapa volcano in northern San Salvador province. Beginning in about 1980, these communities suffered from massacres, often in "hammer and anvil" operations where the army would trap the population between two military units, and also from massive bombings (including the use of white phosphorous and, some Salvadorans claim, napalm). These attacks killed tens of thousands of people and forced many peasants to flee their homes in rural war zones. Many stayed in villages, such as Arcatao in northern Chalatenango or Perquín in northern Morazán, which maintained a civilian population throughout the war despite bombings and the abandonment of most of the nearby villages. A large percentage of the population in the war zones, however, fled to refugee camps in El Salvador and Honduras or to exile in other countries in Latin America, the United States, Canada, Australia, or Europe.

By the late 1980s, many of the refugees living in camps inside El Salvador and in Honduras, as well as smaller numbers in Panama and Nicaragua, decided to return to the areas they had abandoned, even though the war continued. The refugees had educated and organized themselves in the camps and decided to return to the war zones as a collective project. Most of the mass returns were coordinated by the Christian Committee for Refugees and the Displaced (CRIPDES), an organization founded in the mid-1980s by laypeople living in a refugee camp in San Salvador. Beginning in 1986, thousands of refugees came on buses from camps in San Salvador and Honduras to "repopulate" abandoned villages, mainly in Chalatenango, Morazán, San Vicente, Cabañas, and Usulután provinces. Despite continual government harassment and military attacks, the repopulated villages provided models of autonomous, communitarian, and egalitarian political and economic development.[21] Many of the community leaders in the *repoblaciones* (repopulations) had participated in progressive Catholic pastoral and educational projects in the 1970s before leaving their homes.

Throughout the war, the army concentrated on civilian targets, mostly because the FMLN grew fairly quickly into a formidable adversary. The guerrillas probably never numbered more than 12,000 or 13,000 regular combatants, in addition to perhaps 40,000 militia members, part-time soldiers, mostly in rural areas, who joined in special actions and also defended communities against army attacks, especially in areas of FMLN control. A combination of civilian support, careful military strategizing, and government mistakes enabled the guerrillas to maintain a military stalemate against the government for more than a decade. The government forces suffered from extremely low morale in comparison to the guerrillas who, though not always well-armed or well-fed, were generally highly motivated. Most important, despite the exhaustion and fear felt by many in the opposition, the FMLN retained strong popular support, especially in rural areas and in poor urban neighborhoods. As an analyst for the Commission on U.S.–Latin American Relations wrote in April 1990, "Given the army's vast superiority in numbers and firepower, the FMLN could not survive—let alone operate as widely and freely as it does—without a substantial civilian base of support."[22]

The military and political stalemate broke on November 11, 1989, when the FMLN launched a nation-wide offensive, centered in San Salvador, that paralyzed the capital for weeks and led to near-insurrection in at least one provincial city. The November offensive demonstrated the FMLN's military expertise and strength. However, it also revealed the resolve of the government, led since June 1989 by the rightist ARENA party (Republican Nationalist Alliance), to crush the insurgency at all costs. To this end, the government ordered widespread aerial bombings of densely populated urban areas and the arrests of hundreds of opposition activists, and an army battalion assassinated six internationally prominent Jesuit intellectuals at the Central American University (UCA).

Most observers cite the 1989 offensive as the turning point that made successful peace negotiations possible after years of aborted efforts. The offensive demonstrated to the Salvadoran and U.S. governments the continuing strength and popular support of the FMLN. While the guerrillas could not win militarily, neither could the government army. The killings of the Jesuits also prompted international criticism of the Salvadoran government and army, which helped encourage the U.S. government, after years of unwavering support for the Salvadoran army's pursuit of military victory, finally to support serious negotiations. In April 1990, the United Nations entered the Salvadoran conflict to mediate peace talks between the FMLN and the ARENA government. After intense negotiations, an agreement was announced on New Year's Eve, 1991. Representatives of the FMLN and ARENA signed the accord in Mexico City on January 16, 1992, and February 1 marked the start of the formal pacification program, including a cease-fire, gradual demobilization of all guerrilla forces and half the government army, and the incorporation of the FMLN as a legal political party. The war formally came to an end in December 1992, when the last guerrillas and targeted government soldiers entered civilian life.

A Negotiated Peace?

This book finishes, in a sense, with the end of the severe repression that provoked popular religious interpretations of political violence during the 1970s and 1980s. Presently, religion continues to play a central social in Salvadoran society, helping to shape people's understandings of the post-ar processes of economic reconstruction, democratization, and reconciliation.[23] Religious institutions also remain active in the changing political configuration. Many Catholic and Protestant leaders (including Lutheran bishop Medardo Gómez, Baptist pastor Edgar Palacios, and Episcopalian priest Luis Serrano) actively participated in the mobilization of popular support for the negotiations, through the National Debate for Peace (Debate Nacional para la Paz) and other programs. The Catholic hierarchy initiated the National Debate in 1988 as a one-time event to bring together different civil sectors to discuss a negotiated settlement, but then withdrew when the group became a permanent organization.[24] Many individual Catholic pastoral agents and lay activists continued to participate, though. Lutheran leaders played prominent roles in the group, and Rev. Palacios served as the organization's president.

The peace settlement generated optimism, even euphoria, among the political opposition. On January 16, 1992, the day the accords were signed, the FMLN distributed flyers proclaiming "*ganamos la paz*" ("we won peace") and inviting supporters to celebrate their "victory" in San Salvador's central plaza. Since 1992, however, Salvadoran society has not been transformed as rapidly or dramatically as many political leaders and ordinary citizens hoped. The country continues to suffer from economic crisis and from violence, now in the form of crime (petty and organized). By the mid-1990s, "death squads" had re-emerged, this time focusing not on political activists but on suspected criminals, prostitutes, street children, beggars, and gang members.[25] Many Salvadorans in poor and working-class neighborhoods in San Salvador and smaller cities fear crime, and particularly its effects on youth. Gangs have grown rapidly in the country since the war's end, due to the lack of economic opportunity and also to the return of some young Salvadorans who grew up in Los Angeles and other U.S. cities where they came into contact with gangs. (A number of Catholic parishes have initiated sports programs and other projects designed to keep young people off the streets.) Thus, even though the war has ended, violence remains a fact of life for most Salvadorans, and many draw on religion in efforts to understand and cope with the new situation.

Endnotes

1. Figures come from the following sources: Robert Armstrong and Janet Shenk, *El Salvador: The Face of Revolution* (Boston: South End Press, 1982), 6–7; Maxwell S. Peltz, *El Salvador 1990: An Issues Brief* (Washington, DC: Commission on U.S.–Latin American Relations, 1990), 53–55; Americas Watch, *El Salvador's Decade of Terror: Human Rights Since the Assassination of Archbishop Romero* (New Haven: Yale University Press, 1991), 1; Interamerican Development Bank, *Economic and Social Progress in Latin America, 1991 Report: Special Section—Social Security* (Washington, DC: Interamerican Development Bank, 1991), 15; and CENITEC, "La erradicación de la pobreza en El Salvador," *Política Económica* I, no. 4 (December 1990–January 1991).

2. See William Fowler, *The Cultural Evolution of Ancient Nahua Civilizations: The Pipil-Nicarao of Central America* (Norman and London: University of Oklahoma Press, 1989). On sacrifice in Mexica culture, see Burr Cartwright Brundage, *The Fifth Sun: Aztec Gods, Aztec World* (Austin: University of Texas Press, 1979), pp. 195–219.

3. Alistair White, *El Salvador*, 3d ed. (San Salvador: UCA Editores, 1987), 27, 44–45.

4. Rodolfo Cardenal, *El poder eclesiástico en El Salvador: 1871–1931* (San Salvador: UCA Editores, 1980), 23. See also David Browning, *El Salvador: Landscape and Society* (Oxford: Oxford University Press, 1971); and Enrique Baloyra, *El Salvador in Transition* (Chapel Hill: University of North Carolina Press, 1982), 5.

5. Thomas Anderson, *El Salvador 1932*, 2d ed. (San José, Costa Rica: Editorial Universitaria Centroamericana, 1982), 202. See also Baloyra, *El Salvador*, 8–14, on the events and causes of the crisis of 1931–1932.

6. Anderson, *El Salvador 1932*, 200–201.

7. Roque Dalton, *Miguel Mármol*, trans. Kathleen Ross and Richard Schaaf, with an introduction by Manlio Argueta and a preface by Margaret Randall (Willimantic, Conn: Curbstone Press, 1987), 304–305.

8. See Baloyra, *El Salvador*, 15–17.

9. Victor Bulmer-Thomas, *The Political Economy of Central America since 1920* (Cambridge: Cambridge University Press, 1987), 188.

10. Robert Williams, *Export Agriculture and the Crisis in Central America* (Chapel Hill: University of North Carolina Press, 1986), 52–73.

11. James Dunkerley, *Power in the Isthmus* (London: Verso, 1988), 192.

12. Charles Brockett, *Land, Power and Poverty* (Boulder, CO: Westview Pres, 1990), 75.

13. Bulmer-Thomas, *The Political Economy*, 192–199.

14. Jenny Pearce, *Promised Land: Peasant Rebellion in Chalatenango, El Salvador* (London: Latin American Bureau, 1986), 42; Armstrong and Shenk, *El Salvador*, 48.

15. Salvador Sanabria, Democratic Revolutionary Front, lecture, University of California at Berkeley, 20 September 1990. See also Ignacio Martín-Baró, "The Church and Revolution in El Salvador" (keynote speech presented to the Midwest Association for Latin American Studies, University of Missouri, Columbia, 20 September 1985), 13.

16. See Phillip Berryman, "El Salvador: From Evangelization to Insurrection," in *Religion and Social Conflict in Latin America*, ed. Daniel Levine (Chapel Hill: University of North Carolina Press, 1986); Jorge Cáceres Prendes, "Political Radicalization and Popular Pastoral Practices in El Salvador, 1969–1985," in *The Progressive Church in Latin America*, eds. S. Mainwaring and A. Wilde (Notre Dame: University of Notre Dame Press, 1989); Tommie Sue Montgomery, "Christianity as a Subversive Activity in Central America," in *Trouble in Our Backyard*, ed. Martin Diskin (New York: Pantheon, 1984); and T. S. Montgomery, *El Salvador in Revolution*, rev. 2d ed. (Boulder, CO: Westview Press, 1995).

17. María López Vigil, *Muerte y vida en Morazán* (San Salvador: UCA Editores, 1987).

18. See Mark Danner, "The Truth of El Mozote," *The New Yorker* (6 December 1993), 50–133.

19. See Joe Fish and Cristina Sganga, *El Salvador: Testament of Terror* (New York: Olive Branch Press, 1988) and Jack Nelson-Pallmeyer, *War Against the Poor: Low Intensity Conflict and Christian Faith* (Maryknoll, NY: Orbis Books, 1989).

20. "The Sign of Resurrection in El Salvador: A Testimony from Christians who Accompany the People in their Struggle," in *Trouble in Our Backyard*, ed. Martin Diskin (New York, Pantheon Books, 1984), 207.

21. On the repopulations, see Berkeley Sister City Project, *History of San Antonio Los Ranchos* (Berkeley: BSCP, 1990); Beth Cagan and Steve Cagan, *This Promised Land, El Salvador: The Refugee Community of Colomoncagua and Their Return to Morazán* (Rutgers, NJ: Rutgers University Press, 1991); Beatrice Edwards and Gretta Tovar Siebentritt, *Places of Origin: The Repopulation of Rural*

El Salvador (Boulder, CO: Lynne Rienner Publishers, 1991); and Mandy Macdonald and Mike Gatehouse, *In the Mountains of Morazán: Portrait of a Returned Refugee Community in El Salvador* (London: Latin American Bureau, 1995).

22. Peltz, *El Salvador 1990*, 36.

23. See Kathleen Blee, "The Catholic Church and Central American Politics," in *Understanding the Central American Crisis: Sources of Conflict, U.S. Policy, and Options for Peace*, ed. by Kenneth M. Coleman and George C. Herring (Wilmington, DE: Scholarly Resources, 1991) and Guillermo Meléndez, "The Catholic Church in Central America: Into the 1990s," *Social Compass 39*, no. 4 (1992): 553–570.

24. For a thorough discussion of the National Debate, see CAICA, *La iglesia en Centroamérica: Guatemala, El Salvador, Honduras y Nicaragua: Información y análisis* (Mexico City: Centro de Estudios Ecuménicos, 1989), 111–121.

25. See Terry Tracy, "Death Squads Reemerge in El Salvador," *NACLA Report on the Americas XXIX*, no. 3 (Nov./Dec. 1995): 2.

3

Progressive Catholicism in El Salvador

Progressive Catholicism in El Salvador was shaped by a unique conjunction of resources and limitations. Religiously, both the long history of Latin American Catholicism and the more recent innovations of Vatican II and Medellín defined the theological, pastoral, and ecclesiastical boundaries within which Salvadoran Catholics could maneuver. Economically and politically, extreme inequality and violent repression marked the stage on which most Salvadorans, particularly the poor and working classes, could act. Within these constraints, ordinary Salvadorans worked, with creativity and resilience, both to make sense of their lives and, insofar as they could, to make those lives better.

This chapter offers a history and portrait of the popular or progressive church in El Salvador as the context for popular ideas about martyrdom and persecution. I begin with an overview of the evolution of Catholicism in Latin America and then provide some background on Salvadoran religious history. I then describe the Salvadoran *iglesia popular*, the immediate setting for the interpretations of martyrdom that will concern the remainder of this book.

I. The Catholic Church

The Catholic Church's links to the dominant elite in Latin America began in the earliest period of Spain's conquest and settlement of the Americas. While a few clerics, such as bishops Bartolomé de las Casas and Antonio Valdivieso, defended the rights of indigenous people, overall the church shared wealth, power, and prestige with the ruling military and political elites and in a variety of ways buttressed the order that maintained their privileged position. The church also played an ideological role in justifying the conquest and the creation of a political economy based on "the forced expropriation of the best lands and the forced conscription of labor to produce export crops for small local elites."[1] The church's legitimation of the conquest and subsequent Spanish domination relied upon its claim that the unequal political and economic order on earth was divinely ordained and could not be changed by human effort and that earthly problems mattered less than the hope of a better lot in heaven. Ecclesial structure in this period corresponded with and upheld the passivity that this theology encouraged. The priest read the scripture in Latin, with his back to the congregation, and few laypeople participated in official church affairs beyond occasional attendance at mass. Organizationally as well as ideologically, the Latin American Catholic Church taught the poor "to accept the conditions of life that [they] had," i.e., political marginalization and economic inequity.[2]

While the institutional church taught passivity and punished unorthodox or rebellious behavior, however, popular religion encompassed a wide range of groups, ideas, and practices, many of which challenged the colonial order directly or indirectly. In a variety of ways, religion, both syncretic Catholicism and surviving indigenous traditions, provided ordinary people with resources for cultural identity, community solidarity, and ideological and practical resistance to Spanish rule. In rural communities, which usually had little contact with priests or bishops, lay-led brotherhoods (*cofradías*) often dominated religious life. The *cofradías* and other popular religious groups continued to tie religion, including Catholicism, to pre-Hispanic forms of community and cultural identity.

After independence from Spain in 1821, when liberal and secularizing sectors rose to power, the Salvadoran church faced substantial anti-clerical sentiment. In general, however, church leaders retained close ties to the government and oligarchy. By the 1920s, the bishops' fear of socialism supplied another motivation for it to support the status quo. In return for providing doctrinal arguments against new ideologies, the church received freedom to preach and evangelize, government officials attended ecclesial functions, and the state continued to offer favors to church administrators.

While the church hierarchy sought to maintain its privileged position vis-à-vis the liberal state, its relations with the grassroots became increasingly problematic. The link between the hierarchy and local communities had been at best tenuous throughout most of the church's history in El Salvador. The religious orders that had taken charge of different parishes yielded control of most localities to diocesan clergy in the seventeenth century, but the division between local political-religious organization and the official church grew over time. Most bishops visited each parish in their dioceses at best once every five years, many parishes lacked a regular priest, and priests often did not take an active part in community life.[3] Independent lay organizations emerged to fill the pastoral void, and by the late eighteenth century, many local parishes had achieved almost total autonomy from the church hierarchy.

Popular Catholicism

As many scholars have emphasized, popular Catholicism in Latin America has been alienating in many ways, for example, through its insistence on obedience to authority and on resignation to bodily suffering. However, it has also served as a resource for the collective identity and resistance of marginalized groups, especially indigenous people and peasants. Despite often violent methods of conversion, indigenous and mestizo Catholics in El Salvador, and throughout Latin America, managed to create a religion that differed in crucial ways from the Iberian Catholicism of the missionaries and settlers. In many cases, native people renamed and reconceptualized their own deities, holy places, and ceremonies to fit into the new Euro-Christian pantheon.[4] Much of the "folk" Catholicism that emerged from the meeting of Spanish and Amerindian traditions reflected efforts to understand earthly unhappiness and injustice and to find release. While this often resulted in a fatalistic acceptance of the status quo, some indigenous, mestizo, and African communities in the Americas nurtured religious beliefs and practices that questioned European dominance, sometimes even through apparently nonthreatening images like the Virgin or the crucified Christ.

In his account of religion's role in the Nicaraguan revolution, Roger Lancaster contends that the traditional religiosity of the poor in Latin America "promotes an ethical or ideological subsystem that roughly, if unselfconsciously, corresponds to the social interests of the popular classes, and which already suggests a possibility and a direction of departure from the religion of the elites."[5] The seeds of class consciousness, in other words, lurk even in traditional beliefs and practices. Lancaster argues that despite images of passivity, subjugated people will always resist domination, as best they can, and that religion often offers tools for this resistance. In Latin America, continued adherence to indigenous traditions and reformulations of Christian images, especially of Mary and

Jesus, provided resources for indigenous and mestizo resistance to domination by elites.

Religion helped poor and indigenous Latin Americans maintain autonomy in practical, as well as ideological, ways. In many parts of Latin America, especially rural areas, parishes retained a great deal of independence from the central church authorities. *Cofradías* organized most rituals, coordinated many social projects, and might even decide whether a certain priest came to or stayed in the community. Through the *cofradía* system (also known as the *cargo* system, for the hierarchy of ranked offices within the brotherhoods), many indigenous and mestizo communities in Mesoamerica maintained local autonomy as well as distinctive religious beliefs and practices that drew from both pre-Hispanic and Catholic traditions. The *cofradías* also often owned substantial amounts of communal livestock and property, frequently including church buildings, and wielded great influence on political and economic, as well as religious, events.

This was true in nineteenth and twentieth century El Salvador, where "parish life turned in large measure around the political-religious system known as *cofradías*."[6] Salvadoran *cofradías* were hierarchically ordered, male-dominated groups, usually dedicated to a patron saint or virgin, which performed a variety of social and religious tasks throughout the year. Popular religion, organized through *cofradías*, focused on miracles, processions, devotion to Mary, and the celebration of local patron saints. The emotional and ritual aspects took center stage, and piety looked primarily "towards Jesus patiently carrying the cross or dead or suffering the pains and humiliations of the passion, towards the Virgin Mary and some popular saints," according to Cardenal.[7] While this emphasis on resignation and suffering was common, popular practices also included elements, such as rituals of status inversion and levelling, which expressed criticisms of the established order and its rulers.

The often problematic relations between the *cofradías* and the church leadership reflect the general tensions between popular and official Catholicism throughout the colonial and postcolonial period. The conflicts frequently centered less on the unorthodoxy of some popular practices, although those were of concern, than on the autonomy of the brotherhoods and local communities and their frequently anticlerical attitudes. Many *cofradías*, for example, refused to allow local priests or bishops to interfere in their internal affairs. Bishops and priests thus sought increasingly to direct the groups' religious practices, political organization, and property. Efforts in the late 1800s by the Archbishop of San Salvador to gain control of the groups' finances and property met with fierce resistance from both the *cofradías* and local political bodies (municipalities).

During this period, social and economic transformations produced by the rise of coffee intensified conflicts between the church hierarchy and local groups. Political reforms in the late 1800s concentrated land in the hands of wealthy coffee-growers and destroyed the power of local communities. Although local municipalities protested, they failed to stop the transition from small farms to large plantations or the expropriation of most *cofradía* (and other communal) property. The church hierarchy did not oppose the dissolution of villages and communal land, partly because it viewed these changes as a way to end the *cofradías* and thus the problem of local autonomy. The new economic order dealt a devastating and eventually mortal blow to the *cofradías*. Without close-knit villages and communally held property as a base, the *cofradías* lost most of their power. They persisted in many rural and semirural areas, partly as resistance to the perceived aggression of the central church, but without much vitality or strength and generally with ritual responsibilities centered in individuals or families rather than the community as a whole.[8]

After the virtual disappearance of the *cofradías* early in the 1900s, the hierarchy attempted to give popular religiosity a more centralized and clerical form. Generally, however, it had little success in this effort. Personal and local saints remained the focus of piety, and overall church participation gradually declined, especially among adult men. Thus, even though *cofradías* had lost power, "popular religion retained its autonomy and local character" and did not come under the control of the official church.[9]

During the battles with the *cofradías*, the church hierarchy retained its close links to economic and political elites. Church officials rarely took strong positions on social issues, and on the most intensely contested issue, changes in land ownership, they supported the oligarchy, the conservative party, and the government. Even international Catholicism's new interest in social and economic problems, outlined in *Rerum Novarum* (1891) and in several papal encyclicals in the first half of the 1900s, did not lead the Salvadoran hierarchy to address political and economic issues. "Instead of committing itself to the transformation of the established order," according to Cardenal, "the ecclesial organization chose to exalt the message of the cross, understood as acceptance of suffering and a wait for celestial justice."[10] The official church continued, in short, both to ally itself with political and economic elites and to offer theological justifications for continued dominance by this elite and obedience by the poor majority.

While they did not espouse the explicitly oppositional politics of many contemporary *comunidades de base, cofradías* did exercise many of the same religious and social functions. Thus, the transition from traditional "popular religion" to the new "popular church," in Lancaster's terms, was probably not as abrupt as some observers suggest. New pastoral models in the 1960s and 1970s invented neither local lay control over pastoral activities nor the religious expression of economic interests and social resentments, although they often made this institutional independence and class consciousness more explicit than had earlier religious communities.

II. Reforms in Latin American and Salvadoran Catholicism

Beginning in the early 1960s, a combination of intra- and extra-ecclesial pressures pushed the Catholic Church to question its role as a pillar of the status quo. The Second Vatican Council, held from 1962 to 1965, provided the most important impetus for change within the church. The Council's final document, *Gaudium et Spes* (Pastoral Constitution on the Church in the Modern World), affirmed that the church has a responsibility to act in the world on behalf of the poor and weak; that the right "to have a share of earthly goods sufficient for oneself and one's family"[11] takes precedence over the right of the wealthy to accumulate private property; and that poor individuals and poor nations have the right to political equality. *Gaudium et Spes* addressed itself in particular to the church in the developing world and spurred laypeople and clergy in Latin America to seek ecclesial forms that could embody the church's concern for social justice.

Following Rome's lead, the Latin American Bishops' Conference (CELAM) met in 1968 in Medellín, Colombia to examine Latin American reality "in the light of the Council." The Medellín meeting proved a watershed for the Latin American church, opening a new era in both ecclesial structure and the church's social role. The conference encouraged the newly developing *comunidades eclesiales de base* (base or grassroots Christian communities, or CEBs) as "the first and fundamental ecclesiastical nucleus."[12] CEBs helped make the Bible more accessible, especially in rural areas, and encouraged both individual reflection and group discussion. By educating and empowering people at the grassroots level, base communities also encouraged local autonomy, democratization, and economic development.

Another significant outcome of the Medellín conference was the bishops' condemnation of the "institutionalized violence" of poverty. They defined sin as a social phenomenon, embedded in political and economic structures, and concluded that in Latin America, only a transformation of these structures could achieve the social justice demanded by the Bible and the Catholic tradition. The bishops also acknowledged the Catholic Church's culpability in supporting unjust social structures in the past and affirmed the church's present responsibility to work for socioeconomic justice.

Beginning in the late 1960s, the "theology of liberation" elaborated in Latin America further propelled the shifts taking place within Latin American Catholicism at the official level. In 1979, CELAM's conference in Puebla, Mexico reaffirmed the church's responsibility to the oppressed, which it described as a "preferential option for the poor."[13] Thus, during the 1960s and 1970s, a significant portion, although by no means all, of the institutional church in Latin America came not only to address the concerns of the poor majority in Latin America but even to ally itself with them. For pastoral workers in El Salvador, recalls Daniel Vega, a diocesan priest from San Salvador, the conclusions of Medellín, Puebla, and liberation theology made the principles of Vatican II directly applicable to "our reality, not a universal reality, but Latin American reality."

The Catholic Church in El Salvador had begun changing in the late 1950s, with moderate reform projects sponsored by Archbishop Luis Chávez y González (who served from 1939 to 1977). In 1958, Chávez founded the Diocesan Social Secretariat, which coordinated and promoted assistance programs and self-help projects in parishes in the archdiocese of San Salvador. He also encouraged priests in La Libertad province to organize agricultural cooperatives in the 1950s. Because of Archbishop Chávez's efforts, the reforms of the Second Vatican Council encountered ground in El Salvador "already fertilized to receive the idea that faith could call for social and even political action, and that this action could be in opposition to the established order."[14] After the council, Chávez encouraged the reading of its documents and issued pastoral letters focusing on issues in the archdiocese of San Salvador.

The archbishop's support made it easier to apply the principles of Vatican II, and after 1968 those of Medellín, to the archdiocese and motivated young priests and nuns to implement new pastoral methods and address social issues. "The documents [of Vatican II and Medellín] were like the air that we breathed at this time," recalls Daniel Vega. In 1970, about forty priests formed the Grupo de Reflexión Pastoral (Pastoral Reflection Group) to discuss their work "within the historical movement forward of the poor in our country," according to a member of the group.[15]

The "National Pastoral Week" (Semana Nacional de Pastoral de Conjunto) in July 1970 strengthened progressive changes within the church on a national level. Archbishop Chávez, his auxiliary bishops Arturo Rivera y Damas and Oscar Romero, and 123 priests, religious, and laity met for a week to discuss pastoral methods and directions in the archdiocese of San Salvador and in other regions of the country. Because of the hostility of bishops outside San Salvador, a second pastoral week, held in January 1976, was limited to clergy of the archdiocese. At both gatherings, participants criticized the church's traditional work and called for the growth of CEBs, the democratization of church structures, an increase in lay participation and leadership, and the development of a "critical and liberating evangelization" and also concrete projects to combat "social sin."[16] Despite conservative opposition, the pastoral weeks encouraged pastoral innovations throughout the country and especially in the archdiocese of San Salvador.

Comunidades Eclesiales de Base

In El Salvador and throughout Latin America, one of the most important new developments was the formation of grassroots Christian communities in rural and urban areas. CEBs usually began at the initiative of a priest or nun, generally supported by the larger institutional church, who envisioned a religious community emphasizing lay leadership, member participation, and community involvement guided by a commitment to the poor. Typically, the pastoral worker started by visiting and getting to know local residents. After this acquaintance period, members (usually from twelve to thirty per community) undertook a series of courses (*cursillos*) that usually last several months. In rural areas, where many parishes lacked permanent priests, *cursillos* were often offered not by local pastoral agents but by centers serving regions as large as an entire diocese. Laypeople trained in these courses would then return to their own villages, to serve as catechists or as lay preachers (known as "delegates of the word," *delegados de la palabra*) to help form base communities.

In the courses, members would relate the Bible to current events or local concerns, thus developing a critical understanding of their faith and their social reality. After the *cursillos*, leaders and participants would often come together in a retreat, or *encuentro*, where participants would reflect upon the *cursillos*, solidify their bonds with each other, and reaffirm their commitment to energetic involvement in church programs.

Cursillos and *encuentros* provided training for the defining activity of CEBs: *reflexión*, or group Bible study and discussion. Drawing from the "see-judge-act" methodology of Catholic Action developed in Europe in the 1950s and the pedagogy of Brazilian educator Paulo Freire,[17] *reflexión* stressed a critical approach towards the established order, grounded in biblical stories that speak to CEB members' own experiences as an oppressed group. In Central America, for example, CEB members often read Exodus as a paradigm for all people struggling to free themselves from unjust rulers and the Gospels as the story of a poor man who fought for the poor and suffered the same type of persecution as people who denounce injustice today. Participants in this type of *reflexión* often concluded that Christians must follow Jesus' model, working to liberate the poor from an unjust human system.[18]

The awakening of this critical attitude, legitimized by denunciations of injustice in the Hebrew prophets and elsewhere in the Bible, constituted the first and perhaps most important contribution of CEBs to political protest. When poor people concluded that socioeconomic inequities resulted from human actions and not divine will, political and economic leaders could no longer appeal to God as the ultimate guarantee of their authority. As a Salvadoran priest explains, *reflexión* generated an ideological "un-blockade" (*desbloqueo*), which in turn motivated increasingly stronger challenges to the status quo.[19]

In addition to providing a context for Bible discussion, CEBs offered a communitarian, participatory group very different from hierarchical models of organization that prevailed, politically and religiously, in much of Latin America. In certain cases, including many parts of El Salvador, participation in CEBs contributed to political mobilization in at least three ways. First, democratization in the local religious community called into question "institutional structures and existing systems of authority,"[20] often leading to demands for greater democracy and accountability in larger religious and political institutions. The fact that efforts to democratize the church itself often failed, due to opposition from the hierarchy, probably encouraged Catholic activists to turn their attention to secular politics. Second, CEBs often helped people develop leadership and organizing skills that later provided the foundation for political organizing, especially in rural areas. Participation in CEBs taught many people to speak in public, to reach consensus, to act as a group, to share responsibilities, and to practice democratic methods of organization and decision-making—skills that proved invaluable in the formation of peasant and neighborhood associations. Third, base communities strengthened collective identity by bringing together people who might have hesitated to gather for explicitly political purposes. Based on biblical calls to unity and on a postconciliar view of the church as the "people of God," CEBs encouraged group cohesion on a familial and local level, often providing a foundation for more political forms of solidarity later on. In strengthening matrimonial and family ties, asserts a priest who worked with Salvadoran CEBs in the 1970s, "the communities began to develop fidelity to the Salvadoran people."[21]

Especially in Central America, CEB members often expanded their social commitment beyond spiritual and family concerns to larger-scale tasks, such as community building projects, literacy classes, and the formation of cooperatives or savings and loans. Later, some members moved to more clearly political issues, starting with cost-of-living and neighborhood problems and sometimes arriving at conflicts over the nation's economic structure and political system or sympathy with revolutionary political groups.

The concrete actions carried out by base community members usually emerged from a general awareness and commitment rather than a specific political agenda. As Pablo Jiménez, a European priest working in El Salvador, notes, social projects "aren't born because we say we want cooperatives, but because the conscientización and the evangelization carry this message." He continues:

> The CEB doesn't begin with a social project. The CEB begins with the good news of the poor. It's a project of faith . . . As Christians we reflect on this and out of this root are born things like the cooperatives. We see the need for things and we do them.

In many parts of Latin America, *comunidades de base* have provided forums to bring people together, to develop social criticism and grass-roots leadership, and to practice participatory democracy. They can serve, in the words of the priest who initiated the first CEBs in Nicaragua, as a "trampoline" for political practice, "an alternative of organization and of struggle, from which the people [become] conscious and [organize] themselves."[22] Summarizing the political role of base communities in Nicaragua, Michael Dodson and Laura Nuzzi O'Shaughnessy offer a conclusion that applies to El Salvador as well:

> The CEBs helped to fill the political void in *campesino* life by providing space for group organizing and by justifying the struggle for justice. Even though their primary aims had been spiritual, because of their prophetic orientation the CEBs became identified with the interests of the poorest classes.[23]

In the context of political closure, this prophetic message made CEBs in El Salvador, as in Nicaragua, important players in the political conflicts of the 1970s.

CEBs in El Salvador

Most observers identify the first base communities in El Salvador as those in Suchitoto, where Father José Inocencio Alas, a diocesan priest from San Salvador, initiated courses for Delegates of the Word in April 1969. Many priests working in El Salvador visited Alas's parish and replicated his efforts in their own. Other Salvadoran base communities had roots in the neighborhood of San Miguelito in Panama City, where Leo Mahon, a North American priest, began in 1963 to build a new kind of Christian community, a small group that would meet regularly to discuss everyday issues in the light of faith. Mahon developed a series of courses called "the family of God," which included such topics as "the Christian ideal," "sin," "the prodigal son," "sex and marriage," and "the community."

In the mid- and late-1960s, a number of priests and laypeople from elsewhere in Latin America visited Panama to participate in the *cursillos* and learn about the kind of community forming in San Miguelito. Two of the visitors, Rogelio Ponceele and another priest, both from Brugge, Belgium, spent a month in San Miguelito in 1969 before moving to the

Zacamil neighborhood in northern San Salvador. Following Mahon's model, they began by visiting families house by house, inviting residents to meetings, and gradually forming a "Christian group" (the term *comunidad eclesial de base* was not yet used in Central America). From these initial groups in Zacamil and nearby *barrios* emerged other projects, including youth groups, literacy campaigns, and gardening cooperatives.[24]

These two, another Belgian priest, and a Belgian nun constituted one of the most influential pastoral teams in El Salvador. Known throughout the areas where they worked simply as "the Belgians" (*los belgas*), the pastoral agents helped develop CEBs in several working-class and poor neighborhoods on the northern edge of San Salvador. In the late 1970s, when repression made it impossible for them to continue working in the city, two of the priests and the nun left El Salvador, and Rogelio Ponceele went to FMLN zones of control in Morazán province. Even ten years after they left San Salvador, the Belgians' efforts mark the important northern *barrios*. These neighborhoods have been sites of political as well as religious organizing and were among the most active in San Salvador throughout the war and in the 1989 offensive.

In addition to the Belgians and other foreign pastoral agents, a number of other pastoral workers initiated base communities in El Salvador. Salvadoran diocesan priests played an especially important role. (Diocesan priests are those attached to a diocese and bishop rather than to a religious order.) Many young priests in the San Salvador archdiocese had studied liberation theology and new pastoral methods at the San José de la Montaña Seminary in San Salvador, run by the Jesuits. A number of priests also met regularly in the Pastoral Reflection Group to discuss local and international experiences, new theological trends, and the church's relations to political issues. Inspired by these experiences and by pastoral innovations elsewhere in Latin America, Salvadoran diocesan priests initiated a number of important grassroots pastoral projects of the late 1960s and 1970s, particularly in poor areas of San Salvador and the rural areas of Chalatenango and Suchitoto, where "Chencho" Alas's success in bringing peasants together generated considerable hostility among landowners. These rural projects represented a new direction for Salvadoran clergy, who, although often of peasant origin, traditionally lived in the capital city, creating an especially severe shortage of pastoral agents in rural areas.

Diocesan priests were joined by male and female religious, of whom three-quarters were foreign, in implementing pastoral innovations in poorer areas of the country. Among religious communities, the Society of Jesus (the Jesuits) has been the most influential single group, with nearly sixty men in El Salvador by the early 1970s. The Society worked primarily in education, although in 1972 a team of Jesuits began pastoral work in Aguilares, in what became one of El Salvador's most significant rural base community experiences.[25] In other regions, Jesuits and men from other orders, including the Franciscans and Maryknoll Fathers, also worked with CEBs.

A number of women's orders, including both Salvadoran and foreign sisters, helped initiate *comunidades de base* in different regions. The Sisters of Saint Claire ("Clarisas"), a British order, worked in Morazán province and the northern edge of San Salvador, two of the most "conflicted" areas of the country. Missionary sisters from the Maryknoll order and other congregations also worked in the capital and other parts of the country. A uniquely Salvadoran order, the *pequeña comunidad* (little community), began in November 1970 when three young Salvadoran women, aspirants in a more traditional order, left their convent to initiate a new kind of pastoral work, dedicated especially to the poor. Like members of traditional orders, the sisters of the *pequeña comunidad* live together and take vows of celibacy and poverty, but they do not wear habits or otherwise distinguish themselves very much from the laypeople with whom they work. *Las chicas*, the little ones, as they are called, have worked primarily in the northern parts of San Salvador and in rural zones of conflict or guerrilla control.

The CEBs where archdiocesan priests, the Belgians, the Jesuits, the Clarisas, and the *chicas* worked occupy center stage in the history of the "popular church" in El Salvador. These communities generally emerged in the early 1970s and thus had the luxury of developing gradually, before repression became severe. Members of older communities often demonstrate greater group unity, more sophisticated theological understanding, and a stronger social commitment than CEBs born after the intensification of repression and the war. These communities, like early CEBs in Nicaragua, wielded a political and religious influence belying their relatively small numbers.

Centros de Formación Campesina

Although CEBs have received more scholarly attention, probably the most important element of the popular church in El Salvador was the *centros de formación campesina* (peasant training centers, also known as *universidades campesinas* or peasant universities). These centers were not unique to El Salvador, since similar projects existed in Guatemala and Nicaragua, but the Salvadoran program was probably the most extensive. Each of El Salvador's five dioceses (San Vicente, San Miguel, Santa Ana, and Santiago de María, plus the archdiocese of San Salvador) sponsored a center, in addition to several specialized centers. The main *centros*, almost all established in the mid- to late 1960s, were Escuela La Divina Providencia in Santa Ana; Centro Reino de la Paz in El Castaño, San Miguel; Escuela Los Naranjos in Jiquilisco, Usulafter (in the diocese of Santiago de María); and the Centro Rural Itinerante, based in San Salvador, an itinerant team that gave *cursillos* (courses) in rural parishes throughout the archdiocese. Smaller centers included the Centro San Lucas in San Miguel, which focused on health care training, and two centers run by and for women, the Centro de Promoción Rural (CEPROR) in Santa Tecla and the Centro Guadalupe in San Miguel.[26] In the late 1960s another type of center, specializing in agricultural training, was founded in Chalatenango, then part of the Archdiocese of San Salvador, by the Fundación para la Promoción de Cooperativas (FUNPROCOOP), a group established around 1966 by Archbishop Luis Chávez y González.

The centers were especially important in spreading progressive pastoral and social ideas outside the Archdiocese of San Salvador, since most of the other dioceses had conservative bishops who prevented individual pastoral agents from forming CEBs or other parish-based projects. Thus, for example, eastern El Salvador, with relatively little CEB activity, had two of the most active centers, El Castaño and Los Naranjos. The regional *centros* varied according to local needs and conditions, as well as their own purposes and resources. In El Salvador, unlike other countries, the centers had no official national coordination, due mainly to divisions among the bishops. This gave the centers some autonomy but limited their resources and perhaps the overall national impact of their work. The fact that most centers were run by members of religious orders, often foreign nationals, increased both their independence and their relative isolation. Thus, some experiences remained localized, although El Salvador's compact scale facilitated contacts among pastoral agents and the diffusion of pastoral innovations.

Despite the diversity among the centers, they shared similar methods and goals. A staff member from the El Castaño center described the centers' mission in a 1975 meeting with the Salvadoran Bishops' Conference (CEDES):

> to develop leadership qualities in peasants, with knowledge of the value of mutual help and of cooperative work; to train men for change, ready to form part of parish and diocesan pastoral work, putting themselves at the service of bishops and priests. Briefly: the integral training of men [sic] for liberation.[27]

The centers pursued these objectives in a variety of ways, including prebaptismal, prematrimonial, and child catechism; community development projects; and the purchase of land for community financial autonomy. The *cursillos*, however, constituted their core activity. The courses provided a way for laypeople in areas without regular pastoral care (or with pastoral agents uninterested in innovations) to learn about new theological and social themes, to develop leadership skills, and to meet and interact with other laypeople from their region. Most centers gave two or three levels of courses, so that graduates who wished to could continue. Many centers cooperated with each other, sharing resources, teachers, and students.

From the time the first centers were established in the late 1960s until repression forced most to close around 1980, tens of thousands of peasants passed through the centers, and thousands more came into contact with center graduates who served as lay leaders in rural communities throughout El Salvador. A priest who worked at Los Naranjos, for example, claims that "There was no catechist [in the region] who didn't pass through Centro Los Naranjos."[28] The *centros* and *cursillos* provided perhaps the single most important means of diffusing the ideas, practices, and goals of the *iglesia popular*. Certainly no other progressive church program surpassed the *universidades campesinas* in scale, although locally based projects, especially the *comunidades de base*, often provided more intense experiences.

The work of *centros* and CEBs together comprised the base of the popular church in El Salvador. These programs had the greatest impact and reached the most people in the archdiocese of San Salvador (which in the 1970s included the departments of Chalatenango, Cuscatlán, and La Libertad as well as San Salvador) and in the departments of Cabañas, Morazán, and San Vicente. The laypeople and pastoral workers in these areas articulated, in Bible studies, discussions, and ritual, the theology of the popular church, including ideas about martyrdom and persecution. Their ideas were not confined to their own communities, however, but were widely diffused in and through other social and political groups. By spreading the "message" of Catholic reforms and recruiting more laypeople as active participants in the church's official structures, *centros* and CEBs broadened the social and political impact of progressive Catholicism throughout the country (as did similar programs elsewhere in Latin America).

Despite the social and political impact of these educational and pastoral programs, most of them struggled for support from the official church. Bishops in several dioceses, especially San Vicente and Santa Ana, were overtly hostile to progressive pastoral agents and their projects. The lack of support from the institutional church helped push progressive Catholics even closer to political groups, which offered moral and material support and sometimes physical protection. By the mid-1980s in El Salvador, some progressive Catholic programs had spilled beyond the confines of the institutional church. Most notable was the emergence of two left-leaning Catholic groups without official church recognition: the National Coordinator of the Popular Church (CONIP) and Base Ecclesial Communities of El Salvador (CEBES). These developments resulted, at least in part, from the decline in official support for progressive Catholic initiatives, even from the Archdiocese of San Salvador, following the assassination of Archbishop Romero and the increasing political radicalization of many laypeople in the early 1980s.

III. The Church and Political Activism

While political mobilization occurred throughout El Salvador, some of the strongest popular organizations arose in rural areas to the north and east of San Salvador, also the region of greatest base community success. Many rural and urban areas where CEBs thrived also became strongholds of political organizing by peasant groups, neighborhood associations, and other popular organizations. Pedro Henríquez claims that the Popular Revolutionary Bloc (BPR) took root only in areas where base communities had first opened up a space.[29] In Morazán and Chalatenango, especially, strong pastoral work combined with the existing social organization of small farmers led to the development of strong and militant peasant associations during the 1970s. In other areas of El Salvador, as in Nicaragua, the regions of CEB strength often became the centers of progressive political activity. Throughout Central America in the 1980s, as Tommie Sue Montgomery notes, there was a strong correlation between areas of pastoral work and political opposition. This is especially true in El Salvador, insofar as the sites of the oldest CEBs and *cursillos*, such as northern San Salvador, Chalatenango, and Morazán, have also been strongholds of opposition political activity throughout the 1970s and 1980s.[30]

This link was stronger in rural areas, where the nature of religious life and social structure facilitated the growth of CEBs. "In the countryside," asserts Marcelo Quintana, "every village is a natural community, so it's easy to form a [base] community." In rural areas, CEBs find a strong social base in the sense of community centered around the family and *cantón* (hamlet) and a denser concentration of economic power, since all the residents of an area are more likely to be employed by or renting from the same landlord. Intensive pastoral work in rural CEBs, such as the Jesuits' efforts in Aguilares, thus tended to reach a large portion the local population. This "massification" of pastoral work encouraged the growth of popular political organizations as well.[31] In urban areas, on the other hand, both living space and economic power tend to be more fragmented. Weaker social solidarity, combined with greater mobility, can make it difficult for pastoral work to incorporate a large percentage of the residents. Thus, in urban areas such as Zacamil, pastoral workers trained a smaller number of people to serve as the foundation of the CEB and as "ferment" for the larger community.[32]

Despite differences in style and scale, CEBs in both rural and urban areas helped a large number of Salvadorans to develop a critical understanding about the larger political situation, identify their interests, and acquire organizational skills. From there, CEB members often became involved in organizations such as FECCAS and the UTC, which drew many leaders and activists from base communities in areas like Chalatenango and Suchitoto. Despite the participation of many members, most religious communities maintained a religious identity distinct from popular political organizations.

CEBs took on particular importance in societies without other channels for political expression and organization, such as Nicaragua under Somoza, Brazil under the military regime, Chile under Pinochet, or El Salvador throughout the 1970s and 1980s. In such conditions, the religious sphere often provided not only organizational support for people seeking social change, but also a haven from repression. Ironically, the church's traditional privilege and power, emerging from its complicity in oppressive social structures, helped it provide protection, at least initially, for groups challenging those structures.

The church's advocacy of social change and critiques of the status quo attracted new members and renewed its moral legitimacy in many parts of Latin America. Often, however, these changes also cost the church its protected status (as well as its more conservative or fearful members). While church sectors remaining loyal to the traditional order continued to receive protection and benefits from those in power, Catholics who questioned the justice of capitalism and the legitimacy of military rule incurred the wrath of an elite that felt betrayed by its former ally. In many regions, the part of the Latin American church that sided with the poor became as vulnerable as the activists it sheltered. In El Salvador, by the late 1970s, political violence became both an experiential reality and a theological theme for many religious communities. The increasing violence also led sectors within and outside the church to pressure its leaders to take sides.

This pressure created divisions within the institutional church. While grassroots programs and activists became involved in politics in the late 1970s, the bishops debated about how to address the social issues raised by progressive sectors while retaining institutional unity and their own authority. The records of meetings of the Salvadoran Bishops' Conference (*Conferencia Episcopal Salvadoreña*, or CEDES) in the 1970s reveal deep conflicts among the bishops. Only the representatives of the archdiocese, Auxiliary Bishop Arturo Rivera y Damas and Archbishop Chávez, consistently supported progressive pastoral agents and proposals. Oscar Romero was quite conservative until he became archbishop in 1977, when he became Rivera's only solid ally in the hierarchy. Even Chávez, Rivera, and Romero often sought to slow down the pace or moderate the rhetoric of progressive pastoral work, although by the end of his life Romero had become an outspoken supporter of both progressive pastoral agents and the political opposition.

Monseñor

Oscar Arnulfo Romero was bishop of the diocese of Santiago de María in early 1977, when Archbishop Chávez, aging and exhausted by the deepening conflict in the archdiocese and the country as a whole, announced that he would step down as soon as the Vatican could name a successor. Progressive clergy and laypeople hoped that Auxiliary

Bishop Arturo Rivera y Damas, whom they saw as likely to continue Chávez's liberal policies, would replace the outgoing archbishop. Conservatives in the church, government, military, and oligarchy supported Romero, seen as conservative, "bookish," and likely to reverse the trend of pastoral activism and return the church to its historical position as a pillar of the status quo. On February 3, 1977, the Vatican did, in fact, name Romero, and he became archbishop in a quiet ceremony February 22, shortly after General Humberto Romero (no relation) won the hotly debated presidential election.

The subdued ceremony impressed liberal clergy, but they still worried that the new archbishop would limit their pastoral work. Some time later, Romero admitted this motivation behind his selection, when he told progressive priests "my job was to finish you off."[33] Before Romero could move against progressive pastoral work, however, a series of events transformed him into a spokesperson and defender of the very members of the church who had feared him. The archbishop's "conversion" began on March 12, when Jesuit Rutilio Grande, a close friend of Romero's, was killed, along with two peasants who rode with him, by automatic weapons fire as he drove from Aguilares to the nearby village of El Paisnal. Grande and the other Jesuits in Aguilares had incurred the wrath of landowners because their pastoral work had encouraged peasants in the area to organize. Romero later acknowledged that Grande's assassination "gave me the impetus to put into practice the principles of Vatican II and Medellín which call for solidarity with the suffering masses and the poor and encourage priests to live independent of the powers that be."[34]

In the wake of the murder, Romero ordered all the Catholic schools in the country closed for three days, and, in an unprecedented action, canceled all masses in the country on the second Sunday after the killing, except for a single memorial service in the cathedral. The archbishop also sent a letter to the president demanding an explanation for the assassination, which many attributed to the military, and announced that he would attend no government functions until the crime had been solved. Grande's killing, like most of the political murders that followed, was never clarified, and in his three years as archbishop, Romero never attended a government event.

After Grande's assassination, rightist attacks on the church and popular organizations increased, pushing Romero to defend progressive clergy and laypeople and denounce government abuses. He often visited churches in the archdiocese, especially those suffering military harassment in Chalatenango, Aguilares, and other rural areas. Romero's Sunday sermons in the cathedral became famous for his outspoken denunciations of the military's brutality and the oligarchy's greed and for his passionate defense of the people's right to organize. He avoided partisan positions, however, and instructed his priests to do the same. Romero viewed the country's divisions, and the church's part in them, as social, rather than partisan or ideological. "The conflict," he asserted in January 1979, "is not between the church and the government. It is between the government and the people. The church is with the people, and the people are with the church, thanks to God!"[35]

Romero's support for popular movements for social change led rightists in the military, government, and media to call him "subversive." Many also threatened to kill him. At several points, the regime even offered him armed security guards for his own protection (from forces of the very same government, ironically). When the president offered him security and an armored car, Romero noted in his diary in September 1979, the archbishop expressed his thanks, then, in a response that came to symbolize his solidarity with the poor, explained that

> I wouldn't accept that protection, because I wanted to run the same risks that the people are running; it would be a pastoral anti-testimony if I were very secure, while my people are so insecure. I took advantage to ask him [the President] for protection for the people in certain areas where military blocks, military operations . . . sow so much terror.[36]

While Romero expressed fear at the thought of a violent death, he never shied from his duty, as he saw it, to accompany the people in their insecurity. Nor did he seek special protection for his priests. "It would be sad," he remarked in June 1979, "if in a country where people are being assassinated so horribly, we didn't count priests among the victims as well. They are the testimony of a church that is incarnated in the problems of the people."[37]

Violence Against the Salvadoran Church

> Our church is persecuted precisely for its preferential option for the poor and for trying to incarnate itself in the interests of the poor.
>
> Oscar Romero

While repression of popular organizations, peasant leaders, and the secular left have taken place for generations in much of Latin America, attacks on the church are a recent phenomenon, coinciding with the development of the option for the poor and the growth of CEBs. This persecution has occurred on a scale once unimaginable in nominally Christian countries, with thousands of Catholic activists imprisoned, tortured, and/or murdered since the late 1960s. Although laypeople have suffered the most, military regimes have also attacked pastoral agents, perceived as the symbolic and practical leaders of progressive social movements. Between 1968 and 1982, Latin American governments and armies imprisoned, exiled, or killed close to a thousand priests, nuns, and bishops. In Central America alone, at least forty nuns and priests and one archbishop, were murdered between 1971 and 1990.[38] More than half of those killings occurred in El Salvador, the smallest country in Latin America.

Repression was not entirely unknown to the Salvadoran Catholic Church before the late 1970s. In January 1970, armed men kidnapped and tortured José Inocencio Alas, and in late November of that year Father Nicolás Rodríguez was killed in Chalatenango, in what then auxiliary bishop Rivera y Damas called "a political crime committed with the aim of intimidating the entire clergy . . . a warning to abandon our ministry."[39] The Jesuits had also received right-wing attacks beginning in 1973. With the start of Romero's tenure as archbishop in early 1977, however, repression against progressive religious sectors erupted with unprecedented fury. Between February 18 and February 22, 1977, the Salvadoran government expelled or exiled eleven foreign priests, including two Belgian priests and Spanish Jesuit Ignacio Ellacuría (who later returned as rector of the Jesuit university). In that same five-day period, security forces arrested and tortured Rafael Barahona, a Salvadoran priest working in Tecoluca, for the second time. In March, Grande was killed, and on June 21, the White Warriors Union, a notorious death squad, warned all the Jesuits (whom it called "Jesuit guerrillas") to leave the country within thirty days or face death. Throughout that summer, flyers circulated with the slogan "Be a patriot. Kill a priest." In all, between February and July 1977, seven priests were refused re-entry into El Salvador, eight were expelled, two were killed (in addition to Grande, Alfonso Navarro, a diocesan priest of San Salvador), two tortured, one beaten, two imprisoned, and four threatened with death.

The attacks continued throughout 1977 and 1978, and on November 28, 1978, a third priest was killed. Ernesto Barrera, a

Salvadoran diocesan priest popular in his parish in a working-class *barrio* of San Salvador, died, according to the government, in a gun battle between the army and guerrillas. Romero initially dismissed this charge as an attempt to hide official guilt. A short time later, however, the Popular Liberation Forces (FPL) sent Romero a long letter discussing Christian participation in armed struggle, expressing its respect for Barrera, and asserting that the priest had indeed belonged to the group. Barrera's death sharpened existing divisions within the church regarding the position of priests in political and even military organizations. The killing itself remained unclear, since physical evidence suggested that Barrera had not been wielding a weapon when he died. Nonetheless, conservative bishops and priests urged Romero not to give Barrera the same honors accorded to the two priests murdered earlier. After reflecting on the case, Romero decided to say a funeral mass in the cathedral, arguing that Barrera's bishop, like his parents, had a duty to be at the priest's side, "without asking questions about his activities or method."[40]

Less than two months later, Octavio Ortiz, a Salvadoran priest assigned to the working-class suburb of Mejicanos, became the fourth priest killed. On January 20, 1979, Ortiz, a Belgian nun, a laywoman working with the pastoral team, and thirty young men were in Colonia San Antonio Abad, another working-class neighborhood in northern San Salvador, for a weekend retreat. Early in the morning, uniformed National Guardsmen ran a tank through the gate of the parish house (called "El Despertar," the awakening) and stormed into the yard. They shot Ortiz and then crushed his head with a tank, leaving it "completely disfigured," in Romero's words.[41] The Guardsmen also killed four young men participating in the retreat and then placed the bodies on the roof of the parish house, with weapons nearby, as "evidence" of a gun battle. The Guard arrested forty other youths, the nun, and the laywoman.

The fifth priest killed was Rafael Palacios, a Salvadoran who worked in Santa Tecla and, following Ortiz's death, in the San Francisco de Asís parish in Mejicanos. Palacios had received numerous threats, and expressed concern for his safety to Romero shortly before he was shot in Santa Tecla on June 20, 1979. With his death, San Francisco lost its second priest in six months. Two months later, Alirio Napoleón Macías of the diocese of San Vicente was killed in his church as he left the sacristy for the altar.

The attacks, as Romero noted, did not target "just any" priest or nun. Pastoral workers were not killed for being Christian or for representing the church but for their work in progressive pastoral projects and often for their links to popular organizations.[42] Romero often contended that attacks on priests, nuns, and churches only symbolized the greater repression unleashed against the laity. The true victims of persecution, he argued, were the poor and those who defended them, especially activists in popular political organizations and religious communities.

If attacks on priests signified the larger persecution of Christian activists, undoubtedly the most powerful symbol was the murder of Romero himself as he said mass in a hospital chapel in San Salvador March 24, 1980. Numerous observers, including U.S. Ambassador Robert White, named ARENA founder and army major Roberto D'Aubuisson as the one who had ordered the crime.[43] Many identified the immediate catalyst for the assassination as Romero's March 23 homily, in which he ordered soldiers not to obey orders to kill. Clearly, however, his three years of increasingly concrete denunciations of human rights violations and economic injustices had made Romero a target regardless of any single homily or speech.

Subsequent to Romero's murder, an Italian Franciscan, Cosme Spezzotto, was killed on June 14, 1980, followed the next month by seminarian José Cáceres. A few months of calm ensued, as Rivera y Damas, then "apostolic administrator" of the archdiocese, tried to avoid conflicts with the government. (The pope did not name Rivera archbishop until several years later.) Rivera's denunciation of abuses in September inaugurated a new series of assassinations. On October 7, the body of Manuel Reyes, a diocesan priest of San Salvador, was found on the road leading to Mariona. In late November, two diocesan priests from San Salvador, Ernesto Abrego and Marcial Serrano, "disappeared" and were murdered, respectively.

The repression touched even U.S. citizens working with El Salvador's poor. On December 2, 1980, National Guardsmen raped and killed four U.S. religious women: Maryknoll lay missionary Jean Donovan, Maryknoll sisters Ita Ford and Maura Clarke, and Ursuline sister Dorothy Kazel. The murders of the nuns sparked more outrage in the United States than all the killings that had preceded. Robert White vowed that the murderers would be found and brought to justice. ("This time," he reportedly swore, "they won't get away with it.") In May 1984, five Guardsmen were convicted of the killings, but no officers were brought to trial for ordering, financing, or covering up the crime.

On January 17, 1981, six weeks after the killing of the U.S. religious women, Silvia Arriola, a member of the *pequeña comunidad*, died in

Santa Ana as she aided victims of the fighting during the FMLN general offensive. After her death, no priests or nuns were killed in El Salvador for more than eight years, although thousands of lay Christian activists continued to die at the hands of death squads and the military. Then, early in the morning of November 16, 1989, soldiers dragged UCA rector Ignacio Ellacuría, vice-rector Ignacio Martín-Baró, professors Segundo Montes, Joaquín López, and Juan Moreno, all Spanish Jesuits, and Amando López, a Salvadoran Jesuit, from their beds in the Jesuit residence at the UCA and assassinated all six, plus Elba Ramos, their housekeeper, and her fifteen-year-old daughter Celina. Things had not changed much, it seemed, in the nearly thirteen years since Rutilio Grande, a small boy, and an old man were murdered on a lonely road between two dusty villages. The Salvadoran popular church continued to produce its martyrs, and those who survived continued their search for ways to understand the devastation.

The Meaning of Martyrdom

No Salvadoran Catholic, from Archbishops Romero and Rivera to ordinary believers, could entirely ignore the violence that ravaged the church's progressive wing from 1977 to the end of the 1980s. Some conservatives, including many bishops, explained attacks as retaliation for political subversion. Left-leaning Catholics, they claimed, acted out of political motives, thus placing themselves outside the church and bringing upon themselves retaliation from government security forces. The "martyrdom" of the Salvadoran church, in this view, was the justifiable elimination of threats to the social order; its victims suffered for their political ideology, not their faith.

More sympathetic observers also interpreted attacks on Salvadoran Catholics in largely political terms. Repression against progressive Christians, they argued, represented a specific piece of the larger government-military-oligarchy strategy to crush all opposition, religious or secular. The persecution of the popular church resulted from the growth of ecclesial groups that encouraged poor people to organize for better conditions. This type of organization gained significance not because it came from the church but because it challenged the established order. Martyrdom, in this largely secular analysis, represented the religious dimension of a larger conflict, in which popular efforts to transform repressive structures in Salvadoran society met, as they had for generations, with vicious responses from elites who benefitted from the status quo.

Within the *iglesia popular*, however, pastoral agents and laypeople struggled for ways to understand the violence in light of their religious worldview and motivations. If, as religious activists believed, work for social justice was a requirement of true faith, then why were the ones doing God's work suffering so much? How should Christians respond to such extreme violence? Just as they framed the question theologically and ethically, so their answers, while not ignoring political reality, came primarily in religious terms.

Over the course of the late 1970s and 1980s, Salvadoran Catholic activists articulated a distinctive interpretation of martyrdom, building on the resources provided by the centuries-old tradition of Christian martyrdom, Salvadoran popular religiosity, and postconciliar Latin American Catholicism. Pre-Hispanic indigenous views that sacrificial deaths served the good of the entire community probably played a role as well.[44] This enterprise involved many persons, including Archbishop Romero, many priests and nuns, and a few professional theologians (notably Jesuits Jon Sobrino and Ignacio Ellacuría),[45] as well as countless ordinary laypeople. Pastoral workers played particularly important roles as mediators, often communicating church teachings and the ideas of theologians to people at the base. These priests and nuns occupied a central place in the continuum of progressive Catholicism in El Salvador, which, as elsewhere in Latin America, encompassed a wide range of popular and elite expressions. In El Salvador, diverse individuals and groups responded to the events of their lives by reference to the symbolic capital of Christianity. Pastoral agents and theologians, in particular, looked back to martyrdom in the Roman era, especially the experience of the underground or "catacombs" period of the Christian community, as well as new approaches to ecclesiology, Christology, and ethics developed since Vatican II and Medellín.

While church teachings and liberation theology helped shape popular understandings of martyrdom, grassroots ideas about martyrdom arose, above all, out of ordinary believers' readings of the Bible, and especially the story of Jesus' life and passion. For many ordinary Salvadorans, the Bible was not only the most readily available and authoritative source for explaining their own suffering but also the one that rang truest. Thus, it was primarily in and through biblical *reflexión* that Salvadoran Catholics constructed their understanding of different religious and political issues, including assassinations and repression. While this process (and the resulting ideas) certainly received influence from pastoral agents, laypeople approached the Bible and other religious resources and traditions with creativity and relative independence. This creative process of appropriation and innovation—the ways laypeople draw on diverse traditions to respond to their own concerns and experiences—is central to popular religion in both its traditional and "reformed" or progressive variants. This process is, of course, constrained by the guidelines of the religious institution as well as by material and historical circumstances, but ordinary people have striven within these limitations to make their own religion as well as their own history.

Salvadoran Catholics articulated their understanding of repression and martyrdom primarily through interpretations of biblical stories that seemed to speak directly to their own experiences. In addition to biblical *reflexión*, however, religious rituals helped people develop both their general religious perspective and specific ideas about martyrdom. The next chapter will look in more detail at rituals in the Salvadoran *iglesia popular*, focusing on the way that they introduce themes elaborated more fully in reflections and discussions of biblical readings.

Endnotes

1. Phillip Berryman, *The Religious Roots of Rebellion: Christians in Central American Revolutions* (Maryknoll, NY: Orbis, 1984), 57.

2. Margaret Randall, *Christians in the Nicaraguan Revolution* (Vancouver: New Star Books, 1983), 71.

3. In addition to Cardenal, *El poder eclesiástico*, see Jesús Delgado, *Sucesos de la historia de El Salvador, Volumen 1: Introducción a la historia de la iglesia en El Salvador (1525–1821)* (San Salvador: Archdiocese of San Salvador, 1991) and *Volumen II: Historia de la iglesia en El Salvador (1821–1885)* (San Salvador: Archdiocese of San Salvador, 1992).

4. The Virgin of Guadalupe, who appeared in 1531 to an Aztec man on a hill traditionally dedicated to an Aztec goddess, represents the most famous example of this syncretism. See Ingham, *Mary, Michael, and Lucifer*, 2, and Davíd Carrasco, *Religions of Mesoamerica: Cosmovision and Ceremonial Centers* (New York: Harper Collins, 1990), 135–138.

5. Roger Lancaster, *Thanks to God and the Revolution: Popular Religion and Class Consciousness in the New Nicaragua* (New York: Columbia University Press, 1988), 38.

6. Cardenal, *El poder eclesiástico*, 147. See also three works on popular religiosity in El Salvador: Segundo Montes, *El compadrazgo: una estructura de*

poder en El Salvador (San Salvador: UCA Editores, 1987); Miguel Angel Amaya, *Historias de Cacoapera* (San Salvador: Minsterio de Educación, 1985); and Alejandro Dagoberto Marroquín, *Panchimalco: investigación sociológica* (San Salvador: Editorial Universitaria, 1959).

7. Cardenal, *El poder eclesiástico*, 173. See also Espín, "Trinitarian Monotheism," on the importance of Mary and the crucified Jesus in Latin American popular Catholicism more generally.

8. Stephen and Dow, "Introduction," 10.

9. Cardenal, *El poder eclesiástico*, 266.

10. Ibid., 270.

11. *Gaudium et Spes*, in *Documents of Vatican II* (New York: American Press, 1966), ed. Walter Abbott, no. 69.

12. CELAM (Conference of Latin American Bishops), *The Church in the Present-Day Transformation of Latin America in the Light of the Council: Medellín Conclusions* (Washington, DC: National Conference of Catholic Bishops, 1979), 185, 41.

13. CELAM, "Puebla Final Document," in *Puebla and Beyond*, eds. John Eagleson and Philip Scharper, trans. John Drury (Maryknoll, NY: Orbis, 1979) 222, 264–267.

14. Pearce, *Promised Land*, 93. See also Rosa Carmelita Samos Stibbs, *Sobre el magisterio de Mons. Luis Chávez y González: Estudio teológico de sus cartas pastorales* (Guatemala City: Universidad Francisco Marroquín, 1986).

15. Plácido Erdozaín, *Archbishop Romero* (Maryknoll, NY: Orbis, 1981), 1.

16. *Primera semana de pastoral arquidiocesana, 5–10 enero 1976* (San Salvador: Archdiocese of San Salvador, 1976), 5–6, 9–10.

17. On the links between European Catholic Action and progressive Catholicism in Latin America, see David J. Molineaux, "Gustavo Gutiérrez: Historical Origins," *The Ecumenist* 25, no. 5 (July–August 1987): 65–69. The best-known statement of Freire's pedagogy is his *Pedagogy of the Oppressed* (New York: Continuum, 1984).

18. I am describing one of several forms that base communities took throughout Latin America; this model (similar to what Daniel Levine calls the "radical ideal") should not be taken as typical of all CEBs in all areas. This description does, however, typify many communities in Central America, especially El Salvador, during the 1970s and 1980s. See Levine, *Popular Voices*, 45–48.

19. Rodolfo González [pseud.], interview by author, 12 November 1988, Managua. See also Frei Betto, *¿Qué es la comunidad eclesial de base?* (Managua: Centro Ecuménico Antonio Valdivieso, n.d.) on the development of political consciousness in CEBs generally.

20. Michael Dodson and Laura Nuzzi O'Shaughnessy, *Nicaragua's Other Revolution: Religious Faith and Political Struggle* (Chapel Hill: University of North Carolina Press, 1990), 155. See also Levine, *Popular Voices*.

21. Pedro Henríquez, *El Salvador: Iglesia profética y cambio social* (San José, Costa Rica: Editorial DEI, 1988), 177.

22. Felix Jiménez, *Historia de la parroquia San Pablo Apóstol* (Managua: n.p., 1986), 24.

23. Dodson and O'Shaughnessy, *Nicaragua's Other Revolution*, 144.

24. CEBES, *Una experiencia de iglesia: Mística y metodología* (Managua: CEBES, n.d.), 13–14. See also Pablo Galdámez, *The Faith of a People* (Maryknoll, NY: Orbis Books, 1986).

25. Aguilares is by far the best-documented pastoral project in El Salvador. See Henríquez, *El Salvador*, chap. 2; Rodolfo Cardenal, *Historia de una esperanza: vida de Rutilio Grande* (San Salvador: UCA Editores, 1985); *Rutilio Grande, mártir de la evangelización rural en El Salvador* (San Salvador: UCA Editores, 1978); A. Douglas Kincaid, "Peasants into Rebels: Community and Class in Rural El Salvador," *Comparative Studies in Society and History* 29, no. 3 (July 1987): 466–499; and Salvador Carranza, "Una experiencia de evangelización rural parroquial: Aguilares, septiembre de 1972–agosto de 1974," *ECA* (San Salvador) 32, no. 348–49 (1977).

26. Ricardo Urioste, director of the *equipo itinerante*, recalls that there was also a *centro de formación* in San Vicente. I have found little information about this center, perhaps because the conservative bishop of San Vicente, Pedro Aparicio, limited both its work and publicity about it. The only published mention of the San Vicente center I found is in CEDES, *Actas de CEDES*, no. 100 (20–24 January 1975), p. 12, where Aparicio affirms his trust in the *centro* in his diocese, in response to concerns that other centers might not merit the bishops' confidence.

27. *Actas de CEDES*, no. 101 (July 7–11, 1975), 7.

28. Mario Ferrer, interview by author, San Salvador, April 5, 1990.

29. Henríquez, *El Salvador*.

30. Montgomery, "Liberation and Revolution," 92.

31. See Kincaid, "Peasants into Rebels," and Carranza, "Una experiencia de evangelización rural."

32. Henríquez, El Salvador, 147–148, 224.

33. Erdozaín, Archbishop Romero, 1; see also Armstrong and Shenk, El Salvador, 91.

34. Quoted in "Oscar Romero: Archbishop of the Poor," interview by Patrick Lacefield, in El Salvador: Central America in the New Cold War, eds. Marvin Gettleman et al. (New York: Grove Press, 1981), 202–203.

35. Oscar Romero, La voz de los sin voz (San Salvador: UCA Editores, 1987), 455.

36. Oscar Romero, Su diario: del 31 de marzo de 1978 al 20 de marzo de 1980 (San Salvador: Archdiocese of San Salvador, 1990), 75–76.

37. Romero, La voz, 454.

38. Penny Lernoux, Cry of the People (New York: Penguin Books, 1984), xvii; Jon Sobrino, "Espiritualidad de la persecución y del martirio," Diakonía (Managua) 27 (1983): 172.

39. Cáceres Prendes, "Political Radicalization," 113.

40. Galdámez, The Faith of a People, 71.

41. Romero, Su diario, 104.

42. La iglesia en El Salvador (San Salvador: UCA Editores, 1982), 80.

43. White claimed there was "compelling, if not one hundred percent conclusive" evidence that D'Aubuisson was involved in the murder. Later investigations, including the report of the United Nations-sponsored "Truth Commission," supported this charge and confirmed more generally that D'Aubuisson organized some of the country's most brutal death squads. See Philip Russell, El Salvador in Crisis (Austin: Colorado River Press, 1984), 115; James Brockman, Romero: A Life (Maryknoll, NY: Orbis Books, 1989), 249–255; and Universidad Centroamericana "José Simeón Cañas," "De la locura a la esperanza: La guerra de doce años en El Salvador. Informe de la Comisión de la Verdad," ECA XLVIII, no. 53 (March 1993): 153–326.

44. See Ingham, Mary, Michael, and Lucifer, 185; Rowe and Schelling, Memory and Modernity, 71.

45. See, for example, Ignacio Ellacuría, "El pueblo crucificado, ensayo de soteriología histórica." Revista Latinoamericana de Teología (San Salvador) 6, no. 18 (Sept.–Dec. 1989): 305–334 and Sobrino, "Espiritualidad de la persecución."

4

Sacrifice, History, and Ritual

Let's go jubilantly to the Lord's table
The poor and humble are invited by God
This bread that God offers us nourishes our union
Christ makes himself present here when we meet in his love[1]

In most religious traditions, rituals play a major role in constructing and inculcating worldviews and value systems at the popular level. Especially in regions where low literacy rates and the scarcity of books make Bible reading and reflection impossible for most people, rituals serve as the primary locus for both the development and the expression of the worldview, ethical norms, and political assumptions associated with religious belief. Ritual offers a kind of lived (and living) theology, a medium in and through which believers/practitioners see, hear, and often act out defining elements of their faith. In such a context, rituals can assume "the major burden of meaning," more important than written documents in transmitting religious values and worldviews.[2] Through the popular appropriation of organizational forms, rituals, and other practices, religion provides a medium in and through which ordinary people can define the meaning and purpose of their lives.

Laypeople have always played a central, often dominant role, in ritual dimensions of Salvadoran Catholicism, in contrast to their relative (or total) absence in the formulation of official theology, the governance of church institutions, and the performance of the sacraments. The prominence of laypeople in ritual builds on Salvadoran Catholicism's long tradition of lay autonomy through *cofradías* and other devotional groups. Ritual was often central to the religious lives of these groups and of local communities generally. The main religious activities in most communities, especially in rural areas, have been processions, pilgrimages, the *vía crucis* (stations of the cross), and other ceremonies that do not require the presence of a priest the way sacraments do. These rites have been organized traditionally by *cofradías* or other lay groups. Progressive popular Catholicism has transformed these rituals in many ways, but they continue to represent an arena in which laypeople can exercise leadership and shape the meaning of their religion.

In the contemporary Salvadoran *iglesia popular*, a variety of Catholic rituals have played important roles in the formulation and expression of religious and social values and identity. Song lyrics and the symbolism of certain ritual acts reflect and reinforce central theological and ethical assumptions raised in biblical *reflexión*. Like *reflexión*, rituals can link post-Medellín values of equality, human dignity, liberation, and autonomy to participants' own experiences and grant both the values and the experiences special power via a religious source and legitimation. Even when priests or nuns are involved, laypeople in base communities and *cursillos* play a central role in the execution and interpretation of the ceremonies. The importance of lay leadership stems in part from the fact that Medellín and Vatican II both called for greater participation by laypeople, which encouraged pastoral agents in El Salvador and elsewhere to train "delegates of the word" (lay preachers), catechists, and other lay leaders. In contemporary base communities, as in the *cofradías* of earlier times, pastoral agents and official church teachings play an important but usually not determining role in ritual.

Many of the most important rituals in the popular church, as in traditional popular religion, do not require the presence of a priest. El Salvador's chronic shortage of clergy, in fact, makes rituals requiring a priest infrequent in many areas, especially rural villages. Still, the mass continues to hold symbolic power that lay-led "celebrations of the word" cannot match and remains central to popular as well as official Catholicism. In this chapter, I will concentrate on the mass and on another, more lay-oriented ritual, the *vía crucis*. The "stations of the cross," which retrace Jesus' path to the crucifixion, are celebrated every Friday during Lent. These two rites, one sacramental and the other traditionally lay-run, have not always supported the progressive tenets of the post-Medellín "popular" church. Historically, masses in El Salvador and in Latin America often reinforced the passivity, individualism, and obedience to authority that made Catholicism so congenial to the dominant classes.[3] The dictatorial role of the priest, the absence of lay participation, and an emphasis on personal morality drained the eucharist of all notions of "communion." Overall, the rite imprinted a message of universal guilt for Jesus' death, with individual repentance as the only hope for redemption. Since the late 1970s, lay and pastoral participants in base communities and the popular church more generally have transformed this message, converting the mass and other religious rituals into celebrations of the dignity of the poor, community solidarity, and the struggle for social change. *Misas populares*, folk songs written to accompany the mass, have particular power in communicating, in vivid and memorable form, central religious images and values. (It is worth noting that although some *misas*, most notably the *Misa Campesina Nicaragüense*, were written by professional musicians, many, including the Salvadoran popular mass, were written by ordinary laypeople.)

This chapter will explore two major themes or aspects of ritual, focused on the mass and *vía crucis*, in the progressive Catholicism that evolved in El Salvador during the 1970s and 1980s. First, at a more "external" level of analysis, I will look at the specific ways in which rituals express and inculcate theological and ethical ideas, focusing on the ways rituals link sacred and secular history. Second, I will examine the "internal" content of belief, concentrating on the ways that rituals re-enacting Jesus' passion raise the central claims that believers make about contemporary martyrs.

I. Ritual

Rituals construct and express theological and ethical ideas in various ways. They do so in part by presenting an idealized version of real, less than ideal, actions or events. During ritual people represent things—themselves, the world, their own and other people's behavior, and even historical or political events—the way they believe these things ought to be. While these idealized versions may appear quite distant from the way things are actually done, they often influence not only interpretation but also real-life behavior. Jonathan Z. Smith elaborates this perspective: "Ritual is a means of performing the way things ought to be in conscious tension to the way things are in such a way that this ritualized perfection is recollected in the ordinary, uncontrolled, course of things."[4] In progressive Catholicism in El Salvador, the most important religious rituals present both an idealized version of mythical or past events and a model for present events that, to believers, parallel the ritually remembered past. Believers' "recollection" of ritualized events provide guidelines for their behavior in the often chaotic, highly imperfect events of real life.

Some of the most important Catholic rites re-enact turning points in Christian sacred history. The eucharist commemorates the last supper, for example, and the *vía crucis* retraces Jesus' path to the cross. By representing these events, rituals not only present compelling visions of past events but also bring the divine into the present and vice-versa. By inserting Jesus into present events and putting participants into the sacred history of Jesus' own life and death, these rituals give sacred value and transcendence to contemporary events. In the 1970s and 1980s in El Salvador, certain rituals, especially the mass and *vía crucis*, took on particular importance as vehicles linking Jesus' passion and contemporary political killings. Before turning to this specific issue, however, I will discuss some more general features of the ways that Salvadoran Catholic activists connected their lives to Jesus' experiences in and through religious rituals.

Ritual, Poverty, and Collective Identity

Since the colonial period in Latin America, popular Catholicism generally and its rituals more specifically have offered support for a distinctive social identity among poor people. Even traditional rituals "designed to invoke God's protection," as Thomas Kselman argues, often "do not imply fatalistic resignation in expectation of a heavenly reward, nor do they obviate the need for activity in this world," but rather they can "be seen as a form of action through which communities express solidarity and hope."[5] In the progressive Catholicism which has developed since the 1960s, new styles of ritual bring these expressions to the fore, seeking to generate community solidarity and identity. These rituals build on traditional notions of community and human relationships to the divine, to nature, and to each other, while they also raise new themes. For example, they may transform the subtle, often ambiguous critiques of elites found in traditional rituals into an explicit class consciousness.

In El Salvador, rituals in the popular church seek to contribute to collective identity, and especially to poor people's sense of their own dignity and worth in various ways, beginning with the inclusion of everyday items, such as food and tools, as offerings at the altar and in song. Not only objects, but labor itself—"the bread of our work without end" (619)—is symbolically presented in popular masses. Offerings of everyday items and experiences, like the traditional wine and bread, are altered by Christ's presence: "we want to see our sorrow converted/ into your life and your courage/ toppling the oppressor" (524). In these rituals, the eucharist symbolizes the transformation of ordinary things, including hardship and pain, into spiritual weapons against injustice.

Rituals also encourage pride among the poor by portraying Jesus as a poor man who lived with the oppressed and fought for their liberation. The opening song of the *Misa Campesina Nicaragüense*, very popular in Salvadoran CEBs, highlights the identification between Christ/God and the poor:

> You are the God of the poor,
> the simple and human God,
> the God who sweats in the street,
> the God with the weather-beaten face
> This is why I talk to you the way my people talk
> because you are the laboring God, the worker Christ (850)

In contrast to the traditional vision of God as both outside history and "mysteriously responsible for the established order,"[6] the *Misa Campesina* depicts a God who shares the daily activities of the poor and who suffers injustices large and small with them.

A *vía crucis* booklet created by Equipo Maíz, a team that produces pastoral materials used in CEBS in many parts of El Salvador, reinforces the identification of Jesus as a poor person, victimized by the wealthy. Jesus was born poor and died poor, asserts the reflection for the tenth station, when Jesus is stripped of his clothes. "He never had much and the little he had was taken from him: they left him naked." The commentary explicitly links sacred history and current events: "In the same way today they strip the poor of their rights. They leave them with nothing, trying to take even what they don't have." By identifying the oppressors, the commentary stresses the fact that human action, not a divine plan, causes poverty: "The ambition of a few is the cause of the misery of the many. Jesus taught us to share and not to strip others of what they have."[7]

Rituals re-enacting Jesus' passion link Jesus' identification with the poor to a demand for action on behalf of the needy. By explicitly paralleling the class conditions of contemporary society, the presentation of Jesus in ritual encourages participants not only to develop a conscious identity as members of a subordinate class, but also to seek, collectively, changes in unjust socioeconomic structures. Instead of sanctioning a system that marginalizes and represses the poor, popular *misas* and other rites give divine approval to struggles for justice. Not only is Jesus poor, these rituals suggest; he also fights to defend the poor, who are the special recipients of the gospel message, understood as the liberation of the oppressed. The Lord's supper is thus "the table of the poor united", "the table of the poor and oppressed who struggle for equality and justice," motivating and channelling protests against exploitation.[8]

Ritual images such as these provide poor people with a sense of "vocation" as those chosen by God to receive the messiah and to build the kingdom. The notion that Jesus sides with the poor, accompanying and legitimizing, even sacralizing, their struggles, reinforces this calling. Thus the *Misa Salvadoreña* asks for solidarity with the poor: "Lord, injustice hurts and oppresses us/ put yourself on our side/ we are the humble" (698). Catholic activists' faith that God supports the struggle of the poor helps them continue in the face of repression. "We know we're doing nothing bad," explains Vilma, from a poor San Salvador parish. "We're on the path of God." The "Gloria" of the Salvadoran popular mass affirms this conviction:

> The gods of power and money oppose themselves to transfiguration
> Because of this you, Lord, are the first to raise your arm against oppression . . .
> because you are just and defend the oppressed
> because you truly love and care for us
> today all your people come, decided, to proclaim our value and dignity (318)

This understanding of Jesus motivates and legitimizes the struggle against injustice. Rather than the victims of a divinely willed injustice, poor people come to see themselves as "the protagonists of a historical mission, that of struggling for a just society in accord with the divine design."[9] This divine plan entails the lifting-up of the poor and the construction of the harmonious world intended in the creation, reaffirmed by Jesus' announcement of the good news and prefigured in the unity of the mass.

To fulfill this plan and achieve liberation, according to this view, poor people must develop not only a conviction of their dignity, grounded in Jesus' identification with the poor, but also a sense of unity, in action as in outlook. To strengthen this unity, base community rituals incorporate practical claims about the effectiveness of united action with calls to Christian fellowship. To belong to the church, in this perspective, requires a connection with "all the brothers and sisters we call Christians," as Julio, a lay activist from Chalatenango, explains. People must break down the isolation and mistrust that often separate neighbors and co-workers. Achieving solidarity is not easy, but it is necessary, both because the Bible mandates unity, activists insist, and because in a situation of extreme poverty and repression, only collective efforts can be politically effective. Religious rituals, *cursillos*, and CEBs help in this task by demonstrating both the value and the possibility of living in community.

The mass, which has symbolized Christians' solidarity with God and with each other since the early years of the church, plays an important role in establishing this unity. Many centuries ago Ignatius called on early Christians to "Be eager to participate in the eucharist, because one is the flesh of our lord Jesus Christ, and one is the chalice for union with his blood."[10] The eucharist expresses Christian unity for present-day communities as well. "Communion is union with God/ communion is union and truth/ our souls united forge together," assert the words to a popular song (146). Celebrations stress not only solidarity but also the equality of participants. "We share the same communion," says one song; "we are wheat of the same sower" (791). In the mass, the distinctions of everyday life, especially those between rich and poor, vanish as all sit together at the same table: "God invites all the poor/ to this common table for faith/ where there are no profiteers/ and no one is lacking what s/he needs" (821).

By offering images of unity, equality, and abundance in the midst of injustice and poverty, the mass ritually restructures the world in terms of an ideal society.[11] It presents a utopia, a taste of the kingdom, which stands as both a judgment on the present situation and a goal to be sought. A guide to the sacraments used in the Archdiocese of San Salvador describes the role of the mass in these terms: "In meeting fraternally and sharing the same bread, we as Christians announce the love of Christians and denounce the divisions and exploitation that exist in the world that calls itself 'Christian'."[12] Slain Jesuit Rutilio Grande expressed a similar understanding of the eucharist:

> God gave us a material world, like this material mass, with material bread and with a material cup which we raise in celebration

of Christ . . . One day the material world will be for us, like this eucharist . . . This is why Christ described his kingdom like a dinner, a table shared in brotherhood, in which all have a place.[13]

In a society with little sharing of material goods, the mass can symbolize unity, equality, and abundance, criticizing actual injustices while presenting a goal around which struggles for change can organize. More generally, the solidarity and participatory democracy experienced in grassroots rituals comment pointedly on the real political situation while also offering a taste of the improved community to come.

Sacrifice and the Passion

The theology developed in the Salvadoran *iglesia popular* during the 1970s and 1980s sought not only to articulate a vision of the egalitarian world sought by Christians but also to offer guidelines and information about how to achieve this goal. As it evolved in the context of political repression beginning in the late 1970s, popular theology in El Salvador claimed in particular that Christians would not achieve their goals without sacrifice, beginning with and modelled after the story of Jesus' life, death, and resurrection. This story became the model for a narrative, reenacted by progressive Salvadoran Christians, which posited parallels in the actors, problems, goals, and fruits of Jesus' and contemporary deaths and offered explanations for the killings.

This emphasis on Jesus' suffering and death emerged in Latin American Catholicism long before Vatican II or Medellín. Orlando Espín argues that Hispanic popular Catholicism is a "religion of the vanquished."[14] Spanish Catholic missionaries in the early colonial period in Latin America provided contrasting images of a powerful, conquering God and a suffering, innocent, and human Jesus. Indigenous people identified with the latter and shaped their appropriation of Catholicism accordingly. Thus, Espín contends, interpretations of Jesus' passion and resurrection have been central to the emergence of popular Catholic spirituality in the Americas since newly evangelized Amerindians used Catholicism, integrated with existing indigenous traditions, to help make sense of the European conquest.[15] In this light, the centrality of martyrdom in the worldview and rituals of Salvadoran popular Catholicism can be seen as a particular instance of a larger focus on the crucifixion in Latin American popular Catholicism.

This identification with Jesus' suffering, reinforced through ritual re-enactments of the passion, helps imprint the "facts" of events in Jesus' life in the ways present believers interpret their own experiences. Certain "facts" or dimensions of the passion story stand out, often because of their relevance to believers' present experiences. In El Salvador, popular interpretations of Jesus' life and death emphasized the idea that true believers will face death at the hands of the establishment. This idea has existed in Christianity since Roman times, when early believers first understood the eucharist as a celebration of Jesus' martyrdom and a preparation for their own. "If we daily drink the cup of the blood of Christ," wrote Cyprian, "it is in order to be ready to shed our blood for Christ as well."[16] In contemporary El Salvador ritual re-enactments of the last supper and the path to the cross through the mass and the *vía crucis* deliver the message that sacrifice, suffering, and temporary defeat are inevitable parts of sharing Jesus' struggle for justice. These rituals thus help prepare people for the death of religious and political leaders.[17]

As a crucial part of most rituals, religious songs often emphasize the correlation between Jesus' passion and the killings of contemporary Christians. Many of these songs are written by parishioners in honor of murdered priests or layworkers. A song for Father Alirio Macías claims that "Catarina [Macías's church] is the new Calvary/ on its lands a cross is raised/ together with the body of Father Macías/ who died because he followed Jesus" (542). And a song called "Father Rafael Palacios" includes the following lyrics: "Like Christ they beat you with a ferocious rope/ with insults they whipped you to silence your voice/ You walked to the Calvary like Jesus walked . . . / the machine gun was your cross" (551). Although the locale and the weapons change, the meaning for believers remains the same.

Songs and rituals assert not only that Christians today repeat Jesus' death; they also claim, or show, that Christ himself continues dying in the struggle for the kingdom. "You are abandoned on the cross/ massacred by the powerful/ Today you also spill your blood/ in the blood of our fallen," asserts the *Misa Salvadoreña* (159). Thus the dialectic between sacred and secular history flows in both directions. Just as contemporary believers enter into sacred history, divine events and characters "irrupt" into present events. When "the powerful" attack activists today, not only do they kill people "like" Jesus, but they kill Jesus himself again. Thus, popular rituals affirm the continuity of the struggle between good and evil: the battle for social justice in Central America today involves forces that were at work in the death of Jesus two thousand years ago. This dialectical relationship between sacred and secular history reinforces the power and significance of each.

Re-enactments of the passion in the eucharist and vía crucis not only explain contemporary events, but also offer ethical responses to violence, primarily through *imitatio Christi*—following the model response set by Jesus' life and passion. Salvadoran Catholic activists interpret contemporary martyrdoms not just as acts of witness to faith in Christ but primarily as imitations of Jesus' death. The notion of Jesus as the original martyr reformulates classical Christian theologies of martyrdom, which focused on martyrdom as a form of witness to and sacrifice for Christ rather than an explicit imitation of Jesus' own actions. The stress on *imitatio Christi* highlights the humanity of Jesus as a person to be emulated and not simply a divinity to be worshipped. This contrasts with the traditional emphasis on the humanity of Mary in Latin American Catholicism, in which Mary as the exemplar of human faith inspires passivity and resignation is the proper Christian response to suffering. Revised portraits of Jesus also contrast with the dominant popular interpretations stressing his submission and suffering. Progressive Catholic rituals depict Jesus as an active model, encouraging believers to participate in struggles that are seen as continuations of Jesus' own efforts on behalf of the poor and oppressed of his time. By emphasizing Jesus' humanity and his active life and by placing his death in a contemporary, local setting, reworked rituals, such as the *vía crucis*, encourage people to see the repetition of sacred history in current events.

II. Ritual and Imitatio Christi

> I will sit at the table of Christ
> and with him I will be another Christ (146)

In the mass and *vía crucis*, portrayals of Christ's suffering become preparations and models for the deaths of contemporary martyrs. These rituals provide blueprints for how believers ought to live and die. Even though believers cannot follow the model exactly,[18] enacting the passion helps them envision a different course of events and imagine "what might follow from . . . taking up and acting on one set of convictions rather than another."[19] The narrative formulation of contemporary experiences as modelled on the passion expands the range of possible actions and alternative futures available to Salvadoran Catholics. Because of the narrative parallels, the issues raised in rituals regarding Christ's death arise also in relation to present-day killings: the identity of the martyrs, the reasons for the murder, the forces involved, and the consequences for the martyrs, their followers, and society as a whole.

Most simply, popular rituals identify contemporary martyrs as "Christ-like" figures. This identification hinges, of course, on a particular image of Christ. As discussed earlier, progressive popular Catholicism in El Salvador endows Jesus with several distinctive characteristics. It portrays Jesus as working-class, even poor, giving him both humility and solidarity with those who suffer, in his or any time. His bond with the oppressed leads him to defend their rights, to be "the first to raise [his] arm against oppression" (318), as the Salvadoran *Misa Popular* proclaims. Jesus not only fights the abuses committed by the powerful, however, but also provides a model for the oppressed seeking liberation. The last supper, for example, serves as a paradigm of sharing and unity in the midst of deprivation and division. Overall, popular rituals portray Jesus as fully human, joined organically to the poor, and leading them by example and struggle to a better life.

This understanding of Jesus gives rise to a particular interpretation of the reasons for his crucifixion. Salvadoran rituals point to Jesus' prophetic announcement of the truth and struggle for justice as the principal cause of his death. At the first station, where Jesus is condemned to death, Equipo Maíz's *vía crucis* commentary asserts that like Jesus, "Today many are unjustly condemned to death . . . Many are accused for telling the truth."[20] Salvadoran Catholic activists highlight this theme, often linking the fight for social and economic equity to the more theoretical concept of "telling the truth" and especially denouncing existing injustices.

The fact that Jesus was poor and struggled for the poor gave his announcement of the truth special power, popular rituals suggest, but also led directly to his death. A song called "He Was a Worker" tells the story clearly: "He was a worker/ every morning/ he said goodbye to his mother with a kiss./ He worked all day/ broad shoulders, strong hands./ He loved justice above all./ And because of this, they killed him" (247). Being poor and especially defending the rights of the poor are sufficient cause for political killings, in contemporary El Salvador as in Israel during Jesus' time. Catholic activists believe that just as Jesus was crucified for his defense of the oppressed, so contemporary martyrs suffer for their efforts on behalf of the needy of their time. "Today many brothers and sisters who work for the common good and defend the rights of their neighbors are persecuted, imprisoned, tortured, disappeared, or murdered as wrongdoers, just like Jesus," summarizes a 1990 *vía crucis* guide.[21]

The agents of persecution, torture, and murder are those whose interests are threatened by work for the common good. Jesus was killed, according to grassroots theology, because he challenged the exploiters of the poor: "his words bothered them and they killed him."[22] In this perspective, poor people's struggles for dignity and justice today necessarily put them into conflict with the rich, whose actions and wealth itself contradict the message of equality and harmony that is central to the mass and Jesus' mission. As a result of this conflict, the *vía crucis* guide asserts, the powerful today continue to commit murders and "all kinds of evil against the poor and those who take the side of the poor."[23]

According to popular theology, contemporary persecution resembles Jesus' fate not only in the identity of the attackers, but also in the inevitability of death. Progressive Catholics stress that Jesus continued his struggle even though he knew the powerful would probably kill him for threatening their privileges. In their view, this eventuality does not stem from God's will that the innocent suffer, as the traditional interpretation of Jesus' death often claimed. Rather, contemporary ritual and theology in the Salvadoran *iglesia popular* insist that the freely chosen sin of the killers, not any divine inevitability, led to Jesus' death. This reflects progressive Catholicism's contention that evil, including Jesus' death, is something that humans cause and humans must resist. According to this view, contemporary Christians should adopt Jesus' attitude in the struggle against evil: neither a morbid search for death nor a fatalistic acceptance of it, but a clear-eyed knowledge of the likelihood of death and its role in the battle for justice. A popular handbook clarifies this notion at the twelfth station of the cross, when Jesus dies:

> Jesus' death is a consequence of his way of living, the content of his preaching, and his sacrifice for the construction of the kingdom of God. Jesus didn't seek death, because he came to bring life and life in abundance. His death was imposed by the powerful. He accepted it as a consequence of his fidelity to the mission that his father gave him. Jesus gave his life for the love of his father and his brothers and sisters. He obeyed God before men, and because of this he didn't bend before the powerful.[24]

The guilt of the powerful, fidelity to God, and struggle for the kingdom that characterized Jesus' passion also typify the sacrifice of contemporary martyrs, according to many Salvadoran Catholics. They understand Jesus' death not as a result of the moral failings of all people or God's desire for a "ransom," but as the consequence of the injustice imposed by the rich and powerful. Uniting oneself to the death of Jesus does not, as in traditional Catholicism, involve feelings of individual "sin"; rather, it signifies unity with Jesus' struggle to liberate the oppressed. Thus, "every time we eat the bread and drink the wine we renew . . . [our commitment] to do as Jesus did: to give life so that the kingdom of justice and love arrives soon."[25]

Rituals in the popular church call, as the principal inheritance of Jesus' death, for a commitment to continue the struggle for his cause, as followers understand it. This theme is especially clear in the mass. "To participate in the mass is to unite all our work, suffering, struggle, and death to the suffering and death of Jesus," according to a pamphlet from the Archdiocese of San Salvador.[26] In this view, sharing the bread and wine in the eucharist should be a cry against the exploitation of workers who create the wealth: their tables lack bread; their work lacks justice; their communities lack freedom and peace. This inequity demands a commitment to struggle together to transform society so the wealth produced by labor is distributed among all equally, as the bread and wine are shared in the mass.[27] Thus, the Salvadoran Popular Mass claims "God orders us to make of this world/ a table where there is equality/ working and struggling together/ sharing our property" (821).

This effort may require considerable militancy, as well as sacrifice, from believers. According to the Salvadoran *Misa Popular,*

> Whoever accepts the bread and wine accepts communion
> with the struggle and the path of Jesus in his passion
> offering his life in a generous sacrifice,
> giving himself fully and without limit in every step and action
> for the people who raise themselves for their revindication
> Today, Lord, we're hungry for work, a roof, and bread
> give us your body and your blood
> give us combativeness (*combatividad*) (242)

The eucharist should provoke not fatalism and guilt, but class consciousness and "combativeness." Another song from the Salvadoran mass affirms that "Resignation isn't what God wants/ He wants your actions like works of love . . . Today God won't stand for a new Pharaoh/ and he orders all the people to make their liberation" (514). Participation in the mass commits Christians to continue the cause of Jesus, the liberator of the poor. Taking the bread and wine signifies solidarity rather than individualism, commitment to struggle rather than contrition.

The Fruits of Martyrdom

The consequence of this commitment, elaborated in popular theology and rituals, is often suffering and death. However, just as Jesus' own passion brought benefits for himself, his followers, and human society more generally, argues the *iglesia popular*, so the deaths of contemporary martyrs will bear fruit. Progressive Salvadorans' belief that like Jesus', their own suffering serves a larger goal stems from their conviction that they are on God's side and God is on theirs. Thus, they believe that they must continue, as Jesus did, and that their struggle will also bring eventual triumph despite temporary failures.

This conviction of final victory appears in a commentary for the seventh station of the *vía crucis*, when Jesus falls for the second time.

> [Jesus] doesn't feel defeated, and he doesn't abandon his commitment. Jesus knows that what's wrong isn't falling; the real evil is in not getting up. Even though we fall a thousand times, a thousand times we have to raise ourselves up to follow our commitment to give life and happiness to our brothers and sisters.[28]

Despite losses along the way, activists believe their cause will prevail, in part because of their sacrifices. Suffering for the faith, invoked in both the Hebrew Bible and the gospels, can overcome the apparent strength of evil: "Suffering is redemptive: death generates life, death becomes a wellspring of liberation for all humankind."[29]

A conviction that suffering leads to victory helps progressive Salvadoran Catholics maintain their commitment to follow Jesus' struggle despite hardship. Their theology does not, however, advocate resigned acceptance of suffering: "Carrying the cross isn't accepting pain with patience. Carrying the cross is doing something to convert the pain of the humble into joy and happiness."[30] The sacrifices of contemporary martyrs, like Jesus' passion, transform pain into victory, death into life.

While the pain and death may be necessary, they must not be idealized, activists insist; life itself remains the ultimate goal, to be demanded and celebrated.

The eucharist—"the sacrament of [Christ's] death"—expresses the transformative power of suffering with special clarity.[31] The mass affirms that to share in Christ's life, believers must share in his death, as the early church stressed: "It is a grace, not only to believe in Christ, but also to suffer with him" (Phil. 1:29); "We shall live with him only when we have died with him" (2 Tim. 2:11). In this view, initiated by the early apostles and recreated by Christian activists today, the eucharist commemorates not only Jesus' death but also the sacrifices of those who "died with him." Since the early church, writes historian William Clebsch, "The eucharist at once re-enacted the crucifixion and, by association, celebrated the sacrificial victory of martyrdom."[32] Today, popular masses both recall the crucifixion and commemorate the deaths of contemporary martyrs. These rituals make contemporary martyrs themselves into symbols both of Jesus' fate and of the struggle of their contemporary communities.

As the deaths of contemporary martyrs are ritualized, these can come to wield a symbolic power equal to or greater than that of rites such as the eucharist and stations of the cross. Actual martyrdom is the ultimate re-enactment of the passion, a sacrament that guarantees identification with Christ, a call to follow his path, and a supreme contribution to the victory of his cause. The *Misa Campesina* proclaims: "Glory to the one who follows the light of the Gospel,/ the one who denounces injustice without fear!/ Glory to the one who suffers prison and exile/ and gives his life fighting the oppressor" (314). Underlying the politicized meaning given to martyrdom here is a belief in the redemptive power of suffering, grounded on Jesus' own sacrifice.

This redemption is inextricably linked to the promise of resurrection. Popular understandings of Jesus' death and subsequent martyrdoms emphasize the certainty of rebirth after a death suffered in *imitatio Christi*. Salvadoran Catholic activists affirm not a bodily resurrection, however, but the spiritual presence of the fallen, including both Jesus and contemporary martyrs, among those who fight for the same goals. People who have given their lives for the truth, for social justice, for the construction of the kingdom, remain "alive" in those who carry on their fight. Thus, the Salvadoran Popular Mass praises "our God/ who accompanies our people/ who lives in our struggles" (681). And the "Credo" of the *Misa Campesina* vows to Christ:

You are resurrected in every arm that is raised
to defend the people from the exploiter's dominion:
because you are alive on the farm, in the factory, in the school
I believe in your struggle without hesitation,
I believe in your resurrection (165)

In this interpretation, the struggle *is* the resurrection; only by struggling can believers continually resurrect Jesus. They trust that Jesus will accompany and support them in this fight. "With Jesus' resurrection," explains a *vía crucis* booklet, "we know that we're not alone. Jesus Christ is with us and animates us to live and be faithful in the construction of the reign of God."[33]

The living presence of Jesus, accompanying contemporary followers, is invoked explicitly in the eucharist, which recalls the joy of the resurrection as well as the pain of the passion. The bread and wine represent Jesus' rebirth, "the great force of Christians, a fountain of courage and hope . . . a symbol and a guarantee of victory and liberation."[34] In a popular song, believers affirm that "Every time we eat this bread/ we announce the death of the Lord./ Let us proclaim his triumph over hate and evil/ in hope of the heavenly reign" (791).

To progressive Catholic activists, Jesus' triumph over bodily death prefigures and guarantees the final victory of life over death. The resurrection symbolizes for them the inevitable victory of the cause of Christ, i.e., of justice, over the forces of oppression. As Jesus won his battle with death, they insist, so Christians today will defeat the poverty and oppression that bring premature death. Faith in the ultimate victory of life over death motivates believers to continue struggling. They believe that despite the risk of physical death, they do not truly die as long as others continue their fight. "The resurrection of Jesus is the affirmation of the one who lives and dies working and struggling for the reign of God, and his justice triumphs; because of this, the resurrection of Jesus is our victory."[35] Christ's resurrection is repeated, progressive popular theology insists, in every person who "lives and dies working and struggling for the reign of God" because the passion is an exact model and metaphor for the killings of subsequent believers, understood as martyrs for Christ's cause: the cause of justice, thus of life, for the poor. Jesus is also a prototype, the ideal case by reference to which other martyrs can be identified.[36]

This view asserts that some must die, as Jesus did, to build the reign of God, "to generate new life for the next generations."[37] Many

Salvadoran activists believe that like Jesus, those who give their lives are reborn in the unity of those who follow, in the daily battle for justice, and in the ultimate victory of Christ and all "true" Christians. They envision this triumph as the construction of a reign of justice, without poverty and repression. Insofar as this goal is approximated in human history, they believe, the blood of the martyrs bears fruit.

Sacred History, Sacrifice, and Ethics

The power of popular religion relies in large part on an explicit connection between sacred and current history. This link, expressed in reflections on contemporary events, in ritual, and in song, relies in part on parallels between the death of Jesus, the first martyr for the cause of the poor, and the killings of people who work for social justice today. The connection comes not only in the form of parallels, however, but also from the perception that past and present martyrs are "part of the same tree," in Ileto's words.[38] A continuous narrative encompasses sacred and contemporary history, giving a place and a meaning to all events within it.

Because of these links, ritual re-enactments of the path to the cross and the passion endow the deaths of contemporary believers with the meaning and value of Christ's sacrifice and provide guidelines for ethical responses. Rituals in the Salvadoran *iglesia popular*, like the Philippine *pasyon* described by Ileto, make people "aware of a pattern of universal history. They also became aware of ideal forms of behavior and social relationships, and a way to attain these through suffering, death, and rebirth." Especially in times of crisis, these models provide "a set of ideas and images" with which people can make sense of their condition.[39] They provide a language of resistance and also models for behavior, based on the image of Jesus as a tireless and selfless fighter for social justice.

According to this model, following Jesus in his call to build the reign of God requires not just works of justice but willingness to sacrifice innocent blood on the path to this goal. A reflection for the twelfth station of the *vía crucis*, when Jesus dies on the cross, states: "In this station let us learn from Jesus, as the martyrs learned from him, to be faithful even to the point of giving their lives for love."[40] At the same station, another commentary explains:

> The one who came to give life, died as a failure. He didn't seek success, and he didn't go after power. He came to liberate the

poor and for this he died. He was faithful to his mission until the end. Today we must follow the example that Jesus left us.[41]

Rites like the *vía crucis* and the eucharist unite believers' lives to that of Jesus and commit them to follow his model of struggle and sacrifice. These rites construct an ethic that demands as much as the code of the early martyrs: "Survival is not an adequate reason for abandoning the struggle for the upbuilding of the new humanity."[42] Underlying the severity of the demand and the harshness of the consequences is the hope, even certainty, that those who repeat Jesus' passion will share his resurrection. In this perspective, contemporary martyrs, as well as Jesus himself, live on in the community of believers and in individuals who continue working for the same cause. This work is motivated by a desire to keep Jesus and recent martyrs alive and to fulfill the promise of their sacrifices by realizing their goals.

By linking contemporary killings to Christ's passion, grassroots theology validates the new deaths as chapters in sacred history. These events "are not allowed to remain situated in the context of everyday life," in Ileto's words, "but are charged with meaning through juxtaposition with transcendental ideas."[43] In El Salvador, rituals such as the eucharist and the *vía crucis* express and reinforce this connection between the sacred and the mundane through the lyrics of songs and the words of reflections at the stations of the cross. By presenting political and personal crises not in secular terms but in terms of a new kind of relation between people and the divine, these rituals thus help "re-enchant" the world in which people live and suffer.

The next three chapters will explore the ways members of the Salvadoran popular church, building on central themes of rituals such as the mass and *vía crucis*, constructed a theological ethics to make sense of the political killings that they understand as martyrdom. In this popular theology, as in ritual re-enactments of Jesus' passion, sacred history provides potent metaphors for understanding present history as part of an overarching divine plan, in which the forces of evil will take their share of victims, but the sacrifices will eventually bear fruit. Building on biblical stories and images, progressive Catholics in El Salvador constructed a belief system to make sense of the repression shadowing their lives and their nation's history. They sought, in short, to understand the killings of leaders and companions not as arbitrary tragedies shattering people's difficult struggles to improve their lives, but as sacrifices necessary for ultimate liberation and as a guarantee of life in abundance for succeeding generations.

Endnotes

1. *El pueblo canta: Libro de cantos* (San Salvador: Archdiocese of San Salvador, 1987), no. 736. This is the primary Catholic hymnbook used in El Salvador. I will refer to songs in it by noting the song number in parentheses after the quotation.

2. Comaroff, *Body of Power, Spirit of Resistance*, 213. See also Paul Diener, "The Tears of Saint Anthony: Ritual and Revolution in Eastern Guatemala," *Latin American Perspectives* 18, no. 3 (Summer 1978): 92–116.

3. See Cardenal, *El poder eclesiástico*, 165–167 on official guidelines and attitudes about the mass and other sacraments in the Salvadoran church historically.

4. Jonathan Z. Smith, *Imagining Religion: From Babylon to Jonestown* (Chicago: University of Chicago Press, 1982), 4.

5. Thomas Kselman, "Ambivalence and Assumption in the Concept of Popular Religion," in *Religion and Political Conflict in Latin America*, ed. Daniel Levine (Chapel Hill: University of North Carolina Press, 1986), p. 31.

6. Juan Hernández Pico, "The Experience of Nicaragua's Revolutionary Christians," in *The Challenge of Basic Christian Communities*, eds. Sergio Torres and John Eagleson (Maryknoll, NY: Orbis, 1981), 66.

7. *Vía Crucis* (Santa Tecla, El Salvador: Equipo de Educación Maíz, 1990), 23.

8. *¿Qué es la misa?* (San Salvador: Archdiocese of San Salvador, n.d.), 7. See also Robert Stark, "Religious Ritual and Class Formation: The Story of the Pilsen Saint Vitus Parish and the 1977 Vía Crucis" (Ph.D. dissertation, University of Chicago, 1981), 8–9.

9. Andrés Opazo Bernales, "La iglesia y el pueblo como sujeto político," *Polémica* (San Salvador): 2, no. 3 (Sept.–Dec. 1987), 10.

10. Quoted in Luis Ramos, "Obispo, profeta y mártir," in *Signos del Reino de Dios* (Mexico City) 17, no. 49 (Second trimester 1980), 15.

11. Ileto, *Pasyon and Revolution*, 11.

12. *Sacramentos como vida y compromiso* (San Salvador: Archdiocese of San Salvador, n.d.), 38.

13. Rutilio Grande, speech given 13 February 1977, Apopa, El Salvador; quoted in *La iglesia salvadoreña lucha, reflexiona y canta* (León, Nicaragua: CONIP/Ediciones Secretariado Cristiano de Solidaridad "Mons. Oscar Arnulfo Romero," 1983), 243.

14. Orlando Espín, "The God of the Vanquished: Foundations for a Latino Spirituality," *Listening: Journal of Religion and Culture* 27, No. 1 (Winter 1992): 74.

15. See Espín, "Trinitarian Monotheism."

16. Cyprian, *Letters* 6, no. 2, quoted in Lesbaupin, *Blessed Are the Persecuted*, 47.

17. See Ileto, *Pasyon and Revolution*, 80, 311, for a discussion of this issue in popular religio-political movements in the Philippines.

18. Smith argues that the knowledge that ritual perfection is impossible to achieve is in fact precisely what gives ritual its power. See *Imagining Religion*, 4.

19. Michael Goldberg, *Theology and Narrative: A Critical Introduction* (Nashville: Abingdon, 1982), 234.

20. *Vía Crucis*, 5.

21. *Vía Crucis: en compañía de nuestro pastor Mons. Oscar Arnulfo Romero y Galdámez* (San Salvador: n.p., 1990), 15.

22. *Qué es la misa?*, 9.

23. *Vía Crucis: en compañía*, 15.

24. Ibid., 16–17.

25. *Qué es la misa?*, 15.

26. Ibid., 10.

27. Ibid., 24.

28. *Vía Crucis*, 17.

29. Lesbaupin, *Blessed Are the Persecuted*, 94. See also Maurice Bloch and Jonathan Parry, "Introduction," to M. Bloch and J. Parry, eds., *Death and the Regeneration of Life* (Cambridge: Cambridge University Press, 1982), 15.

30. *Vía Crucis*, 9.

31. Karl Rahner, *On the Theology of Death* (Edinburgh and London: Nelson, 1961), 85.

32. Clebsch, *Christianity in European History*, 58.

33. *Vía Crucis: en compañía*, 21.

34. *¿Qué es la misa?*, 9–10.

35. *Vía Crucis: en compañía*, 21.

36. On prototypical and metaphorical moral reasoning, see Mark Johnson, *Moral Imagination: Implications of Cognitive Science for Ethics* (Chicago: University of Chicago Press, 1993), 8–9, 78.

37. *Vía Crucis: en compañía*, 19.

38. Ileto, *Pasyon and Revolution*, 254.

39. Ileto, *Pasyon and Revolution*, 254; see also 11–12.

40. *Vía Crucis: en compañía*, 17.

41. *Vía Crucis*, 27.

42. Lesbaupin, *Blessed Are the Persecuted*, 94.

43. Ileto, *Pasyon and Revolution*, 42.

5

The Martyrs

The individual proves his unity with the people unmistakably
through death alone.

Hegel, *Natural Law*

I. Definitions

The English word *martyr*, like the Spanish *mártir*, comes from the
Greek *martyrs*, "witness." The first Christians called all believers martyrs,
witnesses to faith in Christ. For early Christians, as Origen explained in
the third century C.E., "anyone who witnesses to the truth, whether
through words or through actions, has the right to be called a martyr."
Origen noted, however, that this definition narrowed as the church
developed. Eventually "among the brethren, inspired by their reverence
for those who resisted even to death, the custom was established of calling martyrs only those who witnessed to the mystery of faith with the
spilling of their blood."[1] In *Lumen Gentium*, the Second Vatican Council
reaffirmed this definition, calling a martyr one who "freely accept[s]
death on behalf of the world's salvation."[2]

The criteria for martyrdom outlined in the mid-1700s by Pope
Benedict XIV still guide the official Catholic definition of martyrdom.
Benedict defined a Christian martyr as a believer who dies for the faith
and, specifically, whose killer (the "tyrant") was "provoked into killing
the victim by the latter's clear and unambiguous profession of faith."
Further, the killer must have been motivated by hatred of the faith
(*odium fidei*). Benedict also required witnesses who could attest to the
martyr's steadfastness. It was not enough for a person merely to die for a
noble cause; the victim must also have been seen to refuse to recant.
Such superhuman fortitude under torture proved to believers that Christ

was working within the martyr and thus distinguished the Christian martyr from other people killed by tyrants and/or for good causes.[3]

While death for the Christian cause has been the main criterion for Christian martyrdom, the definition of that cause has varied over the church's history. In cases after the end of Roman rule, including the killings of missionaries in European colonies or of Catholics during the Protestant Reformation, it was not always clear whether the "martyrs" were killed for hatred of the faith or for their links to political causes and forces. In such cases, it was difficult to prove that a martyr died for purely religious reasons. In this century, the death of Polish priest Maximilian Kolbe, killed by Nazis in 1941, expanded the church's conception of martyrdom. Kolbe, a prisoner at Auschwitz, offered his life to save another prisoner. Many Catholics, including the Polish pope John Paul II, hoped to canonize Kolbe. However, his case posed problems for the classical definition of a martyr-saint, because the Nazis did not publicly proclaim their hatred of the Christian faith, but rather pledged to protect it. The Vatican found it difficult to prove, therefore, that Kolbe or other victims of the Nazis were killed for the faith, rather than for political causes. A Vatican commission studying Kolbe's case decided that Kolbe was not a martyr, largely because it was not proven that he had been killed for his faith. Despite this finding, John Paul II canonized Kolbe in 1982 not only for "heroic virtue" (another qualification for sainthood), but as a "martyr of charity."[4] The pope's action introduced the category of "martyrs of charity," Christians who "presupposing a good life, out of great heroicity, offer themselves at a particular point for another."[5] The concept of a "martyr of charity" suggests that a person can die a martyr's death for one element of Christian belief rather than for the faith or the church in general.

Building upon this idea, Jesuit theologian Karl Rahner defines martyrdom as "the free, tolerant acceptance of death for the sake of the faith . . . involv[ing] the entirety of the Christian confession of faith or merely one single truth of Christian teaching on faith and morals . . . understood within the context of the entirety of Christian message."[6] Unlike earlier definitions, Rahner distinguishes between persecution for the entirety of the faith and persecution for a single teaching of it. On this point, Rahner echoes Thomas Aquinas, who asserted that dying for the common good could be considered martyrdom from a theological perspective. According to Thomas: "Human good can become divine good if it is referred to God; therefore any human good can be a cause of martyrdom, in so far as it is referred to God."[7] In this light, a believer who willingly dies for an aspect of the faith, such as charity, justice, or peace, can be considered a martyr "for the faith." Rahner also expands the traditional definition by rejecting the idea that martyrs must exhibit a "free, tolerant acceptance of death." He contends, rather, that death in an active struggle for the faith or an aspect of it also can constitute a form of martyrdom. According to Rahner, the example of Jesus' death provides a model for uniting the two elements, since his active struggle in life brought on a death which he then freely accepted.[8] In this view, active struggle to fulfill all or part of Christian teaching can, no less than a refusal to worship idols, result in a true martyr's death.

Contemporary Martyrdom

The large-scale violence against religious activists in South and especially Central America during the 1970s and 1980s challenged official definitions of martyrdom. While some Catholics believe that many, if not all, of the victims of military regimes and death squads qualify as Christian martyrs, the pope has called only Romero a martyr. The Vatican differentiates between the persecution of Christians in Latin America today and true Christian martyrdom for several reasons.

Rome's reluctance to label Latin American Christians "martyrs" stems in part from the identity of the killers. A simple distinction between "Christians" and "pagans" cannot clarify the conflict, because in Latin America today most of the killers claim to be Christians, usually Catholics. If the killer and the victim belong to the same church, "hatred of the faith" on the part of killers cannot define the victims as martyrs. While the case of Kolbe and other victims of Nazism presented a similar challenge, the official church's unanimous (albeit tardy) condemnation of Nazism made it easier to assert that the Nazis did act in *odium fidei* despite their professions of Christianity. Divisions among Catholics in Latin America and in Rome, however, make a similar condemnation of right-wing regimes or paramilitary groups there problematic. The majority of Salvadoran bishops, for example, believed that Catholics involved in opposition political movements threatened the traditional social order and values to which the church remained committed.

Conservative Catholics have frequently questioned the status of contemporary "martyrs," on the grounds that progressive Catholics are politically motivated or, at best, naively manipulated by political organizations. At an even deeper level, many influential men in the Vatican and in Latin American episcopacies do not merely question the source of progressive Catholics' beliefs but disagree with the ideas themselves. A left-leaning social agenda in Latin America does not attract the same support from church leaders as did, eventually, opposition to Nazism (thus helping justify the canonization of Kolbe). Further, the church would not even consider most Catholics killed in Latin America "martyrs of charity," since they made sacrifices not for a particular individual but on behalf of a social group, i.e., "the poor." Even recent innovations, such as Kolbe's case, then, provide insufficient precedent for qualifying progressive Latin American Catholics as martyrs in official terms.

Against the strict constructionists, Mexican theologian Carlos Bravo argues that Latin American Christians are killed "for believing that the real worship of God is life, a life lived in the service of others."[9] Because service to others and especially to life for the poor is central to Christian faith, in his view, death for this conviction qualifies as martyrdom for the faith no less than death precipitated by refusal to sacrifice to a Roman god. Theologians such as Bravo and Jon Sobrino argue that Latin American victims of repression represent a new kind of martyr, which challenges and expands the church's definition of Christian martyrdom.

Kenneth Woodward summarizes the arguments for a new definition of martyrdom grounded in the Latin American experience by linking it to the early church's emphasis on the reign of God. In this view, Jesus himself gave his life for the sake of the eschatological utopia, which at that time was identified with the Christian community. To die for this cause meant to die for the church, but today many Catholics argue that the reign of God is not limited to the church. Rather, the church is called "to serve and extend God's kingdom . . . Martyrs, by making the supreme sacrifice, witness to the absolute claims of the kingdom over all other values, including the value of life itself."[10] Since Catholic social teaching today clearly asserts that justice and peace are signs of God's reign, dying for these values can constitute Christian martyrdom. Whether or not the Vatican comes to accept this new definition of martyrdom, many Latin American Catholics firmly believe that a death for the liberation of the poor qualifies as genuine Christian, and not just "political," martyrdom.

II. Model Martyrs

Jesus as Model Martyr

Especially after the New Testament era, Christian martyrs offered their lives not in *imitatio Christi* but rather as testimony to Jesus' divinity and to the absolute claim he exercised on their faith. Early martyrs like Stephen, rather than Jesus himself, served as their main models. Contemporary Latin American Catholics, however, have renewed the interpretation of Jesus himself as the original martyr and the model for subsequent martyrdoms. Jesus' crucifixion, rather than the death of Stephen or other witnesses to Christian faith, provides the central reference point. The element of witness to faith in Christ is by no means absent from popular martyrologies, nor is the notion of witnessing to previous Latin American martyrs, such as Archbishop Romero. The idea of self-sacrifice as testimony to Christ's divinity, however, takes second place to a view of martyrdom as following the model set by the human Jesus.

An interpretation of martyrdom as a repetition of the passion portrays Jesus primarily though not exclusively as a human person who can be emulated rather than a divinity who demands witness. Without denying Jesus' divinity, this view stresses his humanity, following the emphasis on what biblical scholars call the "historical Jesus" in liberationist Christologies.[11] Biblical *reflexión* in CEBs and *cursillos*, similarly, often focuses on the events of Jesus' life and the ways he provides a model for human action. This approach, contrasting with the traditional emphasis on Christ as the object of faith, has generated shifts in popular Catholic belief as well as changes in the political commitments engendered by faith.

These elements contribute to a popular martyrology that makes Latin America the most likely place, as Woodward writes, for "a genuine expansion of the Catholic concept of martyrdom" to emerge. This expansion has occurred primarily at the grassroots level, where people tell and retell the stories of contemporary martyrs in "a modern *Acta Martyrum.*"[12] In this new book of martyrs, Jesus represents the original and paradigmatic figure, a prototype in relation to whom others gain significance and legitimacy. As the experiences of martyrs move away from this core, the use of the term *martyr* becomes more controversial and less unanimous.

"Saint Romero"

After Jesus, Oscar Romero represents the *iglesia popular*'s consensus choice as model martyr. The official church appeared to recognize this status when, on March 24, 1990, the tenth anniversary of Romero's death, Archbishop Rivera y Damas announced the initiation of a formal investigation into "the life, virtues, and death of his predecessor—the first step toward canonization."[13] Popular responses to the first official recognition of Romero's holiness varied widely. Many Salvadoran laypeople welcomed beatification as an honor and a validation of Romero's prophetic stance on behalf of the poor. "It's a great light to have a saint of America, a living saint. The things that were mute are now going to be expressed," exclaimed Rosa. Romero's champions realize, however, that not all Christians will be joyful about the news. "We're happy," explains José. "But it will cause conflicts for the conservative church, which will have to honor him like the other saints." He adds, perhaps hopefully, "Maybe they'll go to Protestant churches now." Some laypeople believe that sanctification will force conservatives not to leave the Catholic Church but rather to recognize Romero's saintliness. "People who thought badly of him will have to change their attitudes," declares Elena. Amando concurs. "For the CEBs, he's a saint, but the rich didn't want to recognize him. Now they'll have to."

Many Salvadoran Catholics see official beatification as simply redundant. Popular acclaim has long since beatified "Monseñor" as "Saint Romero of América." A Salvadoran living in Washington, DC, explains: "Monseñor Romero is so important and significant that the pueblo (people) no longer consider him human. For the Salvadoran people Monseñor is a saint and many people with problems will even go to the tomb of Monseñor Romero to plead that he intercede on their behalf."[14] Given the widespread popular "sanctification" of Romero, many laypeople view the official acknowledgement as no more than Romero's due, or even past due. Julia shrugs at the hierarchy's belated recognition of the obvious: "He's already a saint for us." Sister Josefa Avila elaborates this notion: "The people already proclaimed him a saint," especially in the parishes where Romero spent time during his tenure as archbishop. He declared that the people were his prophet, "and the people say that he's their prophet," regardless of the official church's position. Ricardo Urioste, archdiocesan vicar-general under Romero and now Rivera, expressed a similar sentiment. Despite charges that Romero was manipulated by the left, Urioste explained in a 1987 interview,

> For me he is a saint and so I really am not interested in applying for a formal canonization process . . . We are so satisfied with Archbishop Romero that we don't need to have him made a saint. The people have him in mind when they suffer, are persecuted, and are killed. He is the one who gives them strength. So what else do you want from a saint?[15]

Many Salvadorans ask no more; popular acclaim of Romero's holiness is widespread and undeniable. Woodward notes that Romero's tomb "has become a national shrine for pilgrims from throughout Central America" and that already "several hundred cures and other 'miracles' have been claimed through his intercession." Even Pope John Paul II has called Romero a martyr.[16]

The difficulty lies in determining what kind of martyr Romero is. It is not clear that the murdered archbishop is a martyr "for the church," killed, as classical Christian martyrs were, because of a tyrant's hatred of the faith. As Woodward writes, "Romero identified the church with 'the people' in such a way that it would be a falsification of his own convictions to suggest that he was killed out of hatred for the church." Romero's death represents a martyrdom, but for a broader cause than the church or even "charity." Woodward continues: "It was not 'the church' that made Romero an assassin's target, but rather his personal, though not exclusive, identification of the cause of Christ with the cause of liberation for the Salvadoran people."[17]

Jon Sobrino agrees that Romero represents a new kind of martyrdom, and, in fact, a new kind of holiness: "a saint within society, not just within the synagogue," who is "at once a Christian saint and a Salvadoran hero." Although this model of holiness is new to El Salvador, Sobrino claims, it is not unprecedented in Christian history. Romero practiced a pure form of *imitatio Christi*, "not just because he was crucified in the end, like Jesus, but because he was with the people . . . Most saints do not get into direct contact with the people, the way Jesus did. That was not the case with Romero."[18] Mario Ferrer also perceived this quality: "the holiest characteristic of Monseñor Romero is that he accompanied the people, he made himself into a pilgrim with the people in their most difficult time . . . He knew how to walk with the people." Because of his firm commitment to "walk with the people," Romero represents a kind of public saint, or, in Sobrino's terms, a "political saint."[19]

The novelty of Romero's public life complicated the official church's ability to respond adequately to his death and, especially, to popular beatification of him. For years after Romero's assassination, both the Salvadoran hierarchy and the Vatican insisted he could not be beatified until the political controversies surrounding his death had subsided, so the opposition could not make political capital out of official recognition. Such "manipulation" would obscure Romero's status as a martyr "for the church" and quite possibly appear to signal church approval for the political opposition, or at least for politically active, progressive sectors of the church. The hierarchy insisted that "before Romero can be recognized as a saint, he must first undergo a kind of transformation: 'the people's saint' must become 'a martyr of the church'."[20]

Thus, the March 1990 announcement that the hierarchy was initiating steps toward beatification surprised many Salvadorans and led them to speculate about what convinced the bishops to move toward beatifying Romero, given their well-known reluctance to do so as long as the political and religious left in El Salvador invoked his name. Some assumed that members of the hierarchy harbored ulterior motives, perhaps a desire to hasten Romero's "de-politicization" and to manipulate his legacy through the canonization process. José Peña of the archdiocese of San Salvador interprets the move toward beatification an attempt to contain Romero within the institutional church by portraying him as a "man of prayer" rather than an activist. A number of laypeople and pastoral agents agree with Daniel Vega, another priest from the archdiocese, that Rome and the hierarchy hope to "ecclesialize" Romero through the beatification and canonization processes. If, in fact, the official church hopes to diminish Romero's popular appeal, it is not likely to succeed. "The church's proceedings cannot change what Romero is for the people," asserts Vega, "just as it cannot change what Jesus is." Peña adds: "the people aren't afraid of losing Romero."

He is probably right: Romero remains an extraordinarily powerful figure in El Salvador. Visitors crowd around his tomb when the cathedral is open, a huge range of popular organizations invoke his name and likeness, and his writings serve as documents for reflection in numerous parishes and base communities. During the final session of an April 1990 *cursillo* in the San Pablo parish, for example, pastoral agents asked participants what topic or idea raised in the courses had most caught their attention. They answered unanimously: the life and martyrdom of Monseñor Romero. "The *comunidades de base* always have Monseñor Romero present," explained one member. The *cursillo* participants concluded that "we lived a *convivencia* [group celebration] of life and joy in our flesh, and we felt that Monseñor Romero had been resurrected in our community." They believe that Romero's words and deeds "are still alive. Every word he said, every mass he gave. In every meeting we have, we mention them . . . The presence continues among us," Amando asserts. Mirtala López agrees: "Our people continue to live his words. We take his example and continue his work. He lives in the hearts of the people. We can't help but mention his name throughout our whole lives . . . All the people live with the memory of Romero."

It is a dangerous memory. Simply possessing a photo of Romero or a book about him has been sufficient cause for harassment and persecution by the military. Elena recalls that in the early 1980s, "No one talked about Monseñor, because it was subversive." Many Salvadorans, especially in the villages and poor *barrios* that have felt the brunt of repression, hesitate to discuss the archbishop even today. A journalist trying to interview young people who knew Romero ten years after his death found it difficult to persuade them to speak openly about him. "Talking about Monseñor Romero is a sin," one boy told the reporter. In the San Pablo parish, Rosa and Amando used identical phrases, in separate interviews, to echo the youth's fear: "having a picture of Monseñor is a sin." They mean that remembering "Monseñor" is a sin in the eyes of the rich, an offense against the status quo, a threat to the powerful, and thus a source of both strength and danger for the weak.

When they overcome the fear of reprisals and discuss the archbishop, Salvadorans often stress how truly "alive" he remains for them. "Hearing his homilies gave me strength," recalls Jesús. Romero's words are still vibrant, "as if he hadn't died." The words live because they struck home with the people who listened. "He spoke so clearly and certainly," Elena explains. For her, Romero helped to change "the idea that God did everything and we just had to suffer."

Romero often visited rural and urban parishes in the archdiocese of San Salvador, and residents remember his visits vividly. He wrote down what people in the *colonias* and *cantones* told him, they recall, and he ate tortillas and beans, just like them, wanting nothing different. Lucía, a San Pablo resident, affirms that "he saw no differences between people. He would talk with anyone." His willingness to live in a hospital for cancer patients, to eat with the poor, and to listen to them had an impact as great as his words. Because he shared people's experiences, María explains, Romero "saw the injustice that exists . . . and he saw his obligation." Like Romero, other pastoral agents killed by the right are remembered by Catholic activists as those who literally took upon themselves the lot of the weak.

In the view of many progressive Catholics, Romero and other church martyrs died not only because of their solidarity with the poor but also because they told the truth and denounced injustice. Tomasa summarizes the course of events: "[Romero] said we should be free. He told us the truth, and we saw that he was killed for telling the truth, for saying 'No more repression!'" Romero is remembered as a defender of the poor and especially of peasants. "*Campesinos* are never listened to," explains Clara. "Only Monseñor Romero made himself their voice."

With Romero, said Ignacio Ellacuría, "God passed through El Salvador." Laypeople describe Romero in similar terms. "Monseñor Romero was a Christ of the church, a living Christ," asserts Tomasa. Like Jesus, explains Rosa, Romero spread his message through the people who knew him and were inspired by him to continue his work. And like Jesus, many claim, Romero sealed his covenant with the people with his own blood. Elena found the archbishop's steadfastness saintly:

> Monseñor Romero made a pact with God, that he would be faithful to the people and that he wouldn't lie to people who are suffering. These things aren't of this world, but are God's. He wasn't a man like any other, but was chosen by God. He was a prophet, which we may never have again in El Salvador.

Many Salvadorans agree that their country and perhaps the world will never again see "a Romero." "There won't be another prophet like him," repeat both José and Fabio. They found in Romero that rarest of persons in El Salvador: a powerful person willing to defend the dignity and share the fate of the weak. The loss of Romero does not destroy the goals he supported, affirms Ana María, a catechist from San Felipe, Chalatenango: "They tried to silence the voice of the people with his death, but the people are always moving ahead. And there have been other deaths, but the people are always brave, and they always move ahead."

III. Martyrdom, the Church, and the People

Pastoral Workers

Of the nuns and priests who have "moved ahead" with the people, nearly two dozen have been murdered since 1970. Many laypeople have a clear interpretation of why these pastoral agents have been killed: "They killed Monseñor Romero and the other priests for the same reason, because they tried to awaken the people who live oppressed," Clara believes. "They were opening our ears, so that we wouldn't give ourselves up to filth and corruption. The priests that said the poor are worth as much as the rich, that our work has value and we shouldn't sell ourselves, that the poor have the right to demand their rights also" are the priests who have been killed. Conversely, laypeople often add, the priests who did not commit themselves to the poor avoided persecution: "those who didn't put [the principles of Medellín] into practice are very comfortable," a San Pablo resident claims.

In many communities that have lost pastoral agents, residents speak of slain priests and nuns more often than current pastoral workers. People from northern San Salvador remember Octavio Ortiz, murdered in January 1979. Ortiz, who began working with CEBs in San Salvador before his ordination, was well-loved. "We saw him not as a priest, but as a friend," remembers Tomás. He was not "untouchable," like other clerics, but was humble with everyone, recalls Emilia: "For him, everyone was equal." Antonio adds that the priest was "just like Christ" in this respect, treating the poor with respect and making works central to his faith. Thus, Arnulfo, who lived in one of the *barrios* where Ortiz worked, explains that "Octavio didn't hide when things got difficult. He was the first to go out."

Over ten years later, residents of the neighborhood where Ortiz was killed remember the morning of the murders in vivid detail: the sounds of shooting from the parish house, the National Guard swarming the area for hours later, the television and press reports that a "guerrilla training center" had been raided and several "militants" killed. After the attack, a large number of people left the base community and even the neighborhood, and for more than a decade many residents refused to enter El Despertar. The trauma of the killings, however, did not lessen and possibly intensified the affection and respect many felt for Ortiz. People in areas where Ortiz worked recall him as a "prophet" who came

after other priests had left or been expelled and who chose not to abandon them in spite of the obvious danger. Juana asserts that "his example
left us very motivated . . . We've had difficult times, but we always keep
working."

The November 1989 murders of six Jesuits at the Central American
University was the most recent fatal attack against progressive pastoral
agents in El Salvador. Popular reaction to the slaying of the Jesuits, while
strong, differed from the response to the murders of Romero, Ortiz, and
other pastoral figures. Although most of the Jesuits did not work regularly in parishes, they were well-known as critics of the regime and
defenders of human rights. In this capacity, asserts Vilma, "They helped
people to have dignity and the courage to demand what's just." Antonio,
a San Lucas resident, agrees that "the priests came to wake up the people
who were asleep. This was why they killed them. It's not good for them
[the killers] that the people wake up." Jon Sobrino reports that a
Salvadoran woman told him after seeing Ellacuría on television, not
long before he was killed, that "not since they murdered Archbishop
Romero has anyone spoken out so plainly in this country."[21]

Ordinary People

The murders of prominent people like the Jesuits have an impact
beyond the communities where they lived and worked. First, such deaths
affect foreign (and Salvadoran) opinion more than other killings. "If this
[the November 16 murders] hadn't happened," asks Miguel, a university
student; "how long would it take for the United States Congress to realize
this is an army that kills civilians, even priests? Something like this had
to happen for the world to see the reality of El Salvador."[22] While the
killings of well-known figures thus may serve a positive purpose by making clear the brutality of the Salvadoran regime, they also increase the
sense of vulnerability of ordinary people. "If they don't respect a priest,
how will they respect us?" asks Vilma. If even public figures like Romero
and the Jesuits are killed, in other words, how will poor laypeople survive?
Referring to the murder of Romero, Ruth declares that "They don't have
any respect. They'll kill a saint, so of course they'll be brave enough to
kill any ordinary person."

In the past ten or fifteen years, "they" have found the courage to kill
tens of thousands of ordinary persons. The deaths of laypeople raise
anew the question of the cause for which martyrs die. The murder of a

priest or nun, a clear representative of the church, is easier to understand as a death for the faith than is the killing of a Catholic layperson who is also a peasant activist, for example. To understand the latter as a martyr requires a broader understanding of the Christian cause as, for example, social justice. Most progressive laypeople in El Salvador make this connection without difficulty, reflecting the overlap between religious and political values in their worldview.

Many progressive Catholics quickly perceive a martyrlike quality in the killings of ordinary laypeople as equal to those of better-known pastoral workers. While the deaths of priests and nuns may be better publicized, no intrinsic difference separates pastoral workers and laypeople, according to Catholic activists. For example, Fabio, an older man from Chalatenango, asserts that the deaths of laypeople have the same value as those of priests, but receive less prestige because "in this society, people are valued differently." Alejandro Acaya explains that "The blood of peasants is the same as the blood of bishops, physically and religiously."[23] Mirtala López elaborates: "There's no difference between Monseñor Romero and a neighbor, because they're all our martyrs, and we're all human beings. To the degree that we identify with our people, so the people will recognize us as their martyrs." Solidarity with the people's cause, not official status in the church, makes one a martyr, in this view, and no distinction separates clergy and laypeople who give their lives because they believe in and follow the commands of the God of the poor.

Anonymous Christians and Political Martyrs

Not only Catholics who have consciously dedicated themselves to the cause of God qualify as martyrs in the eyes of many progressive Salvadorans. Many argue that commitments and actions may define as "Christian" persons who do not identify themselves as such, or even those who actively reject the church. Just as the popular church finds confessions of Christianity meaningless without praxis on behalf of others, it often considers such praxis sufficient evidence of faith. If commitment to others rather than invocations of the name of God make someone a true Christian, in this perspective, then even nonbelievers can be Christian martyrs, if they give their lives for justice.[24] Thus, political activists who do not claim to be "Christian" but who renounce their families, their homes, and even their own safety for others would qualify as martyrs. "I see [a dead revolutionary] as a testimony, as someone who's died for others, as part of the line of martyrs," says Elizabeth, even if the one who dies would not see him- or herself as a Christian martyr.

In the same vein, many Salvadorans claim that anyone who works for social justice qualifies as an authentic Christian, echoing Karl Rahner's understanding of "anonymous Christians" as nonprofessed Christians who nonetheless live by what Rahner sees as essentially Christian values.[25] In this view, popular organizations and the church do the same work, all grounded ultimately on Christian principles and commitment. According to Mirtala López, "For God, there are no distinctions, because the cause is the same. We're following the same example. So we can't make a distinction, just because you weren't in the church when you died." In this view, action matters more to God than faith. Clara claims, for example, that "a unionist sheds his or her blood so that all will eat, and also because s/he's a Christian. Because if someone weren't a Christian, s/he wouldn't give his life for others." She elaborates her understanding of Christianity by noting that "If they kill a unionist, [it's because] s/he's struggling for everyone, for food and wages. If they kill a priest, he's doing the same thing. He denounces injustice. It's the same thing. For me there's no difference."

Although many Salvadoran Catholics see "no difference," others hesitate to identify nonbelievers as Christians solely because of the content of their actions. They believe that laypeople can properly be called "martyrs" only if they are killed for their religious commitment and actions. In this perspective, not even all murdered Christians are martyrs, since even a committed Christian might be killed as a result of political beliefs or actions, as Pablo argues. People who sacrifice themselves for a political cause may perform a valuable service to the community and deserve recognition, but they do not necessarily qualify as Christian martyrs in the eyes of all Salvadoran Catholics.

Some Salvadorans make a distinction by calling nonbelievers who give their lives for a just cause "martyrs of the people," similar but not identical to Christian martyrs. José contends that when leaders of popular organizations are killed, their professions of faith are irrelevant. "The people recognize them as their own martyrs. They are popular martyrs." The connections between religious and "popular" martyrs reflects, in part, the fact that many Latin Americans do not make the distinction between politics and religion that often seems natural in the United States or Europe. Religiosity, especially popular Catholicism, permeates all aspects of Salvadoran popular culture, and a Christian perspective is often taken for granted. Some Salvadorans even argue that most members of political organizations have made political decisions based on their inherited faith, even if unconsciously.

Commitment and Risk

We know the risks we take in trying to make the word of God come alive.

Elena

The classical Christian definition does not label as martyrs people who die without knowingly taking risks for their faith. A number of Salvadorans, however, argue that the victims of apparently "random" deaths, such as mass killings, qualify as martyrs "despite their lack of consciousness," in Elena's words. This argument identifies victims of "random" political violence as martyrs for a number of reasons. First, they belong to what Jon Sobrino calls "a martyred community," such as the peasantry, membership in which often proves as dangerous as individual activism.[26] Further, an apparent lack of consciousness may hide a deep commitment, since people in war zones and especially in repopulated villages know that simply living in those regions puts them at risk, regardless of their other activities. From this angle, residents of war zones who are killed by aerial bombing or an indiscriminate massacre can be martyrs for the Christian ideal of a just society as much as people like Romero who pursued that ideal more explicitly. Many Salvadorans also point out that the same forces that kill random and "passive" victims also kill better-known martyrs like Romero and the Jesuits, further joining the different types of victims.

While many Salvadorans see connections between selective and random killings, even people with a broad definition of martyrdom generally agree that the clearest followers of Jesus and the early martyrs are people who deliberately choose to work for an ideal and know the risks they take. Elizabeth defines a martyr as "a person who gives his or her life, conscious that one day he'll be killed for his or her ideals." Miguel asserts that "Only people who really discover their role and their commitment are martyrs. Not just any person is a martyr, but only those who really live their commitment." In an effort to retain the force of martyrdom as a distinctly religious term, this perspective resists defining as a martyr anyone who dies in political violence.

Awareness of risk is often linked, in popular martyrologies, to a certainty of impending death. This is especially evident in stories about "protoypical" martyrs, such as priests. Salvador, a member of the pastoral team in San Felipe, Chalatenango, says that "Monseñor [Romero] said he'd die struggling for the poor, and he knew he'd be killed." Tomasa agrees: "Monseñor was very prepared for his death." Noemí, a resident of El Paisnal, Rutilio Grande's birthplace, recalls that Grande told the community "They're going to kill me, and when I die, don't cry. Put out roses." Octavio Ortiz's parishioners also report that he foresaw his death. Although some people wanted Ortiz to return to his home village, the priest "had decided to stay with the people, to give his life if necessary," Angel remembers. Ortiz prepared youths in his parish of Mejicanos to continue his work. "He knew what would happen," believes Emilia, "and because of this he left them prepared." Like Grande, Ortiz did not want his parishioners to dwell upon his death. "Don't look for me among the dead," he told Antonio. "I'm with you."

Not only priests approach death this way, according to popular retellings of the martyrs' lives. The widow of a catechist from Chalatenango recalls that her husband told her: "Don't cry for me . . . be brave, give an example to the rest. I'm not alive for no reason [*sólo por que sí*]. Christ gave me life, and now he'll take it from me. I don't mind dying."[27] The catechist was convinced, as were Grande and Ortiz, that the prospect of violent death is a necessary aspect of struggling for justice in El Salvador today. "Whoever is working for the Gospel, in the service of others, knows what's going to happen to him or her, and that way gives his or her life," argues Norma. The emphasis on "giving" one's life stresses the idea that the martyr rather than the killer ultimately controls the sacrifice. For Arnulfo, "The martyrs . . . don't have their lives taken, but they give them . . . This is the true testimony of the martyrs, that they *give* their lives."

People who risk their lives in the face of evident danger are what Miguel, a student at the UCA, calls "martyrs *en potencia*," potential martyrs. "We don't need dead martyrs now, but potential martyrs, people who accept living with all the consequences of the commitment." The concept of potential martyrs resembles the early Christian category of "confessor," encompassing believers who had been imprisoned or tortured, but not killed, for their faith during the time of the Roman Empire. Confessors "were reverenced for their public witness of faith and their readiness to die for it," according to Kenneth Woodward.[28] In

Christian tradition, confessors, like Miguel's understanding of martyrs *en potencia*, accepted the consequences of their faith and maintained their convictions even in the face of physical suffering.

Accepting the consequences of commitment may include ideas about the ways one's death may contribute to the cause. According to Anita and Eugene Weiner's study of martyrdom, "The martyr's decision to sacrifice his or her life is often based on a rationally grounded belief that the principle he or she represents will live because of the sacrifice." The martyr may not be an "irrational believer" but a "rational social reformer" willing to risk her or his own life for a cause.[29] Without necessarily calculating the results of their own deaths, as the Weiners suggest, Salvadoran activists may indeed realistically evaluate the possibility of their own death and decide to take that risk because of the presumed contribution to their ultimate goal.

Being a martyr *en potencia* requires preparing oneself for the possibility of death, a complex and often lengthy process. For many, as Josefa Avila explains, martyrdom is not one instant, but "a life of conversion and commitment." Laypeople look to well-known martyrs as examples of this attitude. Amanda Campos, a member of the *pequeña comunidad*, explains that people sacrifice their lives gradually, separating themselves from comforts, eliminating prejudices, and losing their fear of insults. Like the early Christian martyrs preparing themselves for death, she believes, Salvadorans today must learn to give themselves day by day. This preparation involves separation from one's family, if not through physical distance then through the potential martyr's decision that not even family attachments can deter her or him from working for an ideal. Elizabeth recalls that her son grew up seeing her and her husband work in a base community and then participated himself in youth groups. The youth greatly admired Romero and a priest in their community who was murdered in 1979. In late 1980, when he was fifteen, he told his mother that he wanted to join the FMLN to participate in the general offensive of January 1981. At first, she told him there were other ways he could contribute, but his response silenced her arguments: "You gave me wings, and now you want to cut my wings."

Estela, a refugee from an impoverished village in Chalatenango, recalls her response to her son's decision to join the guerrillas with a simple question: "What's a person going to do?" If this is heroism, it is born of necessity, of a lack of alternatives. People die regardless, poor Salvadorans often insist; one might as well "die for something." Elena clarifies:

We're going to die anyway, and if I run risks [it is in] doing the
work I should do because the people and God demand it. If I
refuse to do it [it is] in order to take care of myself, to be comfortable. But I prefer to do what God wants and to run the risks.
God has given us our time, and we won't die until he's ready.
We should do what we have to do.

In popular views of martyrdom, self-sacrifice presupposes not only
courage, but also humility, the belief that "We're not the only ones in
the world," as Mirtala López says. This humility, or the subordination of
purely individual interests, stems in part from a close identification with
the community, or what Daniel Vega calls "the spirit of the community
that takes one to the ultimate consequences, which means martyrdom."
This collective sense has roots also in pre-Hispanic indigenous beliefs
that the community transcends (or encompasses) individual lives or
interests. Popular theology closely links the community and the divine
as sources of the spirit underlying their willingness to take risks.

IV. Violence

Progressive Catholics in El Salvador have acted on their commitments in many ways, mostly nonviolent. A significant number, however,
have advocated or adopted violent means of social change, such as guerrilla warfare. The use of violence raises significant questions for both
academic and popular interpretations of martyrdom. Historically, the
Roman Catholic Church has acknowledged the legitimacy of violence
in some circumstances, chiefly in self-defense. In *Populorum Progressio*
(1967), Pope Paul VI offered a cautious legitimation of revolutionary
violence "where there is manifest, long-standing tyranny which would
do great damage to fundamental personal rights and dangerous harm to
the common good of the country."[30] Thus, the church acknowledges the
possibility that a Christian may legitimately decide to take up arms
against a tyrannical government.

In his pastoral letters, sermons, and addresses, Oscar Romero ampli-
fied the discussion on the kinds of violence the church considers justifiable. Although Romero never declared support for the guerrilla
movement, he granted legitimacy to insurrectional violence and to violence in self-defense. In his fourth pastoral letter, written in August
1979, Romero distinguished various types of violence in El Salvador. In

all cases, he wrote, the church condemns the structural violence of poverty and the "arbitrary violence of the state" that represses people who protest structural injustice. Romero also denounced the "violence of the extreme right," meaning the death squads which, like a repressive state, "try to uphold the unjust social order" and which enjoy an impunity "which makes one suspect official connivance."[31]

The archbishop's critique of these kinds of violence follows the teachings of Vatican II and Medellín, which condemn the institutional violence of poverty. Romero departed from official Catholic teaching, however, in his writing about "terrorist violence." Worth quoting in its entirety is his pithy statement on this subject, telling in part for what it does not say.

> The church also condemns the violence perpetrated by politico-military groups or individuals when they *intentionally* victimize innocent persons, or when the damage they do is *disproportionate*, in the short or medium term, to the positive effect they *wish* to achieve.[32]

Notably, Romero did not issue a blanket condemnation of "terrorist" violence, i.e., violence committed by "politico-military groups or individuals," as the church has often done. He also made important qualifications in the nature of the terrorist violence that the church denounces, thus leaving open the possibility of legitimating violence for political ends when it did not intentionally victimize innocent people and when it was meant to achieve benefits greater than the damage it caused.

This laid the groundwork for Romero's defense of "insurrectional violence" in another brief paragraph in the same pastoral letter. The archbishop cited the church's "classic teaching" that legitimizes insurrection in the case of "evident, prolonged tyranny," as recognized in *Populorum Progressio*, and noted that "our own national constitution recognizes the right of just insurrection."[33] At another time, Romero elaborated his position on revolutionary violence:

> When a dictatorship seriously violates human rights and attacks the common good of the nation, when it becomes unbearable and closes all channels of dialogue, of understanding, when this happens the church speaks of the legitimate right of insurrectional violence.[34]

His matter-of-fact tone suggests, rather deceptively, that it is quite ordinary and traditional for the church to justify insurrectional violence.

Romero also described a final type of violence, which he calls the "violence of legitimate defense" and locates "in the same class as legitimate insurrectional violence." Legitimate defense occurs "when a person or group repels by force an unjust aggression that they have suffered," he noted, quoting his own third pastoral letter. He then specified that the violence of legitimate defense is "aroused when changes in the structures of oppressive violence are delayed, and when it is believed that the structures can be kept in being through repressive violence."[35] Violent defense is provoked, in other words, by the violence of the state that seeks to maintain unjust socioeconomic structures by repressing legitimate protest against them.

In delineating his categories of violence, Romero outlined a philosophical justification for certain kinds of violence in the Salvadoran context. Near the end of his discussion of violence, he described the conditions under which the violence of insurrection or defense can be legitimate from a Christian point of view. This interpretation draws on the Christian tradition of justifiable (usually shortened to "just") war, rooted in the thinking of Augustine and Thomas Aquinas. First, Romero wrote, it is necessary "that the violence of legitimate defense not be greater than the unjust aggression" that provoked it. Second, violence may legitimately be used "only after every other possible peaceful means has been tried." Third, violence can be justified only when it does not "bring in retaliation an even greater evil that is being resisted."[36] Violence can best be avoided, according to Romero, by guaranteeing "a truly democratic state, one that defends the fundamental rights of all its citizens, based on a just economic order." Only in this way can a government ensure that legitimate violence of insurrection or self-defense will not be employed by those denied their rights. The archbishop concluded that although Christians should avoid violence whenever possible, ultimately they are "peaceful, but not passive" and not incapable of fighting when necessary.[37]

Romero wrote his fourth pastoral letter at a time when nonviolent doors to change were closing in El Salvador and armed fronts were gathering strength. Many Catholics involved in movements for social justice were wrestling with the question of revolutionary violence in the face of increasingly brutal state repression, which escalated even more sharply after the October 1979 coup. The archbishop's own struggle with the legitimacy of violent response in that situation mirrored the questions of many other Salvadoran Christians, and his conclusions reached receptive ears.

Even before Romero wrote his fourth pastoral letter, many laypeople and pastoral workers had begun debating the legitimacy of revolutionary violence. The experience of the Belgian priests who helped form the CEBs in northern San Salvador is instructive. The priests rejected the use of violence initially and preached passive resistance to their parishioners. This rigid pacifism isolated the pastoral agents from laypeople who found armed struggle, or at least armed self-defense, necessary to continue their work for justice.[38] Representative of at least some of these laypeople is Paco, a member of an urban guerrilla group in San Salvador, who began his activism in the neighborhood CEB. His adoption of armed struggle came from his memory of "all the violence and death . . . it gives you new impetus to keep struggling . . . If they cause violence, they have to know that they'll be met with violence." The increasing repression eventually drove not only laypeople but also a number of pastoral workers, including members of the Belgian team, to abandon their pacifist position. With thousands of other Salvadoran Christians, they decided that government repression left no alternative, and they began, at least in theory, to support the FMLN. Clara summarizes this process: "There were so many massacres. They thought the people would just wait to be killed, and let ourselves be killed, but only to a point. The death squads have caused the people to take up arms . . . The guerrillas struggle for the rights of the people. This is why there is a *guerrilla*."[39]

In a *cursillo* in the San Pablo parish in October 1988, participants discussed the issue of violence in relation to the Medellín document on peace. Their answers to the question of "When can a Christian use arms?" reflect a strong belief that violence is justified as self-defense and a final response to official repression. The use of violence by Christians is justified, they asserted, "when every other recourse has been tried," "when the people demand justice and there's no response," and, finally, when it is necessary "to defend our brothers and sisters." These responses echo traditional just war theory as well as Romero's arguments that violence is legitimate when peaceful means have been exhausted and the violence is employed against a greater evil, i.e., against the structural violence that generates other forms of violence. Traditional just war theory, however, says that violence can only be waged by a legitimate government. Romero's formulation and other justifications of guerrilla warfare (including perhaps *Populorum Progressio*) deviate from tradition on this point.

The view of revolutionary violence as self-defense is so widespread in the *iglesia popular* that even people who reject the possibility of taking up arms themselves rarely condemn others' decision to do so. Elizabeth explains her position:

> I don't think that arms will make a better life. This has to be the fruit of the consciousness of the people. Violence itself won't give birth to a new society, but [this society is born] in the degree that people are born anew and that we're truly brothers and sisters, from the same father.

However, she adds, "I don't ever condemn those who opt for arms . . . Our history has taught us not to condemn it . . . since from the time we're born until the time we die, we're dying slowly." She argues that violence by the poor and by revolutionary groups must be viewed in relation to the much greater violence used by the powerful to kill the poor slowly and, more rapidly, to kill those who defend them. Thus, in her view, "All the rich, who haven't taken up arms themselves, are more responsible for violence and murders against the poor than the [FMLN] combatants who finally saw no alternatives to armed struggle."

Because they believe that revolutionary violence fights against a greater evil, some Christians argue that the guerrillas' decision to take up arms stems precisely from the values that make them good Christians and thus martyrs. Fernando Bermúdez, a priest who worked in Guatemala, writes that people who die as members of revolutionary groups are martyrs also "because they could have lived in comfort, or at least in poverty, without risking their lives, but they have opted instead for the path of sacrifice and love of their people."[40] In this perspective, shared by many progressive Catholics in Central America, all people who give their lives for "love of their people" or "the ideals of the poor" are martyrs; "that they do so as combatants does not eliminate the dimension of martyrdom."[41]

Although many Salvadoran Christians classify combatants as martyrs, this judgment is far from universal. A number of clergy and laypeople would not call those who die using violence, no matter how noble their intentions, martyrs. Rather, they adhere to the traditional Christian definition of martyrs as those who die without resisting, certainly without taking up arms against their enemies. Thus, Elena asserts that people who participate in armed struggle cannot be called martyrs of the church, although they "may be doing more work, greater things, than a church worker, because they've seen the suffering of their people, the cry of the whole people." Elizabeth, whose only son died in 1981 fighting for the FMLN, argues that a martyr can only be a person who "doesn't defend him or herself. S/he can't be violent, even knowing that they'll take his or her life. S/he doesn't offer it foolishly, but at the moment s/he can't be violent against his or her attackers." Her ability to separate her personal experience from her religious ethics reflects the subtlety with which many grassroots activists address theoretical questions. While personal and political ties inevitably enter into the theological claims of lay activists, they, like academic theologians and philosophers, can still arrive at relatively autonomous intellectual positions. These positions sometimes affirm and sometimes reformulate established Christian doctrine such as just war theory. Their novelty often comes less from the content of the ideas than from the context in which they are applied and the consequences of this application.

Endnotes

1. Quoted in Leonardo Boff, "Martyrdom: An Attempt at Systematic Reflection," *Concilium* 183 (1983): 14–15.

2. *Lumen Gentium*, no. 42, in Walter Abbott, ed., *Documents of Vatican II* (New York: American Press, 1966), 71.

3. Woodward, *Making Saints*, 61, 130. Beatification is "a penultimate declaration of blessedness allowing limited public cult," while in canonization the pope declares a person worthy of universal public cult because s/he is definitely with God, and thus can intercede with God on behalf of those who pray to her or him (ibid., 16–17).

4. Ibid., 130.

5. Ibid., 149–150.

6. Karl Rahner, "Dimensions of Martyrdom: A Plea for the Broadening of a Classical Concept," *Concilium* 183 (1983): 9.

7. Quoted in Boff, "Martyrdom: An Attempt at Systematic Reflection," 14.

8. Rahner, "Dimensions of Martyrdom," 9–10.

9. Carlos Bravo interview.

10. Woodward, *Making Saints*, 154.

11. See, for example, Jon Sobrino, *Jesus in Latin America* (Maryknoll, NY: Orbis Books, 1987).

12. Woodward, *Making Saints*, 152-153.

13. Ibid., 49.

14. Recinos, "The Politics of Salvadoran Refugee Popular Religion," 267.

15. Quoted in Woodward, *Making Saints*, 40.

16. Ibid., 37–38.

17. Ibid., 154.

18. Quoted in ibid., 47.

19. Jon Sobrino, *Liberación con espíritu: Apuntes para una nueva espiritualidad* (San Salvador: UCA Editores, 1987).

20. Woodward, *Making Saints*, 43–44.

21. Jon Sobrino, "Companions of Jesus," in *Companions of Jesus: The Jesuit Martyrs of El Salvador*, by J. Sobrino, I. Ellacuría, and others (Maryknoll, NY: Orbis, 1990), 5.

22. After voting more than four billion dollars in aid to El Salvador over the previous decade, on October 19, 1990, the U.S. Congress voted to reduce military aid to El Salvador by half, largely in response to the killing of the Jesuits. Cynthia J. Arnson, "Conscience Vote," *The Nation* 251, no. 17 (November 19, 1990): 584. President Bush ordered the rest of the aid reinstated on January 16, 1991.

23. Alejandro Acaya interview, 12 March 1990.

24. This perspective echoes that of Justin Martyr, who asserted that "Those who lived in accordance with Reason are Christians, even though they were called godless." See Justin Martyr, "First Apology of Justin," in Cyril Richardson, *Early Christian Fathers* (New York: MacMillan Publishing Co., 1970), 272, 244–245.

25. Rahner himself applies this notion to martyrdom in "Martyrdom: A Plea."

26. Sobrino interview, 26 October 1988.

27. María López Vigil, *Primero Dios: Siete años de esperanza (relatos de "Carta a las Iglesias")* (San Salvador: UCA Editores, 1988), 90. This recalls

Ileto's point that Philippine rebels "faced with the certainty of death . . . could live out their final moments in joyful expectation because they had been culturally prepared . . . [to] see beyond the loss of a human life." *Pasyon and Revolution*, 249–250.

28. Woodward, *Making Saints*, 54.

29. Weiner and Weiner, *The Martyr's Conviction*, 71.

30. Paul VI, "Populorum Progressio," in *The Gospel of Peace and Justice: Catholic Social Teaching Since Vatican II*, ed. Joseph Gremillion (Maryknoll, NY: Orbis, 1976), 396.

31. Oscar Romero, "Fourth Pastoral Letter: The Church's Mission amid the National Crisis," in *The Voice of the Voiceless* (Maryknoll, NY: Orbis, 1985), 144–145.

32. Ibid., 144; emphasis added.

33. Ibid., 144.

34. Quoted in Alan Riding, "The Cross and the Sword in Latin America," in *El Salvador: Central America in the New Cold War*, eds. Marvin Gettleman et al. (New York: Grove Press, 1981), 196.

35. Romero, "Fourth Pastoral Letter," 144–145.

36. Ibid., 145.

37. Ibid., 145.

38. See López Vigil, *Muerte y vida* and Galdámez, *The Faith of a People*.

39. While in English guerrilla means a single fighter, in Spanish the term *guerrilla* is a collective term, denoting an army of "irregular" fighters, and *guerrillero/a* is used for a single soldier.

40. Fernando Bermúdez, *Death and Resurrection in Guatemala* (Maryknoll, NY: Orbis Books, 1986), 70.

41. Berryman, "Introduction" to ibid., 13.

6

Reasons for Martyrdom

People understand the reasons for the suffering.

Angélica

Progressive Catholics in El Salvador frequently assert that persecution and martyrdom are necessary. This claim needs explanation, because it has several dimensions and important ethical and political consequences. Explanations of the reasons for and necessity of martyrdom take various forms, including claims internal and also external to religious belief. As noted earlier, "internal" religious explanations understand experiences, such as violence against progressive Catholics, in terms of religious categories, traditions, symbols, and goals. "External" analyses, on the other hand, approach the same phenomena from a secular perspective. Believers do not turn only to internal analyses but often draw on both religious and secular (i.e., political, sociological) interpretations in their efforts to make sense of particular experiences or events. This is evident in the efforts of many Salvadorans to find reasons for the attacks on progressive Catholics.

External analyses usually attempt to explain historically or sociologically why repression occurs, often in terms of political conflict. Carlos Bravo calls this type of interpretation "social-historical."[1] In this view, political and economic conditions require the sacrifice of certain individuals or groups, due, for example, to the greed of elites or to the fact that some sectors must pay the "social cost" of maintaining society.[2] Internal analyses, on the other hand, perceive the reasons for the violence and its necessity from the perspective of believers. Most often, they speak in religious terms, offering what Bravo calls a "social-theological" interpretation of martyrdom. Salvadoran Catholics often claim, for example, that martyrdom is necessary because Jesus' death set the model for redemption and liberation. This chapter will discuss both types of interpretations of the reasons for persecution, with a focus on "internal" explanations and the religious narratives that provide their context.

I. Historical and Political Reasons for Repression

What Bravo calls the "socio-historical" explanation of martyrdom reflects a primarily political analysis of the reasons for repression. I include this as an "external" level of analysis because it requires stepping outside the situation of persecution to identify, with some degree of detachment, its causes. However, this type of analysis need not be and is not done solely by "outsiders." Most Salvadoran religious activists understand repression, at least partly, in political terms that may not differ substantially from the analysis of sympathetic outside observers. Generally, this argument asserts that Salvadoran society consists of structures that benefit a few while excluding the rest and that the state protects the privileges of the minorities at the cost of justice and even physical security for the poor majorities. Any person or group who challenges the status quo, in this view, faces a repressive reaction.

This analysis does not distinguish the church from other groups, such as trade unions or peasant associations, which challenge El Salvador's political and economic system. Insofar as it criticizes the status quo, the church meets with repression, just like any other person or institution. Thus its stance against political and economic inequities, rather than its religious position, provokes attacks. Mario Ferrer elaborates this interpretation, asserting that the powerful in El Salvador concluded that progressive Catholicism posed a serious threat to the established order. Ferrer explains that "the system was right, according to its own logic, to persecute" popular Christian activists, just as it sought to eliminate other organizations seeking social change.

This analysis identifies the political reasoning behind attacks on Christians without precluding or conflicting with theological interpretations. The political and the theological are joined by the idea that since true Christianity requires defense of the weak, the powerful will always persecute true Christians. Members of the *iglesia popular* argue that Christian faith demands a struggle against a government and economic policies that oppress the poor, because, in their view, such projects are anti-Christian. Thus, for example, Marcela asserts that the church must "walk straight" and denounce injustice wherever it sees it. She believes that such denunciations mean that the (true) church "always has to be persecuted." This ethical mandate to defend the weak and suffer the consequences, according to activists, leads the church into conflict with the forces that preserve the interests of the minority over the survival of the majorities, and places the church, along with other groups that defend the poor, under attack from the powerful.

II. The Agents of Persecution

When discussing responsibility for these attacks, activists display less interest in the physical agents, i.e., the ones who pull the trigger, than in the "intellectual authors" of repression, i.e., those who order and benefit from it. Thus, Archbishop Rivera, in response to a question about who killed the six Jesuits in November 1989, answered "It was those who murdered Archbishop Romero and who are not satisfied with 70,000 dead."[3] Obviously, the same persons did not kill all the war victims, yet Rivera and many other Salvadorans believe that the same system and the same holders of power ultimately brought about the deaths.

Such understandings of the agents of martyrdom involve both internal and external levels of analysis. From a relatively detached political viewpoint, people in the progressive church ask who benefits from the killings. This approach assigns ultimate responsibility to powerful classes rather than individual soldiers. From a theological perspective, Catholic activists assert that physical agents are not important in a divinized struggle between good and evil. They see in political conflicts not only the obvious struggles over power and resources but also an ongoing battle between the "true" God, who promises justice, and the "idols" worshipped by the wealthy.

Popular church members often claim that this idolatry blinds the powerful to biblically grounded demands for justice and leads them to murder those, like Jesus, who question the status quo or who present obstacles to their accumulation of wealth and power.[4] The logic behind these attacks hinges on a devaluation and objectification of poor people, according to activists like Elena: "Those people have arms, and so they think that they're the owners of everything, even their brothers' and sisters' lives. They want to own my own heart, my thoughts, my actions." She identifies "them" as the powerful of the time: in biblical times "it was the kings" who ordered persecution of opponents to an unjust order. "Now it's the dominant class that wants to own the thoughts of each one of us." The powerful want to "own" not only the bodies but also the hearts and minds of the poor, she claims, to prevent them from awakening to the injustice of their situation.

Many poor Salvadorans see the most obvious present-day analogy for the "kings" of Jesus' time as their country's oligarchy. Archbishop Romero also blamed the ruling families for much of El Salvador's misery: "The cause of evil here is the oligarchy, a small nucleus of families who don't care about the hunger of the people. To maintain and increase their margin of profits, they repress the people." Romero held the oligarchy responsible for the assassinations of progressive priests, whom he saw as "victims of the effort to maintain an unjust system . . . They grasped reality with great clarity and saw that the common enemy of our people is the oligarchy."[5] Like Romero, many members of the *iglesia popular* understand the ruling elite as the enemy not because of individual flaws or cruelty but because it represents and maintains the nation's structural injustice, or, in religious terms, the deformation of God's plan of abundance and equality for all humankind.

III. Theological Reasons for Martyrdom

While cognizant of the practical political reasons for attacks on progressive activists, Salvadoran Catholic activists often focus on theological reasons for persecution and construct their argument from within the faith, using "insiders'" knowledge. These theological explanations of the inevitability of persecution turn, like much of progressive theology, upon parallels between contemporary events and sacred history, especially the history of Jesus' struggle and death. Progressive Catholics in El Salvador see Jesus' cause and theirs as the same: the struggle for justice, truth, and the rights of the poor. Similarity in goals lead activists to draw parallels between the persecutors, experiences, and sufferings of contemporary activists and those of Jesus. Thus, laypeople in a repopulated village in Chalatenango explain bombings that killed several residents by referring to Christ's travails, re-enacted during Lent: "In Holy Week, we see all the suffering [Jesus] had in his life, and now we're experiencing a little of that."

From this perspective, Christians who suffer today both re-enact and continue Jesus' pain, bringing the passion narrative into a contemporary setting while preserving the structure and meaning of biblical history. Rosa explains that "Some people say they'd like to live in the time of the Bible, but we're living it now . . . We're in the times of the Romans, with the same spying and vigilance." Not only laypeople make analogies between the crucifixion and contemporary events. Guadalupe Mejía reports that after National Guard members tortured and murdered her husband Justo, a peasant activist, Archbishop Romero told her that Justo "suffered the same as the passion of Christ." Parallels between the killings of contemporary activists and Jesus' death provides not only religious but also political legitimacy to the former. Leaders' willingness to sacrifice underlines the absolute value of their cause and enables them to demand similar commitments from followers, as Lancaster explains in reference to revolutionary leaders in Nicaragua:

> In the guerrilla struggle and in the insurrectionary period, the Sandinistas and their partisans suffered imprisonment, torture, execution, and death on the battlefield, thus securing for the Frente a position of revolutionary leadership. This conception of exemplary authority also implied a new egalitarian political culture: the political authority of revolutionaries was necessarily contingent on their acceptance of sacrifice in the name of a cause.[6]

This understanding of and identification with Jesus' fate structures the way Salvadoran Catholics interpret their experiences of violence. While their country's history and their own political realism tell them to expect repression, their religious tradition places this repression in a transcendent framework. Since the colonial period, the image of the suffering Christ has played a central role in Latin American Catholicism, giving meaning to the experiences of pain and loss that have dominated the lives of most Latin Americans since the colonial period. Thus, native and mestizo adaptations of Spanish missionary Catholicism emphasized Jesus' suffering and crucifixion, with an eye also to the crucifixion as a release from these worldly woes. Orlando Espín argues that this experience of suffering and "vanquishment" is central to the popular culture and religion of ordinary Latin Americans: "The story of vanquishment thus became the condition for the promise of their salvation from the real, daily evil they were experiencing."[7] Thus, while the official church in the Spanish Americas may have been aligned with ruling elites and governments, popular Catholicism became, in Espín's words, the "religion of the vanquished."[8]

Attacks on progressive Catholics in El Salvador remind believers how deeply the themes of vanquishment, suffering, and apparent failure are embedded in the Christ story and reinforce the parallels between their lives and Jesus'. This relationship encourages them to understand their suffering as not only a necessary cost of achieving victory for their cause, but especially as an intimate sharing in Christ's life. Insofar as it underscores the parallels between Jesus and contemporary believers, in this view, persecution demonstrates the authenticity of the victims and their community. "If we're persecuted like Christ," claimed a *cursillo* participant in the San Pablo parish in April 1990, "it's because we're doing what's right and we're not mistaken." Amando argues, similarly, that attacks demonstrate truth and vitality. "If the church is alive, there are always problems. If it's stagnant, there's peace." As persecution signifies authentic discipleship, in the view of progressive Catholics, its absence suggests incorrect or insincere convictions.

Ruth contrasts the attacks against progressive Catholics to the situation of evangelical Protestants, who she believes have not suffered persecution precisely because they are not truly Christian. The fact that "they've never killed an evangelical" demonstrates that "it's not the true church," in her eyes. (In fact, political violence has killed many Protestants in El Salvador, including a Lutheran pastor and hundreds of evangelicals in the El Mozote massacre.) Still, evangelicals as a group have not suffered the intense repression directed towards progressive Catholics. Some Catholics interpret the evangelicals' perceived good fortune as indicative not of divine approval but of the wrongness of their religious beliefs and practice. "If a Christian doesn't suffer persecution," asserted a participant in an April 1990 *cursillo* in the San Pablo parish, "I'd doubt that s/he's a real Christian." What does it mean to be a "real Christian," in this view? Progressive Catholics in El Salvador highlight two dimensions: telling the truth and practicing justice.

Telling the Truth

The most common response to questions about why martyrs were killed is a simple phrase: *por decir la verdad* (for telling the truth). People from all parts of El Salvador and all economic and educational strata use the same words to explain the killings of political leaders, loved ones, and pastoral workers. In the words of Angélica: "They killed them for telling the truth, for denouncing. They were clear, and this is the reason they were killed." Elaborating on this point, a peasant delegate of the word explains:

Accepting God isn't a thing to do with the hands, but with the heart, doing good for one's brother, telling the truth, even if we die for it like Jesus, who never lied. And because of this they took his life. Others also, like Monseñor Romero and others who have died for telling the truth and not going around with lies . . . I make an effort to follow Jesus' path . . . I speak the truth, even though for this they may kill me.[9]

The *delegado* highlights the biblical analogy behind this belief: Jesus was killed for telling the truth, and other martyrs, from John the Baptist to Romero, have suffered for the same reason. Other grassroots Christian activists affirm the link between the crucifixion and contemporary sacrifices. A man from Chalatenango, threatened by a soldier, declares: "You can kill me, but for the truth, never for a lie. I owe you nothing." Another *campesino*, describing the incident, comments: "This reminded me of when the Lord told the Jews, 'Why do you hit me? If you have no accusation against me, then why?'"[10]

The emphasis on telling the truth might seem a rather abstract reason for political murder on a large scale. Many Salvadorans, however, link their understanding of "truth" to concrete political and economic conditions. From their perspective, telling the truth involves a positive struggle against injustice and death; it entails, in Jon Sobrino's words, "not just dissipating ignorance, but fighting lies."[11] The biggest lies, in this view, are those that disguise, justify, and maintain unjust political and economic structures. The *iglesia popular* sees the original lie and the original violence as structural injustice, which conceals and twists God's plan for humankind. To maintain this injustice requires further lies, often through the silencing or distorting of critical voices.[12] Thus, for example, the armed forces and death squads in El Salvador call their victims criminals, terrorists, subversives, and delinquents.

In contrast to these official portrayals of political opponents, however, Archbishop Romero called them martyrs. "It was an extraordinary thing for the poor to go to Mass at the Cathedral and hear the archbishop say, 'We have martyrs in this country,'" recalls Sobrino. "Until Archbishop Romero spoke out, the Salvadoran people did not believe that hearing the truth was possible."[13] In a context saturated by lies, as many Salvadorans saw it, telling the truth became revolutionary. As unmasking lies became a political act, the religious sphere became one of the few places where people could commit it.

If the negative dimension of telling the truth entails the denunciation of injustice, for Catholic activists, its positive aspect involves uncovering the biblical promise of genuine justice. Elena articulates this positive nature by linking "truth" to liberation. "We want to be free," she declares, "and God says we'll be free. Truth will make us free." In this view, the promise of victory represents the other side of the truth of prophetic denunciations of injustice. Becoming aware of this "truth" ends the traditional fatalism that attributed suffering to personal fault or God's will. Many Salvadoran Catholics point to their rejection of this fatalism (often through experiences in CEBs or *cursillos*) as both what motivated their activism and what brought repression upon them. Victoria, a resident of the San Juan parish, explains that "People opened their minds here and started to claim their rights, and they [the powerful] don't like it, so the repression began." Clara concurs: "The people began to wake up, then the death squads started."

In the end, members of the *iglesia popular* do not view telling the truth as an abstract philosophical principle. Speaking the truth means denouncing injustice and oppression, pointing out structural violence, naming killers, and describing a more just alternative. Announcements of the truth awaken people to the oppressiveness of the economic and political system and often provoke resistance to it, which the elite seek to crush at all costs. For progressive Catholics, this is the link between truth and martyrdom and between contemporary political murders and Jesus' death.

Practicing Justice

The popular church links authentic faith not only to prophetic words but also to prophetic praxis. In this view, true Christians must share the risks taken by both Jesus and the poor, whose lives are overwhelmingly shaped by insecurity and violence. Thus, martyrs' deaths result not from doctrine itself but from its practical consequences. In the perspective of the popular church, those in power accuse religious activists of manipulating or infiltrating the church because the former fail to see the natural tie between faith and concrete actions. The persecution of priests as political leaders stems from an assumption that political interests motivate believers' struggle for justice. Most church activists, however, cite ethical and biblical reasons for both their activism and the persecution that follows. Although the army claims that all who criticize the status quo are subversives or guerrillas, contends Lucía, "we speak out not because we're guerrillas, but because of the injustice."

Popular theology explains persecution as the natural result of following the religious demand to denounce injustice. In *cursillos* and base communities, people discover the message of the Bible and find that once they begin to preach and practice Jesus' message by telling the truth and defending the poor, they share his fate. Their experiences link the political-historical lesson (repeated many times in Salvadoran history) that people who oppose injustice are repressed to the biblical-theological insight that those who follow Jesus' model will repeat his martyrdom. Progressive Catholic activists incorporate these interpretations of the reasons for persecution into a conviction that the true church, and true believers, will inevitably suffer persecution and martyrdom.

The Necessity of Persecution

This claim is circular: just as being attacked for one's beliefs and actions reveals similarity to Jesus, activists assert, following Christ's model leads to persecution. They base this argument on their reading of the New Testament, linking the necessity of suffering to Christians' relation to Jesus. "Jesus Christ said it," Romero summarized: "'If they have persecuted me, they will also persecute you [John 5:20].'"[4] This biblical claim provides legitimacy and consolation for people who receive neither from the dominant culture. Romero himself demonstrated this principle to many Salvadorans. Elizabeth argues that Romero showed "that to be an authentic Christian follower of Jesus, there's no option. You need to go as far as possible." Because his faith was genuine, she contends, Romero chose to follow Christ and not to turn back even though he knew he would be killed.

The courage necessary to fulfill the demands of this understanding of Christianity is made possible by convictions first that true believers cannot escape martyrdom and second that persecution demonstrates true belief. Understanding sacrifice as necessary in the light of ultimate aims may make suffering easier to accept. If the struggle for a given goal requires suffering, then the choice about whether to suffer or not is subordinated to and included within the more elementary decision to remain faithful to the cause. "Potential martyrs" claim they choose not suffering, but faith; they understand risk not as suicide but as the necessary price of integrity. Further, they believe, sacrifice makes an invaluable contribution toward the triumph of their cause, even though that triumph may not materialize until long after their deaths.

IV. Religious Narratives and Political Action

Explanations of why persecution is necessary often put the experiences of believers into a historical and mythical context, a narrative that provides intelligibility and meaning. Narrative, as Mark Johnson claims, "is a fundamental form of understanding, by means of which we make sense of all forms of human action."[15] Humans experience their lives as historical (i.e., as building on the past and moving forward in some meaningful way) and purposive (i.e., moving toward an end or the fulfillment of some meaning), Johnson contends, and narrative is uniquely capable of capturing these two dimensions.[16]

Although human experience itself may have a narrative character, as Johnson argues, it is also true that narratives are social constructs. In other words, narratives do not simply emerge from experience itself but represent the efforts of an author (who might be the inventor-author of fiction or the observer-author of an ethnography) to bring together the elements necessary for a coherent story. Minimally, these elements include characters, plot, and an ending. For the meaning of the narrative to hold, the plot must be seen as leading to the ending, as Paul Ricoeur claims.[17] The construction of a narrative involves a pool of resources (cultural tradition, earlier stories, etc.) upon which an author (individual or collective) draws to produce a story appropriate to the audience, circumstances, and goals. The socially constructed nature of narrative highlights the fact that every story, no matter who is telling it, is told for a point.

The author of a narrative need not be an outsider to the story (an inventor- or observer-author), but can also be what Janet Hart calls "participant-authors." These are stories constructed and/or employed by ordinary people to make sense of their experiences, articulate collective and personal identities, and mobilize action.[18] Narratives in this sense are not just a tool for scholars, but a resource that provides ordinary people with a language, values, and patterns of thought and behavior. These stories, as David Carr puts it, are not simply told, but are "told in being lived, and lived in being told."[19]

Even participants, however, are never more than the "co-authors" of their narratives, in Alasdair MacIntyre's words.[20] In other words, claiming that people create narratives does not entail the contention that people create them in a vacuum. People make their own narratives, but not in conditions of their own choosing.[21] People live within the constraints of their histories, cultures, and economic conditions, among other limiting factors. However, people's actions are shaped not only by forces beyond their control but also by their understandings of how things are and how they should be—by their models of and for society.[22] These conceptions, in turn, do not spring *ex nihilo* from individual consciousness. Rather, they blend various factors, including cultural tradition and material interest. Often, the resulting worldviews receive force and cohesion from narratives that people tell and are told about their lives and the lives of their community.

The narratives articulated by participants, by people "inside" the story, always have multiple dimensions, of which two are especially relevant to this study. First, many narratives address or reflect participants' concerns with meaning, values, and related issues—what Hart terms their "ontological" dimension.[23] In this perspective, narratives are not only descriptive but also prescriptive, not only heard but internalized. They are constructed and told not only to make sense of events but also to shape them via ethical claims embedded in the narrative itself: critiques of certain actions, praise for others, a vision of how things ought to be and even how they might in fact come to be. Second, many of these narratives are collective, i.e., they are constructed, maintained, and/or diffused by participants in a shared social process. These "social narratives," in Steinmetz's words, order past events, providing a "collective memory" or framework with which to interpret both individual and collective experiences. While social narratives often end in the present, not infrequently they project events into an anticipated future.[24]

A number of scholars recently have applied theories of narrative to processes of identity and class-formation, claiming, for example, that members of social groups understand themselves as part of a continuing story, with a history, plot, guiding themes, and hoped-for end.[25] This work has been important for the study of social movements, insofar as it emphasizes the fact that movements are born not only or mainly from "rational" self-interest or class interest and the strategic mobilization of resources, but from a range of factors, including stories, values, and utopian visions that, while not irrational, correspond to a less instrumental type of rationality. By placing individual experience into a collective and historical context and drawing ethical/ontological conclusions from these experiences, successful narratives suggest that contemporary individuals, facing situations similar to those described in the narrative, might respond in analogous ways. The perceived authenticity and "accuracy" of the narrative helps determine the force of this model for behavior.

Despite this interest in the narrative dimensions of social identity and mobilization, few studies have addressed the role of religion in social narratives. Religious narratives are generally distinguished by reference to the sacred, which transcends and includes human beings: "The sacred cosmos is confronted by man [sic] as an immensely powerful reality other than himself. Yet this reality addresses itself to him and locates his life in an ultimately meaningful order."[26] (Or, as Peter Worsley defines it, religion "refers to, and looks for validation in, a dimension beyond the empirical-technical realm of action."[27]) In other words, conceptions of the sacred, by definition a superhuman reality, provide a context that gives human actions transcendental meaning and legitimacy (or illegitimacy). Like any narrative, then, religious narratives tell a story, but one in which "real" history is linked in some way to sacred history. This link may be allegorical, if secular events are "like" sacred ones, or more direct, if divine forces or figures irrupt into secular events and/or human figures participate in events with transcendent significance. I argue that religion represents a major factor in many narratives, especially those involved in building collective identity and inspiring activism.[28] Social-religious narratives, in fact, represent perhaps the most common and most powerful way that the social and ontological dimensions of narrative come together and provide a model for action.

Reynaldo Ileto's discussion of the role of the *pasyon* in Philippine popular movements elaborates this point. Rituals and stories about Jesus death helped "[narrow] the gap between 'biblical time' and human or 'everyday time.'" Thus, during Holy Week, "the spiritual and material planes of existence coincided . . . the people themselves participated in Christ's passion."[29] In periods of cultural change and socioeconomic hardship, the rite helped Filipino peasants "to maintain a coherent image of the world and their place in it through their familiarity with the *pasyon*."[30] Similarly, Lancaster argues that biblical stories helped motivate rebellion in Nicaragua during the 1970s. Believers found in the record of sacred history "those historical parallels which resonate with the present."[31]

These parallels provide illumination and guidance for believers traversing their own difficult history. This is especially important for poor people, who often lack access to other theoretical frameworks. Sacred history provides one of the few media through which to link their lives to larger forces, to conceive of their experiences as having a logic, meaning, and value beyond the immediate. This relationship between sacred and human history is two-way: just as the human becomes divinized, so the divine becomes humanized. Ideas about the sacred not only place human events in sacred history but also place divine persons and events in contemporary human history. This dimension plays a crucial role in the political impact of popular religiosity. In addition to placing their actions within a sacred narrative (such as the passion story), people identify divine elements and figures within human history. Thus, in the Philippines, "the vitality of the *pasyon* tradition," writes Ileto "made it possible for ordinary folk to recognize the appearance of other Christ-like figures," who promised deliverance in times of crisis.[32]

In El Salvador, similarly, the immediacy and power of martyr narratives enabled Catholic activists both to locate their lives in sacred history and to perceive transcendent dimensions in their own experiences. This is especially evident in people's interpretations of the reasons for martyrdom. Parallels to Jesus' death shaped popular conceptions of the cause and the necessity of persecution and views about correct faith and praxis.

V. Religion and Political Violence

Insofar as religious narratives seek to make sense of people's experiences, they need to explain the existence and meaning of death. While natural deaths from old age and illness are often difficult for survivors to bear, violent killings of well-loved and admired people pose an even greater challenge to efforts to make sense of mortality. In the 1970s and 1980s, most Salvadorans, especially poor and rural people and opposition activists, faced unnatural death on a massive scale. Their religious ideas and practices reflected and responded to this reality in various ways. They sought, especially, to explain the reasons for sacrifice, why it was necessary, and how it helped achieve an ultimate goal and even to fulfill the meaning of Christianity. Many Salvadoran Christians, like believers in other settings, could find death easier to bear when it was meaningful and more meaningful when it was part of a divine plan.

This view of the value of explanatory narratives parallels recent experiences in research and therapy with victims of political repression. Studies of the social-psychological effects of political violence have found that persons with a clear political or religious interpretive framework and value system recover more quickly, with less lasting damage, from political repression. Research in Chile, for example, found that people with well-articulated political commitments recovered from imprisonment, torture, or the death of loved ones more rapidly and completely than their apolitical peers. The Chilean political prisoners saw torture and incarceration as tests of their political maturity and the depth of their commitment. Conversely, people without a political context suffered more when relatives were imprisoned or killed and had the hardest time coming to emotional resolutions regarding the death or disappearance of the loved ones.[33] Terrence DesPres's study of concentration camp survivors also argues that a sense of political purpose helped people to endure: "Political consciousness and contact with others in the struggle against Nazism were necessary conditions of success; it was this that gave people a sense of purpose in life behind barbed wire and enabled them to hold out."[34]

Studies of survivors of extreme conditions, such as Pinochet's prisons or Nazi death camps, reinforce sociological claims that a clear theoretical-symbolic framework can make suffering easier to withstand and survive. The experiences of Salvadoran Catholics suggests, further, that a contextualized understanding of repression may help motivate people to take risks from which others may benefit. Social scientists have not always found such behavior easy to understand. They often assume that people cannot be persuaded to sacrifice themselves for the good of "free riders." This assumption, grounded on abstract models of human behavior, takes only an "outsider's" view of the process. It cannot explain the obvious fact that in El Salvador and elsewhere people risk and often give their lives for the benefit of others or for a cause. In many cases, the key to understanding this behavior lies in the actors' (insiders') own interpretation of the world and their role in it, which, in turn, often rests on a religious worldview and values.

The role of religion in motivating risky resistance to political oppression sheds a new light on the role of theodicies, or theological explanations of evil, usually phrased in terms of an answer to the question of why a good and all-powerful God allows evil. Advocates of social change have sometimes criticized traditional Christian theodicies as efforts to explain and justify suffering so that people accept it as religiously necessary. Popular Catholic interpretations of political killing in El Salvador are theodicies insofar as they explain evil by placing it in a larger religious world-view. They do not, however, encourage passive acceptance of suffering but rather stress action following Jesus' model to achieve social justice.

In discussing theological understandings of political murder, it is important to keep in mind that putting death into a broader context does not make it less painful or unjust to the people involved. Even for the most ardent activists, martyrdom remains "death before its time and against justice," in Carlos Bravo's words, and not something to be sought or idealized.[35] Popular interpretations in El Salvador stress the fact that martyrs, even well-known ones, are still beloved children and companions, and their deaths are tragedies even when they are also understood as victories for the longer struggle or for the church. Even Romero, whose martyrdom is as idealized as any, is mourned by pastoral agents and laypeople. Their overwhelming sense of loss emerges in repeated statements such as "They took from us the best man of the church" and "we'll never have another like him." The credibility he gave to the church and the courage gained from his example cannot erase the pain of his death. The knowledge that a death serves a purpose may make it less difficult to understand and to bear, but it never becomes easy.

Just as survivors strive to make sense of the killings, so "potential martyrs" must come to terms with the possibility and often the reality of their own deaths. This process, like the grief of survivors, seeks to find suffering meaningful without romanticizing it. German theologian Dorothee Soelle offers a helpful way of thinking about this issue. Soelle claims that pain cannot be categorized as right or wrong, but only as meaningless or potentially meaningful. Meaningless suffering destroys people's creativity and ability to act; it may make them bitter, blindly aggressive, or fatalistic. What Soelle terms "meaningful" suffering, on the other hand, impels action and thus helps change the situation causing damage. The key distinction between the two lies not in the nature of the pain, but in the perspective of the sufferer. Suffering meaningfully means "to live conscious of our oneness with the whole of life," and especially of unity with a larger plan or power, be it God or a political movement, contends Soelle.[36] Soelle's discussion helps clarify the ways that Salvadoran Catholics might also understand their experiences of political violence. The key point, for Soelle and for "popular theologians" in El Salvador, is to make of suffering something useful, rather than damaging, to a larger struggle.

To illustrate her claim, Soelle discusses the certainty and even joy with which captured resistance fighters in World War II faced their deaths. The letters of the resistance workers, many of whom belonged to the Communist Party, show "an almost painful sense of self-confidence, the superiority of those who die for a just cause," she writes.[37] Convinced of the value of their goals, the condemned faced death with self-assurance, freedom from fear, and a sense of indestructibility. They found ways to make their suffering productive rather than paralyzing by placing it in a larger context in which personal pain and loss constitute necessary steps towards a meta-individual goal. This parallels the way that many Salvadorans sought to make sense of political violence as part of a larger picture, especially the narrative about Jesus' suffering and the slow march toward the reign of God.

Activists, in El Salvador and elsewhere, sometimes understand their cause not as a conscious choice, but as an integral element of their identity, surpassing the need even for individual safety or survival. A Chilean communist imprisoned and then exiled under Pinochet explained to an interviewer that it never occurred to her to renounce her cause, although she knew her life was in danger. She refused to betray the movement even when soldiers tortured her husband in front of her. Her fortitude did not come from a lack of feeling; when he screamed, she recalls, "it was an enormous suffering, it was as if they took my heart and squeezed it, and squeezed and squeezed." Nonetheless, she continues, "I would be lying if I said that at any time I thought of saying something to save him . . . I couldn't be an informer. I couldn't betray the cause that I have loved all my life, the cause that I have defended since I was fourteen."[38]

Some Salvadoran activists also express the naturalness of their religious and political battle in the face of possible, even probable, death. Their immersion in the world of popular Catholicism, and especially their identification with the passion narrative, make it not only desirable but necessary to follow what they see as the only authentic path. Once they set out on this path, they insist, they no longer consider forsaking it to save themselves. As "true" Christians, in their own terms, they seek not to escape suffering but to confront and grasp it, to incorporate it into an overarching belief structure. Ideally, this helps make pain bearable, because the end of the story is no longer personal agony or death but rather the realization of the ultimate goal for which suffering is borne. Progressive Catholic theology presents this goal in terms of a fuller, even eternal, life for both martyrs and the communities for whom they sacrifice. This conviction that suffering serves a positive end is central to the interpretive framework that makes political violence meaningful.

Members of the Salvadoran *iglesia popular* believe their pain produces a number of beneficial consequences, including practical political effects both on members of the martyrs' peer group and on society more generally. The next chapter explores these perceived "fruits" of martyrdom.

Endnotes

1. Carlos Bravo, "Martirio y pasión." *Christus* (Mexico City) 55, no. 633 (March 1990): 46–50.

2. Pedro Morande, *Cultura y modernización en América Latina* (Santiago: Pontificia Universidad Católica de Chile), 72.

3. Quoted in Sobrino, "Companions of Jesus," 30.

4. Some progressive Catholics in Mexico employed a similar reading of biblical history to make sense of repression following the January 1994 rebellion in the state of Chiapas. A lay preacher in the village of La Estación used terms that echo Salvadoran activists: "If the government comes to kill us, we are not afraid. Jesus also was killed at the hands of the government." Trina Kleist, "Villages are Fertile Ground for Rebellion," *The Gainesville Sun*, 24 January 1994, 4B.

5. Quoted in Erdozaín, *Archbishop Romero*, 76.

6. Roger Lancaster, *Life is Hard: Machismo, Danger, and the Intimacy of Power in Nicaragua* (Berkeley: University of California Press, 1993), 289. Also see Ileto, *Pasyon and Revolution*, 16, 49.

7. Espín, "The God of the Vanquished," 71. See also Espín, "Trinitarian Monotheism" and Carrasco, *Religions of Mesoamerica.*

8. Espín, "The God of the Vanquished," 74.

9. López Vigil, *Primero Dios*, 95–96.

10. Ibid., 62.

11. Sobrino, "Companions of Jesus," 27.

12. From a highly secular perspective, Jürgen Habermas makes a similar point when he asserts that advanced capitalism requires "counter-factual validity claims" to legitimate fundamentally undemocratic structures. *The Theory of Communicative Action, Vol. 2. Lifeworld and System: A Critique of Functionalist Reason*, trans. Thomas McCarthy (Boston: Beacon Press, 1987), 233.

13. Interview with Sobrino, quoted in Woodward, *Making Saints*, 47.

14. Quoted in Brockman, *Romero: A Life*, 32.

15. Johnson, *Moral Imagination*, 11. See also Alasdair MacIntyre, *After Virtue: A Study in Moral Theory* (Notre Dame: University of Notre Dame Press, 1981), 197. I am not arguing that a single "meta-narrative" can explain everyone's experiences; rather, particular narratives make sense to particular individuals and groups at different times and places. To claim that people often see the world in narrative form, in other words, is not to claim that there is only one narrative.

16. Johnson, *Moral Imagination*, 170.

17. Paul Ricoeur, *Time and Narrative*, vol. I (Chicago: University of Chicago Press, 1984), 66.

18. Janet Hart, "Cracking the Code: Narrative and Political Mobilization in the Greek Resistance," *Social Science History* 16, no. 4 (Winter 1992): 633–634.

19. David Carr, "Narrative and the Real World: An Argument for Continuity," *History and Theory* XXV, no. 85 (1986): 126.

20. MacIntyre, *After Virtue*, 126.

21. This repeats Marx's claim in "The Eighteenth Brumaire of Louis Bonaparte," in *The Marx-Engels Reader*, ed. Robert Tucker (New York: Norton, 1978), 595.

22. Clifford Geertz, "Religion as a Cultural System," in *The Interpretation of Cultures* (New York: Basic Books, 1973).

23. Hart, "Cracking the Code," 634.

24. George Steinmetz, "Reflections on the Role of Social Narratives in Working-Class Formation: Narrative Theory in the Social Sciences," *Social Science History* 16, no. 4 (Winter 1992): 491.

25. See Steinmetz, "Reflections on the Role of Social Narratives;" Carr, "Narrative and the Real World;" Hart, "Cracking the Code;" Margaret Somers, "Narrativity, Narrative Identity, and Social Action: Rethinking English Working-Class Formation," *Social Science History* 16, no. 4 (Winter 1992): 591–630; and Hayden White, *The Content of the Form: Narrative Discourse and Historical Representation* (Baltimore: Johns Hopkins University Press, 1987).

26. Peter Berger, *The Sacred Canopy: Elements of a Sociological Theory of Religion* (Garden City, NY: Anchor Books), 26. See also P. Berger and Thomas Luckmann, *The Social Construction of Reality: A Treatise in the Sociology of Knowledge* (New York, Doubleday, 1966) and Geertz, "Religion as a Cultural System," 103.

27. Worsley, *The Trumpet Shall Sound*, xxxv.

28. Two classic studies which do take religion seriously in identity formation, although they do not focus on narrative explicitly, are E. P. Thompson, *The Making of the English Working Class* (New York: Vintage, 1963) and Eugene Genovese, *Roll, Jordan, Roll: The World the Slaves Made* (New York: Vintage, 1976).

29. Ileto, *Pasyon and Revolution*, 21.

30. Ibid., 12.

31. Lancaster, *Thanks to God and the Revolution*, 204. Lancaster claims, further, that poor Catholics retell Nicaraguan history as a series of martyrdoms, in which the martyrs become "icons of class consciousness, emblems of religious hope" (138).

32. Ileto, *Pasyon and Revolution*, 63; see also 14.

33. Eugenia Weinstein et al., *Trauma, duelo y reparación: una experiencia de trabajo psico-social en Chile* (Santiago: FASIC/Interamericana, 1987), 82, 188.

34. Terrence DesPres, *The Survivor: An Anatomy of Life in the Death Camps* (New York: Oxford University Press, 1976), 121, quoting Kraus and Kulka, *The Death Factory*, 27, I. These studies also stress survivors' compulsion to describe and denounce the horrors they witnessed; DesPres, for example, writes that survivors feel compelled to speak for those who cannot; "the survivor allows the dead their voice; he makes the silence heard" (36). For a parallel example in El Salvador, see the story of Rufina Amaya, the sole survivor of a massacre of close to a thousand people in Morazán province, described in Danner, "The Truth of El Mozote."

35. Bravo, "Martirio y pasión," 46.

36. Dorothee Soelle, *Suffering* (Philadelphia: Fortress Press, 1975), 107, 141.

37. Ibid., 137–138.

38. Patricia Politzer, *Miedo en Chile* (Santiago: CESOC/Ediciones Chile y América, 1985), 126.

7

The Fruits of Martyrdom

In addition to explaining the reasons for suffering, narratives of martyrdom in El Salvador outline the ways sacrificial death contributes to individual and collective goals. These narratives seek to make sense of seemingly senseless conditions. They represent people's efforts to find or impose order and meaning on a world made unrecognizable. To this end, believers develop explanations not only of why political murder or martyrdom occurs but also how it ultimately has positive consequences. These consequences, like the reasons for persecution, have both internal and external, as well as religious and political, dimensions.

I. Martyrs and Society

Members of the believing community and outside observers have long noted the ways martyrdom strengthens the commitment of current members and attracts new ones. In the early church, the blood of martyrs provided "the seed of Christians," in Ignatius's well-known phrase; Petilian claimed that "Christianity makes progress by the deaths of its followers."[1] Many contemporary Christians also believe that martyrdom strengthens the church, as Lutheran bishop Medardo Gómez of San Salvador contends: "When the church is persecuted throughout history, it gets stronger. The blood of martyrs gives new life to the church."[2]

Reflecting on the effects of persecution on their community, members of the Salvadoran *iglesia popular* often explain the consequences in terms of a paradox: the enemies thought they would end the movement by killing leaders and activists, but repression instead strengthened the cause, motivating others to continue the struggle the martyrs started. Survivors continue trying to realize the martyrs' goals in their work, because, as Elena declares, "the murderers think that 'We'll kill that Christian and this thing will end,' but for us it's not that way." The anger and pain of losing loved ones often spur people to defy the regime, despite the dangers involved. After her son and two daughters were murdered, Tomasa recalls, "[The killers] thought I'd be quiet then. But with this I haven't silenced my voice. When one loses family, one says 'I'm going to get more involved.'" Elena adds that "We're not going to say 'We won't do this' just because they were murdered for doing this. Rather, we'll continue their work, for which they died."

Repression does not always or only have the negative social effects (fear, withdrawal) intended by its authors. While martyrs show the high cost of resistance, they also demonstrate, *de facto*, that resistance is possible. The sacrifices of members of an oppressed group provide dramatic challenges to the dominant beliefs and can thus help weaken resignation to a status quo that appeared inevitable and untouchable. The Weiners elaborate:

> Martyrs dramatize the feasibility of defying an oppressor. The martyr demonstrates that defiance is thinkable and doable through the challenge of superordinate, oppressive power. He or she breaks through the tacit acceptance of established authority and its right to determine public policy by decree.[3]

Martyrs demonstrate that although the oppressors may win the battle, they can be defied. The memory of this defiance is sometimes stronger and more enduring than the memory of the rebels' defeat. Salvadoran political history contains numerous examples of failed heroes, such as Anastasio Aquino and Farabundo Martí, in whom later generations find powerful images of resistance. The preservation and diffusion of stories about these "martyrs" reinforce the core narrative of repression, loss, and ultimate triumph that Jesus' fate etched into popular Catholicism. The clandestine but potent memory of heroic risks and sacrificial deaths contributes to subsequent struggles; thus a Filipina organizer, quoted by Reynaldo Ileto, insists that "No uprising fails. Each one is a step in the right direction."[4] In this light, Jean Comaroff argues that even failed utopian movements have significant long-term implications for both the dominant and the dominated.[5] Similarly, Jewish and Christian sacred histories frame martyrs' deaths as only apparent defeats for opponents of the dominant structures, temporary setbacks, which, in fact, prove the cause's moral rightness and promise its eventual triumph.

Within this broader framework, as examples of action that runs counter to individual interests, martyrs push survivors to ask themselves why they cannot take similar risks. Their deaths unsettle prior conceptions of self-interest and sometimes inspire similar sacrifice. Hugo summarizes the effect of martyrs on his commitment: "You shouldn't just be celebrating and admiring what the martyrs did, but rather emulating it. If they can do it, so can you: you're young, you have hands and eyes and a voice . . . The martyrs ask you, 'And you, what are you doing? [¿Y vos, qué hacés?]'." His question recalls that of Ignatius of Loyola: "If they could do it, why not I?"[6] A Chalatenango resident elaborates: "I would not stop going; the martyrs of history have always given me strength to confront this kind of situation . . . If they could struggle, why couldn't I risk my life, and so I did."[7] Models of dedication and self-sacrifice dramatize the potential power of ideals over human lives, demonstrating that beliefs may be important enough to conquer the fear of death, that "opinions can and should be fateful."[8] Their examples can give other believers the courage to stake their existence on a conviction. When one believer risks her or his life for an ideal, others may question the depth of their own commitments and consider the possibility of facing similar danger in order to hasten the eventual victory of their cause.

Martyrs' deaths may help legitimize a cause among outsiders as well as believers. Just as early Christian martyrs' demonstrations of courage and conviction strengthened public awareness and appreciation of the nascent church, contemporary persecution can help validate the message of progressive Catholicism. According to the Weiners,

> Through his or her death, the martyr makes believable those abstract principles that lie at the root of human connectedness, such as kinship, religious belief, national or ethnic solidarity, or the more universal principle of 'humanity.' We are forced to take note of the martyr's conviction because it appeared true, valid, and convincing enough to warrant self-sacrifice.[9]

In a Salvadoran example, Jon Sobrino contends that Romero's death gave credibility "to everything he did and said in his life."[10] The fact that one person found a principle worth sacrificing for compels others to contemplate that ideal and perhaps to consider following it despite risks. More generally, Ignacio Martín-Baró claims that rather than eradicating "subversion," the Salvadoran government's repression of religiously grounded opposition in the late 1970s and early 1980s had the opposite effect, because it actually drew new members to CEBs and the political groups associated with them.[11] An account of rural organizing in Chalatenango confirms Martín-Baró's insight, describing the way the killing of a leader of the Popular Liberation Forces (FPL) led other people to join the organization. A peasant activist explains:

> It was the death of the *compañero* [Andrés Torres] which really affected the peasants, especially those who had worked with him and identified with his example, his ideas, his struggle. That was one of the things which helped the FPL make roots among the peasants.[12]

The growth of the popular opposition in El Salvador during the late 1970s despite severe repression suggests that at the very least, persecution did not drive away nearly as many people as intended, or perhaps that it attracted enough to make up for those who left as well as those who died.

The effects of Oscar Romero's death embody the social functions of martyrdom. Ten years after the archbishop's murder, residents of the San Pablo parish declared that "Monseñor Romero left us the example of not being afraid to denounce and tell the truth." Romero helped believers learn "to be sure of ourselves and lose our fear." He left both a challenge "to serve also, not just to be served" and "an example of giving life, with actions and not just with words."[13] For many Salvadorans, Romero showed a way to defend the poor and denounce injustice despite the difficulties corresponding to that role. Like Romero, other martyrs demonstrate to believers that it is possible and perhaps necessary to take the same path. As a man from Chalatenango explains, they offer examples "of how far love for humanity can go, to giving one's life for others."

Martyrs can provide not only models of exemplary dedication to a cause but also a banner under which an opposition movement can appeal to sympathizers. In the Salvadoran civil war, as in other circumstances, many people who kept the faith throughout difficult periods did so "in the name of" those who died. Activists often point to the people who gave their lives for the cause as a primary motivation for their own participation. In a letter addressed to Ignacio Martín-Baró after he was murdered in November 1989, churchgoers in Jayaque, a village where he had celebrated mass most Sundays, wrote: "People like you never last in this life. But we know very well that, with everything that has happened, the church will never give up. We are going to continue your example because God wanted it that way."[14] Other Salvadorans express similar beliefs: "When there's consciousness in the population that there's a person who died in their defense, this itself obliges them to continue the work that [the martyrs] started, to continue the struggle," as Jesús explains.

The memory of the dead may provide one of the strongest motivations to continue seeking social change. César, a young man from Chalatenango currently living in California, says: "With all the people who have died, the living cannot say, 'They've died, and we have nothing to do.' We can't forget." In this view, forgetting would delegitimize the martyrs' deaths, robbing them of meaning. Thus Jesús adds that "So much blood of martyrs cannot be shed in vain . . . If this struggle for the kingdom ends, their sacrifice has been in vain."

For those who survive, continuing this struggle gives meaning to both the martyrs' deaths and their cause. Josefa Avila asserts that "To stop doing what we were doing is to say it was bad." Giving up would entail, in essence, admitting that the killers were right and those who gave their lives were wrong. Echoing this point, Sara, the widow of a catechist, explains what happened after her husband was murdered:

> I had to continue what my husband did, and not just because he was my husband . . . He respected his brother's property, he was humble and affectionate with the children, with the communities . . . With a man like that, living seven years together, I saw I had to continue doing what he was doing when they killed him. His courage gave me strength to continue as a catechist.[15]

As Sara's experience suggests, personal relationships with martyrs generate a particularly strong compulsion to carry on their work. Roger Lancaster makes a similar point when he writes that not just abstract ideals, but rather "Love of real concrete persons—our families, our spouses, our lovers, our friends" leads people to political action, often in defense of loved ones who are "threatened by cruel economies, despotic regimes, and systematic injustices.[16] For many Salvadorans, not only threats to loved ones but the reality of loss motivated resistance to the regime during the 1970s and 1980s.

Loyalty to the dead stems also from an acute awareness that in an extreme situation, the survival of each depends on the assistance and sometimes the lives of others. Salvadorans living through the years of fierce repression know, like survivors of Nazi death camps, that although they survived, and others did not, "all were there together . . . Nobody survived without help." In a very real sense, "the survivor's identity includes the dead."[17] Survivors believe that those who died live on not only in memory but in the ongoing struggle to realize their goals. Martyrdom forges both a community of believers and a tradition of resistance. The deaths create a covenant with survivors who continue working for the same cause. Many Salvadorans see themselves as part of a historical movement with roots in the past and a clear goal for the future, completing the process of reform that the martyrs initiated. "They began it, and we have to continue moving ahead, and not stay asleep," says Clara. This sense of historical continuity is shaped also by the connection between political movements and sacred history, especially progress towards the reign of God. The martyrs join secular and religious goals and communities as well as past and future tenses.

II. Faith and Redemption

Understanding the political implications of religious interpretations of martyrdom more fully requires stepping inside the martyrs' (and potential martyrs') belief system, i.e., inside the theology of the *iglesia popular*. This step makes it clear that Salvadoran activists risk their lives not only because of strong political convictions and interpersonal relationships but also because of loyalty to Jesus and his cause. This loyalty is not unilateral, in their view, since they insist that Jesus walks with those who share his struggle. Salvadoran Christians stress the power of this bond, often attributing their very survival to God's grace. Silvia, a San Salvador resident who fled to Mexico City after the military bombed her neighborhood in November 1989, believes that "We're alive because God is great." Other Salvadoran CEB members use similar language to describe their beliefs. "If I didn't have the word of God, I'd have died," asserts Ruth. Faith in their God and in the truth of God's call to justice and liberation provides motivation to continue in the face of danger.

Religious belief and martyrdom can reinforce each other. Just as faith can make people willing to risk death, sacrificial deaths can deepen faith, survivors argue. "When one lives these experiences," explains Norma, "one's faith deepens, because one sees that God is present, and God is the only one." Sharing this perspective, Julio, a member of the pastoral team in San Felipe, explains that the reason for the recent killings of several community members was to see if we would fail. But no, the Holy Spirit gives us strength to continue, even if words fail us, and it makes us continue working wherever there's a need for work . . . In the end God will touch their hearts, and the grain of wheat will give fruit. But if it doesn't die, it won't bear fruit. We're given a test now, to see if we'll go on. And God has to give us the means we need to continue moving ahead.

Julio's interpretation of political killings as a test, necessary for the struggle for social justice to give fruit, reflects an "insider's" understanding of the social consequences of martyrdom. This perspective is grounded on political convictions and personal loyalties but rests also on a religious faith which, in the end, both motivates and sustains activism. This faith often includes a conviction that believers have received a personal call from God or Christ that helps them work for justice despite repression, fear, and loss. Christians may not be able to respond to this call fully right away, because "often we're deaf or we're blind and don't see," Marcela explains. Slowly, however, believers come to understand what, in their view, God wants of them. Once they understand this, they feel compelled to respond: "If we're called by Christ, we have to be with him."

Many Salvadorans insist that when understood properly, suffering enriches both their faith and their lives. Thus Elena asserts that "In the people, there's a more alive Christianity because of [the martyrs]." Amando explains that "Death is life for us. When we reflect on a martyr, it gives us courage to go on . . . It helps a lot." His simple declaration that "death is life for us" reflects the statement of Julius, a Christian in the Roman Empire: "If I choose life, I choose death. If I die, I live forever."[18]

III. Resurrection: The Dead Who Never Die

In the Salvadoran popular church, martyrdom dramatizes the Christian paradox: ultimate victory can be won only through defeat; death must give way to eternal life; "If I die, I live forever." If the central narrative of the Christian tradition promises that all believers will be resurrected, a martyr's death grants a special guarantee of rebirth. The stories of Jesus' death and other early martyrs drive home the link between martyrdom and "its expected sequel—rebirth," in the words of Reynaldo Ileto.[19] Members of the church in the Roman Empire believed, in fact, that resurrection occurred simultaneously with a martyr's death.

Kenneth Woodward explains: "Because their witness was perfect, their renunciation total, martyrs were believed to be 'reborn' at the moment of death into everlasting life." Believing this, early Christian communities memorialized martyrs not on their birthdays, but on the date of their deaths: their *dies natalis*, or day of rebirth.[20]

Belief in a close connection between martyrdom and resurrection permeates popular Catholicism in El Salvador. Oscar Romero believed, for example, that "If a Christian has to die to be faithful to his or her only God, God will resurrect him or her."[21] In an interview shortly before his death, the archbishop responded to threats on his own life.

> I have frequently been threatened with death. I should tell you that as a Christian, I do not believe in death without resurrection. If they kill me, I will rise again in the Salvadoran people . . . Martyrdom is a grace that I do not believe I deserve. But if God accepts the sacrifice of my life, may my blood be the seed of freedom and the signal that hope will soon be a reality.[22]

In El Salvador and Central America generally, the narrative of passion and resurrection has escaped its original religious locus and suffused popular culture more generally. Nicaraguan leader Tomás Borge, for example, draws on religious categories in recalling the death of friend and fellow guerrilla Carlos Fonseca:

> The commander of the prison of Tipitapa arrives at my small cell, jubilant, with *Novedades* in his hand, to give me the news: "Carlos Fonseca is dead," he tells me.
> After pausing for a few seconds, I respond. "You're wrong, Colonel. Carlos Fonseca is one of the dead who never die."[23]

Many Salvadoran political groups, as well as religious communities, share Borge's insistence on resurrection as an irrefutable fact. Using the notion of life generated from death to press home a political point, the FMLN's Radio Venceremos compared the six Jesuits killed in November 1989 to a tough flower, the *izote*, that reproduces itself very quickly after being cut. The slain priests, asserts the radio, "are like the flower of the *izote*, stubbornly reluctant to die, stubbornly reluctant to stop existing, stubborn in its intent to continue living."[24] José, a member of the San Pablo community, uses a similar image when he compares the base communities to another plant, the *zacate*, "that is cut and comes back."

Ideas about resurrection pervades popular understanding not only in explicitly political and religious settings, but also at an intensely personal level. "We can't deny [resurrection] because we've seen it and lived it," Rosa declares: "One doesn't forget the voice that gives strength." For many believers, the power of their faith in resurrection helps overcome the pain associated with violent death. Fernando, a leader of a severely repressed base community in San Salvador, expresses this perceived link between death and resurrection simply: "There are many mothers who have lost, and gained, their sons and daughters." Elena elaborates the certainty that many Salvadoran Christians feel about the fact of resurrection. The martyrs, she says, "are revived in our people, because now we don't see them, but in all our work and actions, they've been revived. We're very sure of this resurrection." Or, in Daniel Vega's words, "The resurrection is true because there are people like Monseñor Romero who gave their lives. This shows that the resurrection lives and that there is no other hope except that of resurrection."

People who have suffered countless deaths and defeats may indeed perceive resurrection as their only hope: the promise held out when all other expectations crumble. They believe that God's justice guarantees resurrection to those who die for divine goals, regardless of the pain and humiliation they suffer in earthly battles. Salvador explains: "[The martyrs] died in this struggle, and God has kept them alive to see the change we want." In the perspective of the popular church, martyrs' deaths both contribute to and presage the eventual victory. Divine justice promises that they will witness it. This is, in fact, the message driven home by Christianity's narrative of passion and resurrection, the chief resource in the struggle to keep believers committed despite hardship and loss. Unable to guarantee earthly happiness, Christianity (or its charismatic leaders) promises intangible but potent divine goods.

Progressive Catholicism claims that in the struggle for these goods—resurrection and the kingdom—God's promise of victory is not sufficient. "Works righteousness" of a sort still suffuses progressive popular Catholicism in El Salvador, and activists often assert the need for survivors to "make" the martyrs live by continuing their efforts. Daniel Vega says: "This dead man can't say anything to me, but he left his example and his ideals. I have to keep resurrecting him in my work." Rosa agrees: "We make them live. If a community works in their name, they're alive. They are resurrected, as they are converted from one person into another." Progressive Catholics believe that they share with God the responsibility for resurrecting the dead. Without rejecting the role of grace or divine intervention, they highlight the co-participation of human beings in resurrection, as in their salvation and the salvation of their communities. For all its "unorthodoxy" in certain matters, the *iglesia popular* is deeply Catholic (and decidedly un-Protestant) in this understanding of grace and works.

The desire to "make the martyrs live" sometimes motivates activists in a very personal way. In a conversation in the mid-1980s, María, a young catechist from the countryside, recalled the woman who first motivated her to become involved in the popular church. The woman later disappeared, probably at the hands of death squads. "I loved her very much," explains María, "because she taught me the way. That is why, even if my parents are against it, I'm going to go on. Because if I don't, I will betray everything she taught me. So I will show her . . . What I mean is, she will go on living if I follow her example."[25] In this perspective, to continue the work of the dead, to remain true to their ideals and their memory, is to resurrect them.

Forms of Resurrection

Although people work concretely to make the martyrs live, they understand this rebirth in spiritual rather than material form. Despite the emphasis on the practical and the concrete in popular religiosity, a distinctly un-bodily interpretation of resurrection dominates grassroots theological reflection in Central America. Although virtually all Salvadoran Catholic activists attest to the continuing relationship between the martyrs and the community that shares their ideals, they express little concern for physical resurrection. Rather, they understand resurrection as a spiritual presence in those who share their ideals, "a spiritual gift that lives forever in the mind," as Rosa puts it. Tomasa, a human rights activist, explains: "We know that with the priests who die, their bodies are killed, but we believe that their voices live on in all those who do not agree with the persecution . . . When a priest is killed, his voice will never be silenced, because it lives in all of us . . ." In her view, not only priests but all who died fighting for justice share this eternal life: "Our sons and daughters have been murdered, but their spirits live on, in me and in us. We know that all of those who are killed live on in their families and in the Salvadoran people." They live on because others continue their struggle and remember them. Thus Teresa asserts that "They continue living because we remember them. Not just the mothers but the people, because they gave their lives for the homeland, and the people see that it's not just anyone who gives his or her life."

Reference to Christ helps distinguish the people who give their lives as martyrs from "just anyone." José argues that the martyrs are "like Jesus Christ, who died so long ago and still continues." Daniel Vega believes that Christ "now lives in another way," giving believers strength and living within them. In addition to the primary model of Jesus' resurrection, other martyrs also live on in the community's work, according to CEB members. Gilberto, a San Lucas resident, asserts that all the people who gave their lives for "a just cause" are present in those who continue the same struggle, even if they did not belong to the church. "We're all Salvadorans, all brothers and sisters. Like Febe [Velásquez, a union leader killed in October 1989], who isn't in the church, but who gave her life, and we feel that she lives on. And not just her, but all those who give their lives for the people." Progressive Catholic activists often claim that since non-Christians can be martyrs, they can be and are resurrected in those who share their ideals, whether for secular or for religious motives.

Grassroots theology describes martyrs not only as a spiritual presence or memory but also as "seeds" that generate life for Christians and for the continuing work of the community. While the notion of spiritual presence expresses the ongoing nature of martyrs' lives in the community, the idea of a seed points to the maturation of a process initiated by individual sacrifices. The latter image dominates Josefa Avila's memory of the effect of Octavio Ortiz's death on the community near El Despertar, the retreat house where Ortiz and four youths were murdered. "There was a seed left in El Despertar. It dies, but something good has to come up."

What emerges, ideally, is deeper conviction and greater dedication to the ideals for which the martyrs offered their lives. Olivia asserts that "All those who have fallen leave a call to work for peace . . . It's like a seed that they've left for the people." The seed matures not by itself, but through the deepened conviction and redoubled efforts of survivors, who take energy and motivation from the death. Guadalupe Mejía summarizes: those who gave their lives for a just cause "haven't died, because we follow the ideas they left. Some of the fruits we've achieved have been because of them. For us they're still alive, and they will be until the total liberation."

IV. Martyrdom and the Reign of God

To believers, the seed that martyrs leave will ultimately give fruit most clearly in the "total liberation," the triumph of their cause. In the view of many progressive Catholics, death for the faith does not just guarantee eternal life for the martyr but also contributes to the renewal of society and the establishment of the reign of God. While traditional Catholicism (and Protestantism) envisions the reign of God as largely outside human time and geography, progressive theology posits a semi-utopian society that can be approximated or partially realized within human history. The precise characteristics of this ideal take different forms for different individuals and groups, but in general members of the *iglesia popular* understand it as a divinely-directed reign of justice and fullness of life for all, particularly those who suffer most in present conditions. While human efforts for social renewal will not by themselves bring about the reign of God, activists acknowledge, human praxis does contribute to it, insofar as victories for earthly justice represent steps towards the ultimate triumph of divine justice, "the opening of a doorway to the kingdom of God."[26]

In the eyes of many activists, the deaths of martyrs for Jesus' cause or social justice constitute perhaps the most important and unequivocal steps towards the reign of God. Just as Jesus' passion guaranteed the triumph of Christianity, they believe, today the blood shed in "this struggle for the kingdom," in Jesús's words, promises ultimate victory for Christ's cause. Expressing this conviction, Arturo Rivera y Damas asserted in a 1979 homily that "so much pain [is] necessary for redemption, and . . . the deaths of so many priests presages that the hour of liberation [is] near."[27] In his diary during Holy Week of 1978, Romero commented:

> The empty tomb of Christ is an evocation of the definitive triumph, of the consummated redemption. Until then, it is necessary to struggle so that the message of that empty tomb of Christ illuminates all our work on earth until the consummation of the redemption of the Lord.[28]

In El Salvador, where so much defeat and death have surrounded efforts for justice, "the message of the empty tomb" resonates deeply for Catholic activists. Popular theology views political violence in the context of the larger narrative of passion and rebirth, initiated by Jesus, who "gave his life so that others would have life," in Clara's words. In this light, martyrdom not only fulfills predictions of suffering, but also moves inexorably towards an ultimate fruit. Without idealizing martyrdom, many Salvadorans argue that if death is necessary, it should be seen as the road to life. Romero expressed this conviction that martyrdom must bear fruit less than two months before his death:

> I am sure that so much blood and so much pain caused to the families of so many victims will not be in vain. It is blood and pain that will water and make fertile new and continually more numerous seeds—Salvadorans who will awaken to the responsibility they have to build a more just and human society—and that will bear fruit in the accomplishment of the daring, urgent, and radical structural reforms that our nation needs.[29]

Romero's linkage of martyrdom to the "radical structural reforms that our nation needs" highlights the role of sacrificial death in movements for social change. Members of the Salvadoran popular church who faced repression believed that their suffering would bear concrete fruits, ultimately, in increased social justice and a better quality of life. This conviction motivated many Salvadorans to act despite extreme danger. Reflecting upon the political significance of popular Christianity in contemporary Central America, Roger Lancaster highlights the notion that victory will emerge from apparent defeat:

> The price of liberation, then, is the cross; struggle is a cross to bear, but revolution is its ultimate triumph. And echoing the biblical texts, revolution resurrects the dead, for it proves the prophetic vision of the martyrs; in effect, it is also proof of the resurrection, for the body of Christ that was once dead is now resurrected.[30]

The conviction that "revolution . . . proves the prophetic vision of the martyrs" is widespread among progressive activists in Central America. In El Salvador, members of the progressive Catholic group CEBES also believe that the martyrs live in continuing political and social activism. Addressing itself to the government and military, CEBES asserts, "The one that you assassinated is alive in the people. S/he is resurrected in every hand that is raised to defend the people from the exploiter's power. S/he lives in the farm, in the factory, and in the school."[31]

Although grounded in religious belief, CEBES incorporates political analyses and goals in its interpretation of martyrdom and resurrection. The mixture of politics and religion pervades Salvadoran popular culture, especially in visions of communal rebirth—the reign of God or political revolution—gained through sacrificial death. The communitarian traditions of pre-Hispanic Mesoamerica, in which the dead live on in the community, coincide with Catholic moral teaching to make sacrifice possible and resurrection plausible. Mario Ferrer explains this belief: "The feeling of martyrdom, of giving one's life for one's country, one's neighbor, comes I think from a more communal feeling, the need for a common salvation. If we have to die, the community will triumph one day. This coincides with the Christian sense." This conviction explains deaths as the necessary cost of victory and promises eternal life for the dead as the corollary to renewed life for the collective.

During the Nicaraguan revolution, according to Lancaster, members of the popular church saw the link between death and resurrection as "both a real and a figurative relationship." The deaths of individuals became necessary for the renewal of society in two senses:

> Concretely, the revolution requires its martyrs, and death in the defense of the revolution is seen as bringing new, revitalized life to the whole community; figuratively, the death of the individual—in the sense of the death of individualism—signifies the rebirth of the collectivity and the origin of the collectivist "New Man."[32]

As Lancaster's mention of the "New Man" suggests, the classical Christian belief that the deaths of individuals bring new life to the community has ties to Marxist discussions of death. Marx's emphasis on the social leads him to discuss individual mortality in terms of a larger population, history, or historical movement. Death thus negates individual immortality while affirming the immortality of a "meta-individual," in the words of Spanish theologian Juan Luis Ruíz de la Peña.[33] Marxism agrees with Christian theology and indigenous American traditions that individual mortality need not contradict the permanence and unity of humanity as species or as spirit. The deaths of individuals can renew the larger community. The promise of continued life in and for something larger makes the call to sacrifice compelling in contemporary Central America, as it did for Christians in the Roman Empire and for irreligious revolutionaries elsewhere. Whether the ultimate goal is a political revolution, the reign of God, or (as Lancaster suggests) a vision that blends the two, the deaths of martyrs gain public meaning from the renunciation of individual survival for something greater, a utopian horizon orienting efforts towards earthly justice.

This utopian vision may be the most important of the various ways martyr narratives contribute to social change. It is not the only way: narratives can help generate and strengthen collective identity, for example, by presenting members as part of a group with a history (and a future) that resonates with their individual histories. In El Salvador, for example, stories of Jesus and other martyrs help generate collective identity by linking the goals and actions of contemporary Christians to each other via a shared tie to Christian origins. In addition, social narratives often retell histories of heroic action and momentous victories, encouraging contemporary hearers to repeat the deeds of past heroes. Sometimes the narrative spurs action especially by invoking loyalty to the heroes of past stories, such as Jesus, Romero, and other martyrs.[34]

Nonetheless, the ability to present an alternative vision of the future may be the most potent mobilizational dimension of narratives.[35] Narratives often motivate activism, in other words, not primarily because of their vision of the past or critique of the present but because they project a compelling future. Of course, to be compelling a vision of the future must be coherent with people's understanding of the past and present. It must, further, seem possible—a utopia that is truly "no place" cannot motivate people, at least not many, to struggle for its realization.[36] A story that builds on the past, accurately assesses the possibilities of the present, and presents an appealing future, however, enlarges people's views of their possibilities; it can thus motivate them to remake the "narrative" they are living so that it resembles more closely the narrative they want to live.

In El Salvador, stories about Jesus and other martyrs provided a utopian horizon, reasons for hope, and evidence that human history holds room for the unexpected (heroic virtue, self-sacrifice, visions of a new earth) as well as the expected (repression and suffering). Narratives of martyrdom and resurrection not only described the suffering that activists encountered, but also proposed a new and better way to live. Ethicist Stanley Hauerwas elaborates this dimension of religious narratives:

> Our moral language does not just describe what is; it describes
> how we ought to see and intend the world . . . Our metaphors
> and stories entice us to find a way to bring into existence the
> reality that at once should be but will not be except as we act as
> if it is. Morally the world is always wanting to be created in cor-
> respondence to what is but is not yet.[37]

The classic case of the "already, not yet" in Christian history, of
course, is the reign of God. Salvadoran Catholic activists seek this reign
as a goal that lies beyond their proximate grasp but still orients and
motivates their efforts for social change. Images of the reign of God, as
well the stories of those who have struggled for it, help people
"redescribe our human reality in such disclosive terms that we return to
the 'everyday' reoriented to life's real—if forgotten or sometimes never
even imagined—possibilities," in David Tracy's words. For this reason,
Tracy argues, "Human beings need story, symbol, image, myth, and fiction to disclose to their imaginations some genuinely new possibilities
for existence; possibilities which conceptual analysis, committed as it is
to understanding present actualities, cannot adequately provide."[38]
Without conceptions of alternatives to their present situations, people
cannot challenge the established order. Human action is shaped not
only by "real" conditions, but also by visions of a future to be realized.

Without a desired future, in fact, much human action, especially acts
of opposition to the status quo, remains implausible. Even the most prag-
matic of ethicists, Reinhold Niebuhr, insists that a utopian vision is necessary to motivate the effort and risks necessary to work for social change.
Even though the utopia may never succeed, faith in its possibility is necessary to impel activism that may achieve smaller gains. "Without the
ultrarational hopes and passions of religion," writes Niebuhr, "no society
will ever have the courage to conquer despair and attempt the impossible;
for the vision of a just society is an impossible one, which can be approximated only by those who do not regard it as impossible."[39]

It is not enough, further, simply to know that a movement had some
vision of the future. To understand popular actions and statements, we
must know something about the particularities of this vision. These
details about matters such as salvation, the reign of God, and other perceived fruits of political action are often embodied in social-religious
narratives. To describe their hoped-for society, narratives draw on particular sets of symbolic resources, including historical events and religious

parables, to frame a particular way of seeing and acting in certain conditions in a certain time and place. Not only symbolic capital, of course, but also real economic and political factors make possible the rise of one set of ideas and narratives and/or the collapse or delegitimation of others. In the case of the Salvadoran *iglesia popular*, these factors include international and local changes in Roman Catholicism during the 1960s and 1970s and political and economic trends in El Salvador and internationally. Among certain sectors, these developments weakened the case for conservative interpretations and made possible the radical revision of key articles of faith, including a new vision of the future.

Idealized visions of the future raise the question of whether narratives represent merely an imaginary solution imposed upon "real" problems and chaos. This question echoes, on the one hand, Marx's critique of religion as an "opiate" that directs attention away from real suffering.[40] On the other hand, it echoes the frequent post-modernist claim that human history lacks an overarching order, as historian Hayden White suggests:

> [The] value attached to narrativity in the representation of real events arises out of a desire to have real events display the coherence, integrity, fullness, and closure of an image of life that is and can only be imaginary. The notion that sequences of real events possess the formal attributes of the stories we tell about imaginary events could only have its origin in wishes, daydreams, reveries. Does the world really present itself to perception in the form of well-made stories, with central subjects, proper beginnings, middles, and ends, and a coherence that permits us to see 'the end' in every beginning?[41]

White's answer, of course, is "no." I believe that the issue is not so much whether the world *is* a particular way, but rather whether people see the world that way and the consequences of that way of seeing the world. If people not only change their stories to accommodate events, but also, in David Carr's words, "change the events, by acting, to accommodate the story,"[42] then narrativized visions of a better future can serve not to anesthetize but rather to activate.

Endnotes

1. Quoted in Frend, *Martyrdom and Persecution*, 520–521.

2. Medardo Gómez meeting.

3. Weiner and Weiner, *The Martyr's Conviction*, 56; see also 58, 64.

4. Ileto, *Pasyon and Revolution*, 5.

5. Comaroff, *Body of Power*, 262.

6. Quoted by Alberto Iniesta, Auxiliary Bishop of Madrid, in the Introduction to *La sangre por el pueblo: Memoria de martirio en América Latina*, by the Instituto Histórico Centroamericano (Bilbao, Spain: Descleé de Brouwer, 1983), 8.

7. Pearce, *Promised Land*, 177.

8. Weiner and Weiner, *The Martyr's Conviction*, 61, 53.

9. Weiner and Weiner, *The Martyr's Conviction*, 52.

10. Sobrino interview, 26 October 1988.

11. Martín-Baró, "Religion as an Instrument of Psychological Warfare," in *Writings Towards a Liberation Psychology*, eds. Adrianne Aron and Shawn Corn (Cambridge, MA: Harvard University Press, 1994), 140. Church growth and the reasons for such growth are difficult to pinpoint in El Salvador during the 1970s and 1980s, when many people moved and/or left the country. One sign that persecution attracted members, however, can be seen in the fact that vocations in the Central American Province of the Society of Jesus rose during the period of extreme persecution in El Salvador and Guatemala. Another indication might be the fact that the Salvadoran Lutheran Church, whose progressive stance has caused it significant repression was in the early 1990s the fastest-growing Lutheran church in the world. Of course, the 1980s also witnessed rapid growth in evangelical and Pentecostal churches in El Salvador, as elsewhere in Latin America, a trend that may reflect a different type of religious response to the insecurity created by war and economic crisis. See Luis Samandú, ed., *Protestantismos y procesos sociales en Centroamérica* (San José, Costa Rica: Editorial Universitaria Centroamericana, 1991).

12. Pearce, *Promised Land*, 156.

13. *Cursillo*, San Pablo parish, 1 April 1990.

14. Cantón de Jayaque, "La voz del pueblo cristiano salvadoreño," *Diakonía* (Managua), no. 53 (March 1990): 90.

15. López Vigil, *Primero Dios*, 91.

16. *Life is hard*, 207. Lancaster adds the important caveat that love for concrete persons does not always motivate "revolutionary" action; "Such love may

also cause us to lie low when violence threatens to sever these real human connections."

17. DesPres, *The Survivor*, 37, 38.

18. Workman, *Persecution*, 31.

19. Ileto, *Pasyon and Revolution*, 243.

20. Woodward, *Making Saints*, 55.

21. Quoted in *La iglesia en El Salvador*, 68.

22. Romero, *La voz de los sin voz*, 461.

23. Tomás Borge, *Carlos, el amanecer ya no es una tentación* (Managua: Editorial Nueva Nicaragua, 1985), 61–62.

24. Radio Venceremos, "Homenaje de Radio Venceremos," *Christus* (Mexico City) 55, no. 632 (March 1990), 51.

25. María [pseud.], interview with Jim Carney, tape recording, San Salvador, cited in Elizabeth Berguer, "Voices from Latin America: Encounters with Church-Related Grassroots Groups Involved with Social Change," presented at the First International Conference on Liberation Theology, Simon Fraser University, Burnaby, British Columbia, 6–8 February 1986.

26. Carlos Zarcos Mera, Leonor Tellería, and Carlos Manuel Sánchez. "The Ministry of Coordinators in the Popular Christian Community," in L. Boff and V. Elizondo, eds., *La Iglesia Popular: Between Fear and Hope*. New York: Seabury Press (*Concilium* 176), 1984, p. 70.

27. Quoted in Romero, *Su diario*, 260.

28. Romero, *Su diario*, 10. The image of the "empty tomb" also arises in the claim of Nicaraguan priest Ernesto Cardenal that "the tombs of all those who have loved their fellow human beings are empty." See *The Gospel in Solentiname*, vol. 4, 256.

29. Quoted in Brockman, *Romero: A Life*, 223.

30. Lancaster, *Thanks to God and the Revolution*, 91–92.

31. "Monseñor Romero vive! Viva Monseñor Romero!," *Mártires de El Salvador* (Mexico City), no. 61 (January–February 1990): 5.

32. Lancaster, *Thanks to God and the Revolution*, 91.

33. Juan Luis Ruíz de la Peña, *Muerte y marxismo humanismo: Aproximación teológica* (Salamanca, Spain: Ediciones Sígueme, 1978), 15.

34. See Ileto, *Pasyon and Revolution*; Hart, "Cracking the Code;" Lancaster, *Thanks to God and the Revolution*; and Eric Selbin, "Revolutionary Traditions and Revolutionary Reality: People's Narratives of Revolution and Rebellion in Latin America and the Caribbean." Presented to the meeting of the Latin American Studies Association, Atlanta, March 1994.

35. Both E. P. Thompson and Eugene Genovese highlight the political importance of working-class and enslaved people's religious view of an after-life or kingdom. See Thompson, *The Making of the English Working Class*, 34; and Genovese, *Roll, Jordan, Roll*, 165–166, 251.

36. To say that this vision must seem possible does not, of course, mean that it must reflect people's real lives. As Selbin notes, ideals such as justice or freedom can "remain powerful and compelling in a world where many people's daily lives" do not reflect them. Eric Selbin, *Modern Latin American Revolutions* (Boulder, CO: Westview Press, 1993), 139.

37. Stanley Hauerwas, *Vision and Virtue* (Notre Dame: Fides Publishers, 1974), 73.

38. David Tracy, *Blessed Rage for Order: The New Pluralism in Theology* (New York: The Seabury Press, 1978), 207.

39. Reinhold Niebuhr, *Moral Man and Immoral Society* (Charles Scribner's Sons, 1960), 81; see also 221.

40. Karl Marx, "Contribution to the Critique of Hegel's Philosophy of Right: Introduction," in *The Marx-Engels Reader*, ed. Robert Tucker (New York: W. W. Norton, 1978), 53–54.

41. White, *The Content of the Form*, 24.

42. Carr, "Narrative and the Real World," 126.

8

Conclusions: Religion and Political Protest

Religious narratives about martyrdom helped many Salvadorans make sense of political violence during the years of civil war and motivated activist responses to it. Their interpretations and their responses, I believe, can shed light not only on Salvadoran history but on more general understandings of religiously motivated political action. This case suggests that studies of religion and politics will benefit from efforts to take religious ideas and practices seriously. Such an approach would highlight the ways religious narratives provide explanatory and normative frameworks not only for everyday life but also for extreme conditions.

I. The Culture of Fear

These extreme conditions provide the context in which Salvadoran religious narratives and religiously grounded social movements should be understood. One of the most important factors shaping religion in El Salvador is the country's turbulent political history, which has generated a sharp awareness of the possibility of political violence. The powerful, for their part, have always believed, in Enrique Baloyra's words, that "if necessary, they could repeat the 'lesson' of 1932."[1] Less privileged members of Salvadoran society have known, as Pablo puts it, that "repression can come at any moment." Poor people have lived, at least since 1932 matanza and arguably since the conquest, in a "culture of fear." This culture includes limitations of legal and individual rights; vagueness of legal definitions for criminal activity; lack of access to information and difficulty in communication; fragmentation of community and collective efforts (especially via impediments to social organizations); and open physical coercion, including torture, death, and the impunity with which these crimes are committed.[2]

In El Salvador during the late 1970s and 1980s, a particularly important dimension of the culture of fear was not just the massiveness but
also the randomness of repression. No one, including persons without
political affiliation or those loyal to the regime, could feel secure. The
1981 massacre of approximately one thousand people in and near the
village of El Mozote in northern Morazán province testifies to this fact.
Residents of the village offered less support to the FMLN than people in
surrounding areas, in part because many people in El Mozote were evangelical Protestants. Because of their confidence that the army would
know their sympathies and thus leave them in peace, most residents did
not flee when guerrillas warned them that the government's Atlacatl
Battalion was launching a "hammer and anvil" operation in the vicinity.
Their confidence was tragically misplaced; after the soldiers finished,
only one person remained alive, and she survived only by chance.[3] The
massacre at El Mozote points to the lack of absolute security for any person or group, while underlining the special danger faced by poor people,
particularly in or near "conflicted" zones.

In this context, any link to the political opposition, even simple acts
such as claiming a dead relative, made people vulnerable: "Here if you
went to see a body, you were marked," recalls Sara, a resident of El
Paisnal, near Aguilares. Family members often did not hold funerals or
even look for bodies because of their fear that their relation to the dead
person would identify them as "subversives."[4] Personal grudges also
helped spread the violence, as people "took advantage of the situation to
take vengeance" on personal enemies, in Marcela's words. Through
apparently random, or at least unpredictable, violence like this, rightist
paramilitary groups and the government military diminished trust within
families and among neighbors and dissuaded many potential activists
from opposition activities.

To intensify fear, the army and death squads often tortured victims,
disfigured the bodies after death, and left corpses or body parts in symbolic locations. Many people feared not death itself but the torture that
might precede it. Death threats, arbitrary captures and detentions, and
constant military harassment in "conflicted" areas contributed to the climate of fear and suspicion, as did public insults and slander. The
Salvadoran media routinely labeled opposition activists "delinquent,"
"terrorist," and "subversive." Oscar Romero, a frequent target, admitted
that the insults hurt. Like many other Catholics, he sought to make
sense of the attacks within the context of sacred history, especially Jesus'

experiences. "My only consolation," Romero said in July 1979, "is that Christ . . . was also misunderstood and called rebellious and sentenced to death."[5] While people like Romero found consolation in the knowledge that earlier prophets suffered similar attacks, defamation nonetheless intimidated many people beyond its immediate targets and generated greater danger for all activists.

This climate of fear led many people to leave church programs, their neighborhood, and even the country. Those who stayed to face the risks rarely condemn people who left, but point to a lack of *conciencia*, or an understanding of the situation and its requirements. "People who are not *consciente* feel afraid, and because of this fear they are silent. Not because they're not in agreement, but because of [fear], they don't denounce injustice," says Lucía. Like many other progressive Catholics, she feels sympathy for people who do not join political struggles but refuses to acknowledge the legitimacy of opposing views. Popular church ideology may accept diverse responses to fear and loss, but rarely does it openly consider the possibility of error in its own analysis of the political situation or God's will.

Taking for granted, at least publicly, the correctness of their political and religious stance, popular church activists attribute their own staying power to their awareness of what is "right" and "necessary." Jesús recalls that "When the repression came, only the most *consciente* stayed." In this perspective, people without a "true" understanding of the political situation are the most frightened by repression. Thus Vilma explains that "We're not so afraid, because we're a little *consciente*, but with new people it's hard to get them to participate." Many people, including sympathizers as well as critics of progressive Catholicism, are in fact frightened by *conciencia* itself, since a heightened awareness of injustice seems to carry inevitable risks. In these and other ways, as Marcela notes, "Fear conquers us."

II. Forms of Protest and Resistance

Given the high level of violence and risk in El Salvador during the 1970s and 1980s, it is no surprise that fear "conquered" many activists and potential activists. The question, rather, is how so many people managed, if not to defeat fear, then at least to keep it at bay and to commit a wide range of acts of protest. Before describing some of the forms of protest employed by progressive Catholics in El Salvador, it is important to understand the ways their activism was constrained by fear, by "beliefs about the probability and severity of retaliation," and by "the existing forms of labor control," as James Scott notes.[6] In addition, Salvadoran political culture, developments and personalities within the Catholic Church, and the nature of leftist organizations all influenced the forms of action taken by progressive Catholics. Many people sought, for reasons that included not only fear but often personal responsibilities, to avoid more risky forms of open protest. On the other hand, the massiveness and randomness of repression led some people to take greater risks than they might have in a less extreme situation, due either to outrage or to the belief that since nothing guaranteed safety, open defiance was as feasible as any other stance.

Recent scholarship has highlighted the fact that "resistance" against a regime or a policy is not limited to obvious acts of protest but involves what Scott terms the "everyday forms of resistance." Even in the midst of a civil war, subtle acts of protest are more widespread than militant acts of rebellion. "If we confine our historical scrutiny to the zero-sum heroics of revolution successfully achieved," as Jean Comaroff notes, "we discount the vast proportion of human social action which is played out, perforce, on a more humble scale."[7] Salvadorans have employed everyday forms of resistance, including "footdragging," dissimulation, and ritual reversals or negations of the status quo prior to, during, and since the civil war. The drama of more explicit acts of defiance should not blind us to this fact. Nor ought we to assume that apparent compliance signals real agreement. Finally, we should not forget that close to a million Salvadorans, including many who disagreed with the government and resented the ruling elite, chose to leave the country during the war. In exile in the United States, Honduras, and elsewhere, Salvadorans chose among the same options that faced their compatriots at home, including political organizing, self-help and community projects, and/or religious activities, all taking place within the daily struggle for subsistence.

Without denying the existence and importance of mundane acts of resistance, I am interested here mainly in relatively clear-cut and explicit ideas about and acts of opposition to the Salvadoran government and military, and especially those actions that entailed risk. I am interested, in other words, in the actions of *mártires en potencia*. (It is important to keep in mind, though, that in the late 1970s and 1980s violence was so widespread in El Salvador that almost anyone was at risk. Thus one did not need to be a "hero" to risk one's life, and even "everyday" forms of resistance might create danger.) Concentrating on the more self-conscious and organized forms of protest among progressive Catholics in El Salvador at this time, I identify a continuum of possible actions through which Salvadorans resisted economic and political injustices and sought to construct a different kind of society.

Perhaps the most subtle level of resistance entailed religious ideas and action. Under conditions of extreme repression, popular theological and ethical convictions that challenge the dominant ideology can constitute a form of resistance and not only a precondition for it.[8] The claim, for example, that the selfishness of the wealthy and not God's will maintains the poverty of the majority defies the moral foundation of El Salvador's socioeconomic status quo. Popular church activists recognize the power of ideas and words when they assert that people were murdered, most often, simply for "telling the truth." On a practical level, some religious activities, such as prayer and attendance at meetings or Bible study groups, appear innocuous. At times, however, even apparently harmless actions take on clearer political significance, as for example the "clandestine" meetings of CEBs in northern San Salvador or masses in zones of guerrilla control.[9] Still other religious acts, particularly rituals such as the *vía crucis* or funeral masses, can become overt expressions of defiance.

A second form of resistance is community service, i.e., actions to meet people's immediate needs. These may not appear to challenge political structures, but in El Salvador in the 1980s both the government and its opponents understood many types of "charity" as expressions of opposition to the established order. Work with refugees from war zones became especially politically charged, and the repopulation of entire villages in areas such as Chalatenango and Morazán in the late 1980s became the largest-scale example of "humanitarian" aid as protest. On a smaller scale, projects such as soup kitchens, assistance with housing and repairs, and medical care could constitute protest insofar as they aided victims of government repression, criticized the government's failure to meet people's needs; and/or circumvented official channels to address these needs. CEBs and other types of religiously identified groups engaged in these actions on a regular basis throughout the war.

Attendance at demonstrations and marches constituted a third and increasingly "political" form of protest. Participation in such public acts came most often from secular political organizations, which included many active Catholics, and from individuals, rather than from CEBs or religious groups *per se*. However, in many cases religious processes such as *reflexión* played decisive roles in motivating decisions to take public stances. This was true also with a final and most dramatic form of opposition, participation in political-military groups. The choice to join the guerrillas was often intensely individual, although in some cases, especially in rural areas of conflict, the decision encompassed the wider community. Religion often influenced the decision process, primarily insofar as religious convictions helped convince people of the need for radical social change. The extremities of repression and the apparent viability or necessity of armed resistance then pushed many Salvadorans into guerrilla organizations. Repression in turn shaped religious ideas about the ethics of armed resistance itself. While the *iglesia popular* never identified as completely with the FMLN as the government (or some guerrillas) suggested, thousands of Catholic lay activists, as well as a number of priests and nuns, did join or support the armed opposition.

Militant political resistance played the role it did because of distinctive features of Salvadoran political culture and history. Salvadoran politics have been characterized by extreme political closure and repression, leading to "a radicalization of the opposition and an increased polarization of the political process," as Baloyra notes.[10] The exclusionary nature of Salvadoran politics drove many reformers, including peasant federations, trade unions, and guerrilla groups, to develop more militant forms of activism than were common elsewhere in Latin America. Salvadoran groups drew on memories of rebellions led by Anastasio Aquino, Farabundo Martí, and other popular heroes, all of which made revolutionary politics less far-fetched and more broadly supported than in many other parts of Latin America.

Both El Salvador's unique political heritage and the extremity of repression during the 1970s and 1980s make generalizations based on Salvadoran experiences difficult. The distinctiveness of the Salvadoran situation, however, also puts certain issues in sharp perspective, including the question of why and how many people resisted not only socioeconomic injustices but also brutal repression intended to end protest. This leads to more general questions about the reasons act on political convictions, even when they require risks and sacrifices. These questions will not be answered by defining defiance in the face of repression as "irrational." Rather, we should look at protest in the light of its own logic, which is readily apparent from inside the believing community and not entirely inaccessible to outside observers. Describing religiously grounded popular movements in the Philippines during the nineteenth century, Ileto argues that the use of terms like "fanaticism," "nativism," and "millenarianism" only alienate observers from the movements' actors. Instead, scholars need "a set of conceptual tools, a grammar" with which to understand such movements in light of their own rationality, the "intentions and hopes" of the participants themselves, as well as the political, cultural, and economic constraints within which they operated.[11]

III. Rationality, Sacrifice, and Self-Interest

Ileto challenges us to find movements' own rationality. Discovering this logic is not always easy, however. The insistence of many Salvadoran activists that they simply recognized the demands of authentic faith in the light of the immediate political situation may seem insufficient motivation for high-risk activism. Religious motivation poses a difficulty for social scientists, who often look for more "rational" reasons for dangerous activities than claims of loyalty to a "higher cause." The guiding thesis of many approaches to social action, as Laurence Iannaccone summarizes, is that "Individuals weigh the anticipated costs and benefits of their actions and act so as to maximize net benefits." In this strategic-instrumental view, individuals rarely act against their own interests, particularly if such action would endanger their own survival. Rather, people will "sit back and 'free-ride' rather than strive to serve the corporate interest," i.e., they will try to maximize their personal benefits without carrying their share of the (perceived) burden.[12]

Applying this economistic approach to religion, particularly in an extreme situation such as that of El Salvador, raises many problems. While cost-benefit analyses may guide people's (or consumers') approaches to some issues, religions differ in crucial ways from other types of "commodities." In a critique of rational choice approaches to religion, Steve Bruce argues that in choosing or adhering to a religion, people measure not utility, but "salvational truth."[13] In other words, they may rationally consider costs and benefits, but these factors, and the rationality that takes them into account, differ from the instrumental consideration of tangible benefits and costs that rational choice theory views as the only type of rationality.

In an example that is relevant to the Salvadoran case, Bruce notes that high costs (i.e., persecution) and/or relatively few tangible benefits do not necessarily ruin a religion as they might a business. Religious believers, in fact, may even see attacks upon them as proof of ideological purity, as occurred among many Salvadoran Catholics. Herein lies a crucial difference between religion and business: "the management of Ford did not persist in making the Edsel and console themselves with the belief that the lack of consumers just proved that it was too good a car for ordinary Joes."[14] In the end, a range of reasons, understood differently by insiders and outsiders, influence people's decisions about religious commitment and praxis. Because these decisions concern intangibles such as salvation, truth, and ultimate meaning, the rational weighing of material costs and benefits cannot fully explain the choices believers make. Nor does the notion that rational analysis takes place in an intellectual and moral "free market" where all options are equally accessible. In real life, people face limited options in a context that is far from truly free. This is especially true for poor people, in El Salvador and elsewhere, whose access to alternative actions, lifestyles, and worldviews has been severely constrained. They choose rationally, but among limited options and in conditions not of their own choosing.

Without explicit recourse to theories about rational choice, some observers have argued, in effect, that economistic concerns have driven Latin Americans away from activist Catholicism and towards more quietistic Protestant churches. David Stoll claims, for example, that progressive Catholicism's commitment to social justice "carr[ied] a price which was too high for most." Traditionally, this analysis states, the Catholic Church appealed to many people because of its ability to protect the weak. This ability declined as the church challenged institutional injustice. The church's post-Medellín activism put its members in danger, even forcing them to choose among taking up arms, going into exile, or retiring to refugee camps—"not a choice likely to attract more followers." A more appealing choice for "hard-pressed Catholics" in places like El Salvador and Guatemala, according to Stoll, was membership in an evangelical church. In the end, "calls for revolutionary commitment were not engaging the religiosity of the people and sustaining them through long, hard, years of struggle for survival, at least not in the way that evangelical sects could." Ultimately, he contends, "revolutionary visions faded into the grim reality of endless political violence."[15]

Stoll is correct that progressive Catholicism has, in practice, "been forced to carry the highest hopes in the most hopeless situations."[16] However, this analysis misses the mark on several important points. First, claiming that progressive Catholicism's social commitment has "been suicidal in many times and places"[17] fails to reflect sufficiently on the question of who is doing the killing: few observers could deny that political repression, at least in El Salvador, has constituted not suicide but murder. Progressive Catholicism in Latin America called not for self-immolation by the poor but rather for the fulfillment of basic human rights. Claims that such demands are "suicidal" lay the blame for violence with the victims rather than the agents of repression. Further, fear or self-interest may drive people to abandon a group perceived as dangerous, such as the progressive church, without necessarily holding it responsible for the repression it has suffered.

Second, Stoll, along with a number of other observers, claims that the Catholic Church's activism has driven away believers, primarily towards evangelical churches. While this may hold some truth, we must also look at other factors that pushed people towards Protestantism. Many observers argue that evangelical churches provide intimate, quasi-kin networks of moral and material support. Such support is increasingly necessary in the face of economic and social dislocation that has diminished the possibility of resolving economic or personal problems in other ways.[18] The growing conservatism of the Vatican, further, has in some cases had local-level effects of limiting more participatory programs in Catholic parishes.[19]

Third and finally, Stoll argues that liberation theology has been produced largely by "more or less safely situated intellectuals," who have called the poor to risk their lives while remaining protected themselves. "Christianity is about sacrifice, of course," Stoll admits, "but it is not about putting other people on the line."[20] The accusation that Latin American theologians are "safely situated" rings false in the light of the 1989 killings of six Jesuits in San Salvador. More important, however, is the charge that intellectuals, safe or not, have called on the poor to take risks. This accusation comes in the context of Stoll's larger argument that progressive Catholicism (which he defines in shorthand as liberation theology) remained distant from the poor for whom its leaders claimed to speak. While this critique may be appropriate in some situations, to apply it generally denies agency to the subjects (or objects?) of the debate. Poor people in El Salvador, at least, have proven themselves capable of interpreting their experiences in the light of their faith, coming to conclusions based on that faith, and acting on those conclusions. Although many of them endangered their lives, very few did so because a well-protected intellectual urged suicide. They took risks, rather, because their analysis of the situation and their convictions demanded it. In this sense their dangerous behavior was neither naive nor fanatical, but as logical as any other course of action open to them.

While ideas about cost-benefit analysis and self-interest may explain social action in other cases, they cannot explain the experience of popular movements in El Salvador: the undeniable fact that something "engag[ed] the religiosity" of tens of thousands of people "and sustain[ed] them through long, hard, years of struggle." I suggest that a more fruitful approach would focus on religious commitments and religiously grounded interpretations of political events and conditions. In El Salvador, and in many other places, religious engagement and political struggle have been not contradictory but mutually reinforcing. Further, both are often sustained by rational analysis and commitments set within a narrative framework and nurtured within the believing community, rather than by strategic-instrumental calculations or "calls for revolutionary commitment" from afar. Understanding the actions of Salvadoran Catholic activists, or at least understanding them as other than the result of religious fanaticism, suicidal tendencies, or misguided obedience to out-of-touch intellectuals, requires reference to the internal logic of popular world-views, the ways that "*religious* motives and values undergird other aspects of group life and keep them going in the face of possible adversity."[21]

This internal logic often remains unseen to scholars and other outside observers. This failure to see stems as much or more from the guiding assumptions of social scientific approaches as from the supposedly mysterious or opaque nature of religious belief. While as outsiders we can never entirely grasp a culture's or group's dynamic ("do an ethnography of witchcraft as seen by a witch," in Clifford Geertz's words), surely we can come closer than most standard approaches (which often have been the equivalent of ethnographies of witchcraft done by geometers).[22]

Efforts to understand the religious dimension of politics (and vice-versa) are further complicated by the fact that religious images, ideas, and stories usually have more than one meaning, depending on the identity of the practitioner-believer. Each side has its own rationality, which may appear irrational from another angle. Not only secularists and outsiders but fellow believers from different sectors of the religious community may find very different meanings in the same symbol or story. Reynaldo Ileto offers a helpful example of the political implications of religion's multivalence in his description of the Philippine *vía crucis* or *pasyon*. Ileto notes that the powerful believed that the *pasyon's* claim that "social status based on wealth and education has no real value" discourages peasants from improving their lots. "But from the perspective of the mass audience, the identification of wealthy, educated pharisees . . . with Christ's tormentors could not fail to have radical implications in actual life."[23] The *pasyon* provides images which elites believe inculcate passivity but in which the poor may find cause for rebellion.

Ileto's example, which has numerous parallels in Latin America, demonstrates the weakness of defining religion's "social function" in terms of secular instrumental rationality or even from the perspective of elite believers. Understanding religion's political implications more fully requires examining what religious images and stories mean for different sectors of the believing community. To less privileged members of a community, "folk religious traditions and cultural values . . . which usually promote passivity and reconciliation rather than conflict, have latent meanings that can be revolutionary," as Ileto puts it.[24] These meanings, "whether the *pasyon* encouraged subservience or defiance, resignation or hope," Ileto notes, "were not fixed, but rather depended on social context."[25] More generally, the meaning of any religious idea or symbol depends ultimately on the history and narrative settings in which it emerges and to which it is applied.

From the perspective of a secular observer, religious faith that demands action in the face of tremendous risk appears irrational, "fanatical," and/or suicidal. However, from the standpoint of a believer, "rationality" may center not upon self-interest or even self-preservation but on the sacred meanings of secular history and on the believer's own relationship to God. This approach "ask[s] God to give me strength to do what God wants, not what I want for myself," as Clara puts it. In this perspective, the struggle for social justice fulfills divine as well as human goals. If rationality requires behavior consistent with the truth about a situation and the goals sought, then rationality itself demands participation in this struggle. From this perspective, arguments about self-interest, suicide, and free riders miss the point entirely.

IV. Narrative

The question, then, is how to find out what is the point. I argue that the rationality behind both popular ideas about martyrdom and high-risk activism in El Salvador is embedded in religious narratives about perse-cution. These narratives provide a larger context that shows believers the reasons for and the necessity and benefits of persecution. These nar-ratives drew on a pool of already-existing story lines, characters, values, images, and other elements in the collective memory. These resources exist in oral and written stories, songs, art, theater, and also in perhaps unexpected forms such as posters, graffiti, gossip, and other "under-ground" sources. In the formation of any social narrative, different indi-viduals and groups select, reject, and reshape these resources, adding their own imaginings and longings for the future.

The most important resource for progressive Catholics in El Salvador was the "symbolic capital" of Christianity, and particularly the Bible, which post-Medellín reforms and especially the practice of *reflex-ión* made more accessible to ordinary people. Episodes from Salvadoran and Latin American political history, including the *matanza* and other rebellions, also provided material that resonated in a popular imagina-tion. In addition, people drew on local and familial traditions, especially tales of heroic loved ones, often passed on orally in stories and songs. Popular songs about martyrs provide an especially rich primary source; most slain priests, for example, are the subjects of at least one song writ-ten by parishioners. Often song lyrics are not written down (often their authors cannot write) but preserved orally and performed at community celebrations. Especially among physical reminders of repression—in a clandestine meeting in a poor neighborhood or in the bombed ruins of a church in a war zone—the performance of these songs works powerfully to bind participants to each other and to their shared cause.

Once formed, a narrative has to circulate in order to be effective. This means that people must find it compelling enough to retell. Even when a leader formulates a narrative that others find compelling enough to pass (and perhaps act) on, the story that they retell is rarely identical to the one they heard. Different points are emphasized, different mean-ings gleaned, depending on the teller, the circumstances, and the audi-ence. It is important to investigate the ways and reasons mutations occur: the process by which hearers select and reject different elements of the narrative so it resonates with, makes sense of, and/or provides comfort or hope to their own lives.

Further, different narratives resonate with particular groups in par-ticular times and circumstances. In El Salvador in the early and mid-1970s, popular opposition narratives seemed to highlight political closure and censorship. The public high point and perhaps the end of this type of narrative came in February 1977, when Salvadoran Jesuit Rutilio Grande gave a speech responding to the government's expulsion of Colombian priest Mario Bernal. "I'm afraid," proclaimed Grande,

> that if Jesus of Nazareth came back, coming down from Galilee to Judea, that is from Chalatenango to San Salvador, I daresay he would not get as far as Apopa, with his preaching and actions. They would stop him in Guazapa and jail him there.
> . . . They would accuse him of being a rabble-rouser, a foreign Jew, one confusing people with strange and exotic ideas, against democracy, that is, against the minority. Ideas against God, because they are a clan of Cains. They would undoubtedly crucify him again.[26]

Grande makes a political point by reference to the story of Jesus' life. The narrative differs, however, from later Salvadoran stories of martyrdom. In Grande's speech, the theme of crucifixion emerges, but in a speculative way. His main concern lay with the freedom to criticize, to organize, to "tell the truth." Grande's killing in March 1977 marked the beginning of the rise of narratives focused on the passion and resurrection of contemporary martyrs. This change stemmed largely from the dramatic increase in political killings in the late 1970s. It also emerged from the growing radicalization of both secular and religious activists, due partly but not only to the intensified repression, and from the growing ties between these two sectors. Some sort of convergence between political and religious themes and groups was probably necessary, at least in El Salvador, for any social narrative or political ideology to take root as deeply as did the progressive Catholic narrative of passion and martyrdom.[27]

In addition to links between religious and political dimensions, successful narratives must bring together collective and individual narratives. George Steinmetz points to the difficulties that arise when individual and collective narratives fail to mesh. Sometimes social narratives formulated by a leader or a group fail to mirror or resonate with the lives of the individuals to whom they want to appeal. Other times individuals or collectives fail to "narrativize" their lives, or more precisely to understand them as echoing the terms of the narrative being offered.[28] Such narratives rarely achieve significant explanatory or mobilizational power. This does not mean that in such cases people see their lives in entirely non-narrativized form but rather that the narrative in question has failed and other stories will emerge and perhaps achieve greater resonance.

Here we might turn to questions about whether narratives about martyrdom in El Salvador echoed individuals' experiences and whether people understood their lives in light of these stories. As repression affected tens of thousands of Salvadorans, many found clear echoes of the martyr narratives in their personal lives as well as on the national political stage. Christian narratives about persecution seemed to mirror their own experiences and to offer a framework for "narrativizing" those experiences. For many, these narratives provided not only a way of making sense of their lives but a sacred truth about the course of those lives. This not infrequently motivated continued activism in the face of personal loss and danger.

Progressive Catholic narratives of martyrdom were not the only narratives current in El Salvador in the 1970s and 1980s, of course. Not only marginalized or oppositional communities make sense of their experiences, histories, and hopes via social-religious narratives. Rightist governments, like their opponents, construct and circulate narratives that draw on common cultural values and resources, embody people's goals for the future, and present often idealized versions of significant events and characters. In the Salvadoran civil war, the narratives encouraging opposition activism directly challenged the narratives created by and for dominant groups, which presented very different interpretations of the political conflicts of the 1970s and 1980s, with different dead heroes as martyrs. Progressive activist Mirtala López recognizes that hers is not the only side justifying its actions in religious terms, although she does not acknowledge any legitimacy in the government version.

> The government uses images and symbols of Jesus Christ. Since it knows that all the people here are religious, it uses this means to infuse its message in the people. It tries to attract people with the Bible . . . They also say that they'll do what Christ did, give his life for the people. They use his words to mislead the people that it's a Christian government.

The Salvadoran government not only claimed martyr status for its own dead heroes but also characterized progressive/left Catholics (including many church officials) as outside the church or even as atheists. Newspapers, television, and official rhetoric hammered home an image of activists as those who incited violence and chaos against the law and order represented by the status quo. Similarly, of course, progressive Catholics described government soldiers and officials as unchristian agents of selfish and even diabolical interests.

In the face of powerful dominant group narratives, counter narratives require some type of "institutional" support to enter the public imagination on anything other than a tiny scale. In El Salvador, a turning point occurred with Romero's characterization of activists. Earlier, I quoted Jon Sobrino's recollection: "It was an extraordinary thing, for the poor to go to Mass at the Cathedral and hear the archbishop say, 'We have martyrs in this country.'"[29] This public acknowledgement did not start the popular identification of activists as martyrs, since a largely oral and underground tradition identified them as martyrs before any public figures did. This tradition endured especially in stories and songs about murdered activists and crushed uprisings, seen not as mere failures, but as "latent forms of empowerment, waiting to be animated either by the population themselves or by leaders."[30] For this underground tradition to "be animated," in fact, leaders and followers require both catalyzing events (a historical parallel or crisis) and some social-symbolic capital or resources on which to draw in order to propel their story into a larger public arena.

Social narratives help shape people's perceptions not only of the past (i.e., whether a dead activist is a bandit or a hero) but also of their options for the future (i.e., what they can do and whether it will matter). Counternarratives can help convince people that defiance is feasible, even required and that it can lead to a better future. In El Salvador, notions about the possibility of protest rested especially on Christian notions of sacrifice as a requirement of authentic faith and a necessary step towards the reign of God, or at least an approximation thereof. These conceptions helped instill a willingness to take risks, as did the conviction that martyrdom would bring fruits, including both a better society and the martyr's own rebirth in the community of believers. This conviction stemmed primarily from a reading of Jesus' resurrection as a precedent for the "return" of all subsequent martyrs.

The importance of resurrection and the reign of God highlights the distinctive nature of social-religious narratives in contrast to other types of narratives. Uniquely compelling visions of the future are part of what sets religious narratives apart. Other important elements often include reference to an original prophet, as seen for example in the parallels to

Jesus' passion in Salvadoran narratives of martyrdom. The passion provides the "model martyrdom," the original master-narrative without
which, in El Salvador's highly Catholic popular culture, interpretations
of contemporary political killings might have fallen flat. The link to the
passion, and more generally to ideas about divine will, the reign of God,
and other religious symbols and values, gave political killings a transcendent meaning and, perhaps even more crucially, provided divine justification for political opposition. Protest became a sacred struggle;
abandoning the cause meant abandoning one's faith; holding firm in the
face of danger guaranteed supernatural rewards.

The influence of martyr stories in Salvadoran popular Catholicism
illustrates the uniquely compelling power of religious narratives to influence the ways people understand their experience, respond to them, and
envision alternative futures. In this and other cases, social-religious narratives have played a distinctive and crucial role in struggles for political
change. The content of the narratives varies, of course, according to religious and cultural traditions, political histories, economic circumstances,
and individual imagination and leadership. No single narrative makes
sense of and resonates with the experiences of all people or even of all
members of a relatively small group such as Salvadoran Catholics.
Further, in no case will "just any" narrative plot suffice. Some narratives
undoubtedly tend to encourage fatalism rather than activism. However,
with the right plot, among other factors, religious narratives play a vital
role in integrating experiences and granting those experiences meaning
and motivational force, particularly to those who find themselves with
few powerful allies except, in their view, the most powerful of all.

The importance of this faith is vital for understanding religiously
motivated activism. Salvadoran Catholics understand human history as
shot through with divine significance: God acts in history, and human
actions have ultimate consequences. The task of believers is to discern
God's will for human history and to act in accord with that will. Many
activists interpret conflicts between rich and poor as battles between
God and "those who aren't on God's side and who are on the side of
those who cause suffering," as Elena puts it. A Salvadoran base community member explains:

> I understand that we have to recognize the true road of God, the
> God of life, of justice, and not the false gods of money, of the
> riches that make us blind and [make us] deviate to the road of

ambition, selfishness, envy. Thus we have to work for this justice and this reign of God if we want to be true Christians.[31]

Pursuing justice in situations such as El Salvador in the 1970s and
1980s almost always involved risk. What helped sustain people struggling
to follow their religious principles was often a personal relationship with
God, especially the confidence that God was on their side although the
world seemed weighed against them. Medardo Gómez, the often-threat-
ened Lutheran bishop of San Salvador, insists that God sides with those
who struggle for social justice, even though God may not always protect
them from risk. "In a situation of danger," he asserts, "you need to understand that if you lose your life, it doesn't mean that God has abandoned
you."[32] Even believing that God cannot or will not always save their lives,
activists insist that their faith in God sustains their continued, risky work.
Thus, Julio, a lay leader in Chalatenango, contends that "Whoever does-
n't feel fear, like Monseñor Romero, has been given strength by Christ."
Jesús agrees: "It's God that maintains us. Our time hasn't come yet. And
if this time has been given to us to live, we have to take advantage of it
and not waste it on things that aren't God's."

In El Salvador, doing "things that are God's" by this definition has
for much of the past twenty years presupposed a decision that the goal or
ideal is worth more than physical survival. This decision is not fanatical
or naively utopian. Most often, it reflects careful analysis of the present
situation, of desired changes, and of the possible means to achieve them.
This analysis looked for ways to put fear into a larger context, to give
meaning to danger and loss, and to encourage believers to continue
struggling despite risk. Toward this goal, a *novenario* booklet written for
the tenth anniversary of Romero's death answers the question of
whether fear is a sin by explaining that all people feel fear, even Jesus
and Romero. Christians cannot escape fear of death, the guide emphasizes, but should realize that

> if life is lived in accord with Christian ideals, not even death
> will be an obstacle to thinking, living, and acting as God wants
> and [our] brothers and sisters need. We will all be able to say
> 'Death, where is your victory?'[33]

Juan, a lay preacher in Chalatenango, expresses this concept pastorally in
response to a community member's confession of fear as a sin. "Feeling fear

isn't a sin," Juan replies. "The sin is letting oneself be carried by fear, the absence of will, the absence of hope that is God within."[34] This hope gives a single-mindedness to many activists. Clara expresses a sense of urgency: "I'm conscious and I know what the struggle is for. I'm not alone, but there are thousands of us, and with so many risking their lives, we can't wait."

Prudence

While they may feel they cannot wait, activists insist that enthusiasm should not lead to foolhardiness. Again, their decisions to take risks mean not fanatical embracing of danger for an impossible goal but rather rational consideration of the risks worth taking. The frequency with which activists cite the value of prudence reflects the rationality of martyr narratives. They contend that while Christians should not run from death, neither should they seek it out. Unlike stereotypes of morbidly obsessed would-be martyrs, Salvadoran activists on the whole do not scorn "the business of living," nor do they believe "that life is justified only by things which negate it," in Terrence DesPres's words.[35] Life itself remains their ultimate goal and criterion, and they view death not as a triumph but as an often-necessary cost of the struggle for a society that respects life.

Here again, Jesus serves as a model. Catholic activists argue that Jesus did not wait passively for death but rather sought to understand and change his situation and also to distinguish when it was time to flee and when it was the moment to sacrifice his life. Contemporary believers insist they also must learn to escape while the hour still has not arrived, although they should ultimately be disposed to give their lives and not always to run from danger. Rosa asserts that "Every person has to give his or her life [eventually], but it's good to escape if you can." She cites the example of Jesus, who fled to different cities to escape his persecutors prior to his death. Amando expresses the same notion when he asserts that "A Christian has to be both flexible (*suave*) and astute," knowing when and how to escape until the final hour arrives. Daniel Vega agrees that activists must try to prolong life, for themselves and others. "We have to avoid more deaths. If everyone is dead, who will do the work?" He adds, though, that "No one wants martyrdom, but sometimes it comes."

With full knowledge of the risk involved, "potential martyrs" decide to continue working for what they understand as religiously mandated social goals, knowing this activity may lead to their own deaths. Their attitude is not suicidal, but reflects a hard-won acceptance of the possibility of death as an inevitable correlate of the activism they believe they must undertake. Ethicist Sharon Welch calls this attitude "strategic risk-taking," in which

> Martyrdom is not encouraged, yet the willingness to risk physical harm, and even death, is acknowledged as sometimes necessary. The measure of an action's worth is not, however, the willingness of someone to risk their [sic] life but the contribution such an action will make to the imagination and courage of the resisting community.[36]

In El Salvador, the "resisting community" of progressive Catholics seeks an alternative to a system that many of its members see as a sort of living death. They often contrast the present situation with the abundance and justice they say God wants for human beings. Death may not seem much worse than the way they currently live; "life" may mean not just existing, but rather working to create a fuller kind of life. Thus, many people insist risky activism is not choosing death but deciding to die, as Clara says, "doing something, not waiting for someone to die for us." Inhabiting a world that is already full of suffering and death, they ask how to act rationally and faithfully in the face of that reality. Their choice, they believe, lies between being paralyzed by fear or grief, on the one hand, and taking risks with an understanding of the reasons behind it and confidence in the eventual victory, on the other.

V. Theodicy and the Use of the Pain

I have argued that Salvadoran martyr narratives explain political violence and even motivate people to risk their lives. This poses the question of whether this religious worldview, by reconciling people to the possibility of violent death, constitutes a form of resistance to the forces of repression or merely a novel accommodation to the dying they cause. In other words, do Salvadoran martyrologies differ in more than superficial ways from the traditional Christian theodicy that taught people to accept suffering as their lot and to set their hopes on rewards in a future life? Progressive Catholic ideas about martyrdom in El Salvador certainly echo traditional Roman Catholic ideas in many ways. Perhaps popular interpretations of martyrdom and especially the emphasis on the need for sacrifice to achieve a distant goal merely give a new face to the essentially conservative function of Latin American Catholicism in general and its theodicies in particular.

Even more seriously, perhaps sacrifice constitutes not just resignation, but a twisted form of participation in the "project of death" that the church criticizes. In an attack on glorifications of sacrificial activism, Terrence DesPres argues that in the late twentieth century, "except for special cases the martyr and his tragic counterpart are types of the hero unfit for the darkness ahead. When men and women must live against terrible odds, when mere existence becomes miraculous, to die is in no way a triumph." DesPres criticizes the equation of "heroism and death," which idealizes "the grandeur of death." To replace this masochistic ethic, DesPres writes, "We require a heroism commensurate with the sweep of ruin in our time: action equal to situations in which it becomes less self-indulgent and more useful to live, to be there."[37] DesPres's critique recalls Stoll's claim that liberation theology encourages people to seek death and not life.

While romanticized views of sacrificial death certainly pose a danger, particularly when life is difficult, I argue that members of the Salvadoran *iglesia popular* do not, in general, embrace or idealize death. They frequently speak of the pain generated by violent death, which inspires both grief and anger. In their experience, martyrdom, first and foremost, is "death before its time and against justice."[38] Facing this fact, they ask the classic questions of religious theodicy: why do the innocent suffer? How can a just God permit so much pain? They do not always arrive at clear answers. A European priest working in San Salvador remembers the anguish felt by Silvia Arriola, a sister of the *pequeña comunidad*, who told him,

> I'm just in agony. Sometimes I think it would have been better not to preach the gospel. If people's consciousness hadn't been raised at least they wouldn't have died. I feel sad, I feel deathly sad, when I think of all we've done, and how many people committed themselves, and now they've been killed.[39]

Repression generated vast emotional and also practical costs for progressive Salvadorans. The murders of countless activists and experienced leaders have diminished the morale as well as the efficacy of popular political organizations and the *iglesia popular* and will have repercussions on the country's political and religious life for years to come. Most progressive Catholics are well aware of these costs. Their efforts to explain political violence by references to Christian martyrdom represent not an embrace of death but rather an attempt to make it useful. In this effort, they draw on a religious tradition which claims that no sorrow lacks hope because God does not permit great suffering without the promise of ultimate victory.

Postconciliar Catholicism in Latin America has built on this traditional conviction to encourage not passive acceptance of suffering but activism to end it and to achieve an earthly goal of "peace, but with justice," as Clara puts it. Thus, people who have lost loved ones can believe that their pain helps to achieve a larger good, that they "give life by dying," in the words of Julio, a Chalatenango layworker. This faith reflects the concrete ways in which theology resonates at the grassroots level, where its most important political impact may lie.

Many Salvadoran Catholics see Jesus' death not as a distant event but as an ongoing story that makes sense of apparently meaningless happenings. Sacred history is their own history, divine goals their goals. For members of the Salvadoran *iglesia popular*, as for the Philippine popular movements that Ileto describes, the passion "was not simply sung, heard, or celebrated . . . It was lived, both individually and socially."[40] Confidence that they were re-enacting Jesus' story helped Salvadoran Catholics endure and act in the face of tremendous losses. Their religious perspective convinced them that because Jesus' death was not without meaning, contemporary deaths also serve a larger purpose. Cristina summarizes: "There's pain and suffering, but also the hope of resurrection . . . It's a pain that's full of hope, a pain for living, not for dying." This pain became, as Daniel Vega explains, a reason to work for a society that respects all life: "We don't want more deaths. There have already been too many. They've given us motivation, and now we have to work so that there are no more [deaths]." For Clara, similarly, the martyrs call for struggle to change the situation that they risked their lives to oppose. "If this continues the same," she asks, "what would be the value of all the deaths? What would be the use of all the pain?"

VI. The Impact of Religious Activism

The effort to make use of the pain caused by political violence involved many Salvadorans, including especially poor people, who suffered the brunt of the violence. Not all of them participated in CEBs or *cursillos*, but many were influenced by progressive Catholicism through contact with activists and participation in masses and other rituals. In El Salvador, as Roger Lancaster notes for Nicaragua, progressive Catholic ideology

> had appeal far beyond the borders of the base communities proper. Because it grew out of widespread Christian symbols of sin and redemption, liberation theology provided both a powerful language for talking about social injustice and a moral paradigm for those who acted as revolutionaries.[41]

In El Salvador during the 1970s and 1980s, progressive Catholicism influenced a wide range of people beyond those involved in base communities, *cursillos*, and other church projects. The worldview, values, pedagogies, and approaches to social change developed in the popular church influenced political organizations and many local communities, especially in poor urban and rural areas. This influence makes El Salvador a good focus for explorations of the ways religion can influence politics, and vice-versa, at the grassroots.

Some scholars contend that progressive values and activism were limited to a small minority of Latin American Catholics.[42] Others claim that "radical" religious ideas were in fact far from revolutionary, since they divided "elite" activists from ordinary people, who were involved in "everyday" resistance or simply in struggles for survival. These arguments dismiss the impact of religiously grounded activism as wishful thinking. I want to argue, however, that grassroots religious organizing did make a political difference, at least in El Salvador, and further, that the ways it mattered in El Salvador point to ways it might matter in other contexts.

During the 1970s and 1980s in El Salvador, high-risk activism was not limited to a handful of would-be heroes. Tens of thousands of people engaged in open, generally dangerous forms of protest. Their willingness to take risks emerged from neither suicidal wishes nor naive idealism but from a situation of extreme violence and inequality and a particular way, strongly shaped by popular Catholicism, of understanding this situation. In this context, ordinary people pursuing relatively tangible interests (a better standard of living, greater political freedom) and/or religious ideals (*imitatio Christi*, the reign of God) often had no choice other than to commit extraordinary deeds. A closed and brutal political and economic system pushed even the most cautious realists to take risks. Not infrequently, simple survival—the choice between certain starvation or possible assassination— demanded "heroism." In this situation, popular support for and participation in political opposition was not limited to a tiny minority, but spread to broad sectors of the population (i.e., in the twenty or thirty percent of the national territory held by the FMLN for most of the war).

Given this reality, we cannot dismiss the Salvadoran *iglesia popular* as a tiny group of disaffected students, hopeless dreamers, and/or fanatical guerrillas, out of touch with or uninterested in the real interests and hopes of the poor. While many ordinary Salvadorans certainly were caught "between two fires," in Stoll's words,[43] many others actively participated in the conflict. Most of them acted not out of naive utopian dreams but out of the very real material and moral interest they had in changing the basic economic and political structures of their society.

In most settings, religiously grounded activism does not spread as quickly and widely as it did in El Salvador. El Salvador's compact size and the intensity of political mobilization and repression undoubtedly intensified the political impact of progressive Catholicism there. I believe, however, that the Salvadoran *iglesia popular* is not just an interesting exception. Its experiences illuminate a truth about religiously grounded social movements that pertains even where such movements do not achieve national prominence. This truth is that social movements do not emerge only from strategic cost-benefit analysis and the marshalling of resources. Many people formulate their critiques of the political-economic status quo and their hopes for the future out of religious commitments. These religious commitments are reworked in and through ritual and community, which build on tradition while expanding it to encompass new models, values, and standards for action. The most successful social movements do not reject religion and "disenchant" the world but rather enlarge religious worldviews and values to confront contemporary political challenges.

Rowan Ireland suggests what might have to happen for religion to have a significant political impact:

> . . . if the pantheon of saints should expand to include some of the saints of liberation, if old saints be invested with new characters, and if myths and miracle stories should include the triumphs of collective action, then a deep religious transformation with profound consequences for the political action of the faithful will have occurred.[44]

This is precisely what happened for many Salvadoran Catholics during the 1970s and 1980s. The transformation of their understanding of Jesus, in particular, as well as other dimensions of their faith and religious practice, provided a framework within which they interpreted and responded to political violence. Understanding and taking seriously this religious framework is vital to understanding social movements in settings such as El Salvador. While we do not yet know the historical verdict regarding the long-term effects of El Salvador's popular movement and civil war, the experience of the Salvadoran *iglesia popular* offers many lessons. Most pointedly, for students of religion and politics, this experience argues that religious ideas can, in fact, be momentous, that people can and do act in pursuit of ideals, and that in so doing, they can change history.

Endnotes

1. Baloyra, *El Salvador*, 31.

2. María Helena Moreira Alves, "Cultures of Fear, Cultures of Resistance: The New Labor Movement in Brazil," in *Fear at the Edge*, 191.

3. Danner, "The Truth of El Mozote." The massacres at the Río Sumpul and the Río Lempa are widely documented; see Americas Watch, *El Salvador's Decade of Terror* and Fish and Sganga, *El Salvador*.

4. Six relatives of Ernesto Abrego were murdered or disappeared in the process of looking for the priest after he disappeared. See Americas Watch, *El Salvador's Decade of Terror*, 34.

5. Romero, *La voz*, 460. Similarly, Ileto notes that Philippine rebels were denigrated as "bandits, ignoramuses, heretics, lunatics, fanatics," but that Philippine popular culture "anticipated" these characterizations, in part through reference to Christ's own fate; see *Pasyon and Revolution*, 256.

6. James C. Scott, *Weapons of the Weak: Everyday Forms of Peasant Resistance* (New Haven and London: Yale University Press, 1982), 34.

7. Comaroff, *Body of Power*, 261–262.

8. Irene Silverblatt makes a similar argument for native people under Spanish rule in colonial Peru: "By maintaining idolatrous and heretical beliefs . . . indigenous peoples were subverting colonial power." *Moon, Sun, and Witches: Gender and Class Ideologies in Inca and Colonial Peru* (Princeton: Princeton University Press, 1987), xxx.

9. An interesting example of religious event as resistance occurred in eastern Managua in the late 1970s, during the last days of the Somoza regime. Repression was so harsh in the eastern neighborhoods, and CEBs so clearly identified with opposition to the dictatorship, that members of one CEB could not meet together. Rather than abandon their *reflexión* entirely, however, they held synchronized Bible readings, when all members would, in the greater safety of their own homes, read the same biblical passages at the same time.

10. Baloyra, *El Salvador in Transition*, 2.

11. Ileto, *Pasyon and Revolution*, 2, 5, 7. See also Todd Diacon, *Millenarian Vision, Capitalist Reality: Brazil's Contestado Rebellion, 1912–1916* (Durham, NC: Duke University Press, 1991), Ch. 7 passim.

12. Laurence Iannaccone, "Religious Markets and the Economies of Religion," *Social Compass* 39, no. 1 (1992): 124, 126. See also Iannaccone, "Religious Practices: A Human Capital Approach," *Journal for the Scientific Study of Religion* 29 (1990): 297–314.

13. Steve Bruce, "Religion and Rational Choice: A Critique of Economic Explanations of Religious Behavior," in *Sociology of Religion* 54, no. 2 (1993), 202.

14. Ibid., 203.

15. David Stoll, *Is Latin America Turning Protestant? The Politics of Evangelical Growth* (Berkeley: University of California Press, 1990), 39, 314.

16. Ibid., 312.

17. Ibid., 313.

18. See Samandú, *Protestantismos y procesos sociales*; Bárbara Boudejwinse et al., eds., *Algo más que opio: una lectura antropológica del pentecostalismo lati-noamericano y caribeño* (San José, Costa Rica: Editorial DEI, 1991); and Cecília Mariz, *Coping With Poverty: Pentecostals and Christian Base Communities in Brazil* (Philadelphia: Temple University Press, 1994).

19. See Ralph Della Cava, "Vatican Policy 1978–1990: An Updated Overview," *Social Research* 59, no. 1 (1992): 171–199.

20. Stoll, *Is Latin America Turning Protestant?*, 313–314.

21. Levine, *Popular Voices*, 15–16. Emphasis in original.

22. Clifford Geertz, *Local Knowledge: Further Essays in Interpretive Anthropology* (New York: Basic Books, 1983), 57.

23. Ileto, *Pasyon and Revolution*, 15. Orlando Espín discusses a similar duality in colonial missionary images of the suffering Jesus; see "Trinitarian Monotheism."

24. Ileto, *Pasyon and Revolution*, 10.

25. Ibid., 18.

26. Berryman, *The Religious Roots of Rebellion*, 120–121.

27. Cristián Parker argues that politics in Latin America always requires religion; *Otra lógica en América Latina: Religión popular y modernización capitalista* (Santiago: Fondo de Cultura Económica, 1993), 302. See also Lancaster, *Thanks to God and the Revolution*, 21.

28. Steinmetz, "Reflections on the Role of Social Narratives," 491–492.

29. Woodward, *Making Saints*, 47.

30. Selbin, "Revolutionary Traditions," 2.

31. CEBES, "Ganando la paz con el pueblo salvadoreño" (Managua: CEBES, n.d.), 96.

32. Gómez meeting.

33. *Novenario en memoria de Monseñor Oscar Arnulfo Romero, 10º Aniversario* (San Salvador: Archdiocese of San Salvador, 1990), 22.

34. López Vigil, *Primero Dios*, 67.

35. Despres, *The Survivor*, 5.

36. Sharon Welch, *A Feminist Ethic of Risk* (Minneapolis: Fortress Press, 1990), 22.

37. DesPres, *The Survivor*, 5–6.

38. Bravo, "Martirio y pasión," 46.

39. Galdámez, *The Faith of a People*, 79.

40. Ileto, *Pasyon and Revolution*, 22.

41. Lancaster, *Life is Hard*, 4.

42. For example, see David Stoll, "Introduction: Rethinking Protestantism in Latin America," in *Rethinking Protestantism in Latin America*, eds. D. Stoll and V. Garrard-Burnett (Philadelphia: Temple University Press, 1993), 6.

43. David Stoll, *Between Two Armies in the Ixil Towns of Guatemala* (New York: Columbia University Press, 1993).

44. Rowan Ireland, *Kingdoms Come: Religion and Politics in Brazil* (Pittsburgh: University of Pittsburgh Press, 1991), 196.

Bibliography

Primary Sources

Interviews

Acaya, Alejandro [pseud.]. Interview by author, 8 October 1988, San Salvador.

———. Interview by author, 12 March 1990, San Salvador.

———. Interview by author, 20 June 1994, San Salvador.

Adela [pseud.]. Interview by author, 14 March 1990, La Paz province.

Alas, José Inocencio. Interview by author, 4 July 1994, San Salvador.

Amalia [pseud.], San Pablo parish [pseud.], San Salvador. Interview by author, 1 November 1988.

Amando [pseud.], San Pablo parish [pseud.], San Salvador. Interview by author, 20 March 1990.

Ana María [pseud.], pastoral team, San Felipe [pseud.], Chalatenango province. Interview by author, 25 March 1990.

Andrés [pseud.], village directorate, San Felipe [pseud.], Chalatenango province. Interview by author, 25 March 1990.

Angel [pseud.], San Lucas parish [pseud.], San Salvador. Interview by author, 1 April 1990.

Angélica [pseud.], San Pablo parish [pseud.], San Salvador. Interview by author, 9 April 1990.

Antonia [pseud.], San Pablo parish [pseud.], San Salvador. Interview by author, 4 April 1990.

Antonio [pseud.], San Lucas parish [pseud.], San Salvador. Interview by author, 1 April 1990.

Arnulfo [pseud.], San Lucas parish [pseud.], San Salvador. Interview by author, 1 April 1990.

Augusto [pseud.]. Interview by author, 8 February 1990, Oakland. Tape recording.

Avila, Josefa [pseud.], San Pablo parish [pseud.], San Salvador. Interview by author, 16 March 1990.

Bravo, Carlos, Center for Theological Reflection, Mexico City. Interview by author, 30 May 1990.

Campos, Amanda [pseud.], San Juan parish [pseud.], San Salvador. Interview by author, 6 November 1988.

Cecilia [pseud.], San Pablo parish [pseud.], San Salvador. Interview by author, 23 March 1990.

César [pseud.]. Interview by author, 7 February 1990, Berkeley. Tape recording.

Clara [pseud.], San Pablo parish [pseud.], San Salvador. Interview by author, 6 April 1990.

Claudia [pseud.]. Interview by author, 7 April 1990, San Salvador.

Cortina, Jon. Interview by author, 24 October 1988, San Salvador.

———. Interview by author, 25 March 1990, Chalatenango province.

Cristina, Mothers of the Heroes and Martyrs. Interview by author. 15 November 1988, Managua. Tape recording.

Cuadra, Adán, Pastoral Center, Central American University, San Salvador. Interview by author, 31 October 1988.

Del Valle, Luis, Director, Center for Theological Reflection, Mexico City. Interview by author, 31 May 1990.

Diana [pseud.]. Interview by author, 28 May 1990, Mexico City.

Edgar [pseud.]. Interview by author, 1 May 1990, Mexico City.

Elena [pseud.], San Pablo parish [pseud.], San Salvador. Interview by author, 23 March 1990.

Elizabeth [pseud.]. Interview by author, 9 April 1990, San Salvador.

Emilia [pseud.], San Lucas parish [pseud.], San Salvador. Interview by author, 1 April 1990.

Espinosa, Anita [pseud.], San Pablo parish [pseud.], San Salvador. Interview by author, 13 March 1990.

———. Interview by author, 1 July 1994.

Esteban [pseud.], village directorate, San Felipe [pseud.], Chalatenango province. Interview by author, 25 March 1990.

Estela [pseud.]. Interview by author, 27 July 1986, Estelí, Nicaragua.

Fabio [pseud.]. Interview by author, 14 March 1990, La Paz province.

Fátima [pseud.], San Pablo parish [pseud.], San Salvador. Interview by author, 8 March 1990.

———. Interview by author, 9 April 1990.

Fernando [pseud.], San Juan parish [pseud.], San Salvador. Interview by author, 20 March 1988.

Ferrer, Mario [pseud.]. Interview by author, 29 March 1990, San Salvador.

Francisco [pseud.], village directorate, San Felipe [pseud.], Chalatenango province. Interview by author, 25 March 1990.

Gilberto [pseud.], San Lucas parish [pseud.], San Salvador. Interview by author, 1 April 1990.

Gómez, Medardo, Lutheran Bishop of El Salvador, La Resurrección Lutheran Church, San Salvador. Meeting with a religious delegation, 22 March 1990.

González, Rodolfo [pseud.]. Interview by author, 10 July 1986, Managua.

———. Interview by author, 12 November 1988, Managua.

Hector [pseud.], Coordination of Communities [CONIP]. Interview by author, 19 July 1986, Managua.

Hugo [pseud.], San Pablo parish [pseud.], San Salvador. Interview by author, 25 October 1988.

Javier [pseud.]. Interview by author, 7 February 1990, Berkeley. Tape recording.

Jesús [pseud.], San Pablo parish [pseud.], San Salvador. Interview by author, 17 April 1990.

Jiménez, Pablo [pseud.]. Interview by author, 26 July 1986, Estelí, Nicaragua.

Jirón, María, Mothers of the Heroes and Martyrs. Interview by author, 13 November 1988, Managua. Tape recording.

José [pseud.], San Pablo parish [pseud.], San Salvador. Interview by author, 17 April 1990.

Juana [pseud.], San Lucas parish [pseud.], San Salvador. Interview by author, 1 April 1990.

Juanita [pseud.], village directorate, San Felipe [pseud.], Chalatenango province. Interview by author, 25 March 1990.

Julia [pseud.], San Pablo parish [pseud.], San Salvador. Interview by author, 19 March 1990.

Julio [pseud.], pastoral team, San Felipe [pseud.], Chalatenango province. Interview by author, 25 March 1990.

López, Mirtala, Christian Committee for the Displaced of El Salvador (CRIPDES). Interview by author, 26 March 1990.

Lucas [pseud.], pastoral team, San Felipe [pseud.], Chalatenango province. Interview by author, 25 March 1990.

Lucía [pseud.], San Juan parish [pseud.], San Salvador. Interview by author, 7 April 1988.

Lupe [pseud.], San Lucas parish [pseud.], San Salvador. Interview by author, 1 April 1990.

Marcela [pseud.], San Pablo parish [pseud.], San Salvador. Interview by author, 4 April 1990.

Marcos [pseud.]. Interview by author, 25 July 1986, Estelí, Nicaragua.

Margarita [pseud.], Santa Rosa [pseud.], Chalatenango province. Interview by author, 1 November 1988.

Marta [pseud.]. Interview by author, 28 May 1990, Mexico City.

Martín-Baró, Ignacio, Vice-Rector, Central American University, San Salvador. Interview by author, 20 October 1988.

McKay, Ellen [pseud.], San Pablo parish [pseud.], San Salvador. Interview by author, 21 October 1988.

———. Interview by author, 9 March 1990.

Mejía, Guadalupe, Committee of Families (CODEFAM), San Salvador. Interview by author, 28 March 1990.

———. Interview by author, 28 June 1994.

Mercedes [pseud.]. Interview by author, 8 April 1990, San Salvador.

Miguel [pseud.]. Interview by author, 28 May 1990. Mexico City.

Moisés [pseud.], San Pablo parish [pseud.], San Salvador. Interview by author, 23 March 1990.

Muñoz, Ronaldo. Interview by author, Simon Fraser University, 7 February 1986, Burnaby, British Columbia.

Noemí [pseud.]. Interview by author, 5 April 1990, El Paisnal, San Salvador province.

Norma [pseud.], San Pablo parish [pseud.]. Interview by author, 20 March 1990.

Olivia [pseud.]. Interview by author, 28 May 1990. Mexico City.

Ortega, Carlos. Interview by author, 14 November 1988, Managua.

Oscar [pseud.]. Interview by author. 28 May 1990. Mexico City.

Pablo [pseud.], San Pablo parish [pseud.], San Salvador. Interview by author, 17 March 1990.

Paco [pseud.], San Pablo parish [pseud.], San Salvador. Interview by author, 8 April 1990.

Patricio [pseud.], San Pablo parish [pseud.], San Salvador. Interview by author, 25 October 1988.

Paula [pseud.], village directorate, San Felipe [pseud.], Chalatenango province. Interview by author, 25 March 1990.

Peña, José [pseud.]. Interview by author, 27 March 1990, San Salvador.

Quintana, Marcelo [pseud.], San Lucas parish [pseud.], San Salvador. Interview by author, 5 April 1990.

Ramón [pseud.]. Interview by author, 20 April 1990, Cuernavaca, Mexico.

Ramos, Luis. Interview by author, 10 May 1990, Mexico City.

Robinson, Lucy [pseud.], San Pablo parish [pseud.], San Salvador. Interview by author, 18 March 1990.

Romero, Isabel, Mothers of the Heroes and Martyrs. Interview by author, 15 November 1988, Managua. Tape recording.

Rosa [pseud.], San Pablo parish [pseud.], San Salvador. Interview by author, 17 March 1990.

Rubén [pseud.]. Interview by author. 28 May 1990. Mexico City.

Ruth [pseud.], San Pablo parish [pseud.]. Interview by author, 20 March 1990.

Salvador [pseud.], pastoral team, San Felipe [pseud.], Chalatenango province. Interview by author, 25 March 1990.

Sara [pseud.]. Interview by author, 5 April 1990, El Paisnal, San Salvador province.

Saúl [pseud.], village directorate, San Felipe [pseud.], Chalatenango province. Interview by author, 25 March 1990.

Sequeira, Julio. Interview by author, 12 August 1986, Managua.

———. Interview by author, 10 November 1988, Managua.

Sergio [pseud.], Santa Rosa [pseud.], Chalatenango province. Interview by author, 1 November 1988.

Silvia [pseud.]. Interview by author. 28 May 1990. Mexico City.

Sobrino, Jon, Pastoral Center, Central American University, San Salvador. Interview by author, 26 October 1988.

———. Interview by author, 30 December 1989, Santa Clara University, Santa Clara, California.

———. Interview by author, 3 April 1990, San Salvador.

Susana [pseud.], San Pablo parish [pseud.], San Salvador. Interview by author, 17 April 1990.

Tamayo, Luisa [pseud.], San Lucas parish [pseud.], San Salvador. Interview by author, 4 November 1988.

———. Interview by author, 28 March 1990.

Teresa, Mothers of the Heroes and Martyrs. Interview by author. 15 November 1988, Managua. Tape recording.

Thomas, Diana [pseud.]. Interview by author, 16 June 1994, San Salvador.

Tobar, Pedro [pseud.], Archdiocese of San Salvador, San Salvador. Interview by author, 19 October 1988.

———. Interview by author, 9 March 1990.

Tomás [pseud.], San Lucas parish [pseud.], San Salvador. Interview by author, 1 April 1990.

Tomasa [pseud.], Committee of Families (CODEFAM), San Salvador. Interview by author, 4 April 1990.

Ungerleider, David, La Resurrección Parish, Mexico City. Interview by author, 25 April 1990.

Urioste, Ricardo. Archdiocese of San Salvador. Interview by author, 29 June 1994.

Valiente, Laura [pseud.], San Juan parish [pseud.], San Salvador. Interview by author, 16 March 1990.

Vega, Daniel [pseud.]. Interview by author, 27 March 1990, San Salvador.

———. Interview by author, 15 June 1994, San Salvador.

Victoria [pseud.], San Juan parish [pseud.], San Salvador. Interview by author, 7 April 1988.

Vilma [pseud.], San Pablo parish [pseud.], San Salvador. Interview by author, 4 April 1990.

Yolanda [pseud.], San Pablo parish [pseud.], San Salvador. Interview by author, 20 March 1990.

Unpublished Primary Sources

Cortina, Jon. Sermon, 25 March 1990, Chalatenango province.

Cursillo, San Pablo parish [pseud.], San Salvador, 23 October 1988.

Cursillo, San Pablo parish [pseud.], San Salvador, 11 March 1990.

Cursillo, San Pablo parish [pseud.], San Salvador, 1 April 1990.

Gutiérrez, Gustavo. "The Poor as the Body of Christ." Lecture. University Christian Church, Berkeley, 22 January 1985.

Memorial service for Herbert Ernesto Anaya, El Rosario Church, San Salvador, 26 October 1988.

Missionary team meeting, San Pablo parish [pseud.], San Salvador. 31 March 1990.

Sanabria, Salvador, Democratic Revolutionary Front. Lecture. University of California at Berkeley, 20 September 1990.

Sánchez, Daniel. Lecture. St. Joseph the Worker Church, Berkeley, CA, 8 December 1989.

———. Lecture. Central American Refugee Comittee (CRECE), San Francisco, 9 December 1989.

Sobrino, Jon. "Peacemaking in Times of War." Workshop. Saint Mary's Cathedral, San Francisco, 22 February 1991.

Vía Crucis, San Juan parish [pseud.], San Salvador, 16 March 1990.

Vía Crucis, San Pablo parish [pseud.], San Salvador, 30 March 1990.

Vía Crucis, San Pablo parish [pseud.], San Salvador, 6 April 1990.

Published Primary Sources

Actas de CEDES (Conferencia Episcopal de El Salvador). San Salvador: Episcopal Conference of El Salvador, various issues.

Cantemos hermanos. Managua: El Tayacán, 1987.

Carta a las iglesias. San Salvador: Centro Pastoral de la Universidad Centroamericana "José Simeón Cañas," various issues.

El pueblo canta: libro de cantos. San Salvador: Archdiocese of San Salvador, n.d.

Mejía Godoy, Carlos and Pablo Martínez. *La misa campesina nicaragüense.* Managua: Ministry of Culture, 1984.

Monseñor Romero: 1980-1990, Décimo Aniversario. Santa Tecla, El Salvador: Equipo de Educación Maíz, 1989.

Novenario en memoria de Monseñor Oscar Arnulfo Romero, 10º Aniversario. San Salvador: Archdiocese of San Salvador, 1990.

Pascua y resurrección de Cristo en su pueblo. San Salvador: n.p., n.d.

Primera semana de pastoral arquidiocesana. San Salvador: Archdiocese of San Salvador, 1976.

¿Qué es la misa? San Salvador: Archdiocese of San Salvador, n.d.

Sacramentos como vida y compromiso. San Salvador: Archdiocese of San Salvador, n.d.

Vía Crucis. Santa Tecla, El Salvador: Equipo de Educación Maíz, 1990.

Via Crucis: en compañía de nuestro pastor Monseñor Oscar Arnulfo Romero y Galdámez. San Salvador: n.p., 1990.

Vigil, José María, and Angel Torrellas. *Misas Centroamericanas.* Managua: Centro Antonio Valdivieso and Comunidades Eclesiales de Base de El Salvador (CEBES), 1988.

Secondary Sources

Aman, Kenneth, and Cristián Parker, eds. *Popular Culture in Chile: Resistance and Survival.* Boulder, CO: Westview Press, 1991.

Amaya, Miguel Angel. *Historias de Cacoapera.* San Salvador: Ministry of Education, 1985.

Americas Watch. *El Salvador's Decade of Terror: Human Rights Since the Assassination of Archbishop Romero.* New Haven and London: Yale University Press, 1991.

Amnesty International. *El Salvador: 'Death Squads'—A Government Strategy.* AI Index 29/21/88. London: Amnesty International, 1988.

Anderson, Thomas. *El Salvador 1932.* 2d ed. San José, Costa Rica: Editorial Universitaria Centroamericana, 1982.

Armstrong, Robert and Janet Shenk. *El Salvador: The Face of Revolution.* Boston: South End Press, 1982.

Arnson, Cynthia J. "Conscience Vote." *The Nation* 251, no. 17 (19 November 1990): 584.

Baloyra, Enrique. *El Salvador in Transition.* Chapel Hill and London: University of North Carolina Press, 1982.

Berger, Peter. *The Sacred Canopy: Elements of a Sociological Theory of Religion.* Garden City, NY: Anchor Books, 1967.

Berger, Peter, and Thomas Luckmann. *The Social Construction of Reality: A Treatise in the Sociology of Knowledge.* New York: Doubleday/ Anchor Books, 1966.

Berguer, Elizabeth. "Voices from Latin America: Encounters with Church-Related Grassroots Groups Involved with Social Change." First International Conference on Liberation Theology, Simon Fraser University, Burnaby, British Columbia, February 6–8, 1986.

Berkeley Sister City Project. *History of San Antonio los Ranchos.* Berkeley: Berkeley Sister City Project, 1989.

Bermúdez, Fernando. *Death and Resurrection in Guatemala.* With an introduction by Phillip Berryman. Maryknoll, NY: Orbis Books, 1986.

Berryman, Phillip. *The Religious Roots of Rebellion: Christians in Central American Revolutions.* Maryknoll, NY: Orbis Books, 1984.

———. "Introduction" to *Death and Resurrection in Guatemala,* by Fernando Bermúdez. Maryknoll, NY: Orbis Books, 1986.

———. "El Salvador: From Evangelization to Insurrection." In *Religion and Social Conflict in Latin America,* ed. Daniel Levine. Chapel Hill: University of North Carolina Press, 1986.

Betto, Frei [Carlos Alberto Libanio Christo]. *¿Qué es la comunidad eclesial de base?* Managua: Centro Ecuménico Antonio Valdivieso, n.d.

Blee, Kathleen. "The Catholic Church and Central American Politics." In *Understanding the Central American Crisis: Sources of Conflict, U.S. Policy, and Options for Peace,* eds. Kenneth Coleman and George Herring. Wilmington, DE: Scholarly Resources, 1991.

Bloch, Maurice, and Jonathan Parry. "Death and the Regeneration of Life." Introduction to *Death and the Regeneration of Life*, eds. M. Bloch and J. Parry. Cambridge: Cambridge University Press, 1982.

Boff, Leonardo. "Martyrdom: An Attempt at Systematic Reflection." *Concilium* 163 (1983): 12-17.

Borge, Tomás. *Carlos, el amanecer ya no es una tentación*. Managua: Editorial Nueva Nicaragua, 1985.

Boudewijnse, Bárbara; André Droogers; and Frans Kamsteeg, eds. *Algo más que opio: Una lectura antropólogica del pentecostalismo latinoamericano y caribeño*. San José, Costa Rica: DEI, 1991.

Bravo, Carlos. "Martirio y pasión." *Christus* (Mexico City) 55, number 633 (March 1990): 46–50.

Brockett, Charles. *Land, Power and Poverty*. Boulder, CO: Westview Press, 1990.

Brockman, James. *Romero: A Life*. 2d ed., rev., of *The Word Remains: A Life of Oscar Romero*. Maryknoll, NY: Orbis Books, 1989.

Browning, David. *El Salvador: Landscape and Society*. Oxford: Oxford University Press, 1971.

Bruce, Steve. "Religion and Rational Choice: A Critique of Economic Explanations of Religious Behavior." *Sociology of Religion* 54, no. 2 (1993): 193–205.

Brundage, Burr Cartwright. *The Fifth Sun: Aztec Gods, Aztec World*. Austin: University of Texas Press, 1979.

Bulmer-Thomas, Victor. *The Political Economy of Central America Since 1920*. Cambridge: Cambridge University Press, 1987.

Burdick, John. "The Progressive Catholic Church in Latin America: Giving Voice or Listening to Voices?" *Latin American Research Review* 29, no. 1 (1994): 184–197.

Cáceres Prendes, Jorge. "Political Radicalization and Popular Pastoral Practices in El Salvador, 1969–1985." In *The Progressive Church in Latin America*, eds. Scott Mainwaring and Alex Wilde. South Bend: Notre Dame University Press, 1989.

Cagan, Beth and Steve Cagan. *This Promised Land, El Salvador: The Refugee Community of Colomoncagua and Their Return to Morazán.* Rutgers, NJ: Rutgers University Press, 1991.

CAICA (Colectivo de Analisis de Iglesias en Centroamerica). *La iglesia en Centroamérica: Guatemala, El Salvador, Honduras y Nicaragua: Información y análisis.* Mexico City: Centro de Estudios Ecuménicos, 1989.

Candelaria, Michael R. *Popular Religion and Liberation: The Dilemma of Liberation Theology.* Albany: State University of New York Press, 1990.

Cantón de Jayaque. "La voz del pueblo cristiano salvadoreño." *Diakonía* (Managua), no. 53 (March 1990): 89–91.

Cardenal, Ernesto. *The Gospel in Solentiname,* 4 vols. Translated by Donald D. Walsh. Maryknoll, NY: Orbis Books, 1976–1982.

Cardenal, Rodolfo. *El poder eclesiástico en El Salvador (1871–1931).* San Salvador: UCA Editores, 1980.

———. *Historia de una esperanza: vida de Rutilio Grande.* San Salvador: UCA Editores, 1985.

Carr, David. "Narrative and the Real World: An Argument for Continuity." *History and Theory* XXV, no. 85 (1986): 117–131.

Carranza, Salvador. "Una experiencia de evangelización rural parroquial: Aguilares, septiembre de 1972–agosto de 1974." *ECA* (San Salvador) 32, no. 348–349 (1977).

Carrasco, Davíd. *Religions of Mesoamerica: Cosmovision and Ceremonial Centers.* New York: Harper Collins, 1990.

Carroll, Michael P. *Madonnas That Main: Popular Catholicism in Italy Since the Fifteenth Century.* Baltimore and London: Johns Hopkins University Press, 1992.

CEBES (Comunidades Eclesiales de Base de El Salvador). *Una experiencia de iglesia: mística y metodología.* Managua: CEBES, n.d.

CELAM (Conference of Latin American Bishops). *The Church in the Present-Day Transformation of Latin America in the Light of the Council: Medellín Conclusions.* Washington, DC: National Conference of Catholic Bishops, 1979.

————. "Puebla Final Document." In *Puebla and Beyond,* eds. John Eagleson and Philip Scharper, trans. John Drury. Maryknoll, NY: Orbis Books, 1979.

CENITEC. "La erradicación de las pobreza en El Salvador." *Política Económica* I:4 (December 1990–January 1991).

Centro Pastoral de la Universidad Centroamericana "José Simeón Cañas." "Tiempo de pasión en El Salvador: quince estaciones en el Vía Crucis salvadoreño." *Christus* (Mexico City) 55, no. 632 (February 1990): 5–27.

Christian, William. *Local Religion in Sixteenth Century Spain.* Princeton, NJ: Princeton University Press, 1981.

Clebsch, William A. *Christianity in European History.* New York: Oxford University Press, 1979.

Comaroff, Jean. *Body of Power, Spirit of Resistance: The History and Culture of a South African People.* Chicago: University of Chicago Press, 1985.

"Conmemorando a nuestros mártires." *Mártires de El Salvador* (Managua), no. 61 (Jan.–Feb. 1990): 7–9.

Dalton, Roque. *Miguel Marmol.* Translated by Kathleen Ross and Richard Schaaf. With an Introduction by Manlio Argueta and a Preface by Margaret Randall. Willimantic, CT: Curbstone Press, 1987.

Danner, Mark. "The Truth of El Mozote." *The New Yorker* (December 6, 1993): 50–133.

Delgado, Jesús. *Sucesos de la historia de El Salvador, vol. I: Introducción a la historia de la iglesia en El Salvador (1525-1821).* San Salvador: Archdiocese of San Salvador, 1991.

————. *Sucesos de la historia de El Salvador, vol. II: Historia de la Iglesia en El Salvador (1821–1885).* San Salvador: Archdiocese of San Salvador, 1992.

Della Cava, Ralph. "Vatican Policy 1978–1990: An Updated Overview." *Social Research* 59, no. 1 (1992): 171–199.

DesPres, Terrence. *The Survivor: An Anatomy of Life in the Death Camps.* New York: Oxford University Press, 1976.

Diacon, Todd. *Millenarian Vision, Capitalist Reality: Brazil's Contestado Rebellion, 1912-1916.* Durham, NC: Duke University Press, 1991.

Diener, Paul. "The Tears of Saint Anthony: Ritual and Revolution in Eastern Guatemala." *Latin American Perspectives* 18, 5, no. 3 (Summer 1978): 92–116.

Dodson, Michael and Laura Nuzzi O'Shaughnessy. *Nicaragua's Other Revolution: Religious Faith and Political Struggle.* Chapel Hill and London: University of North Carolina Press, 1990.

Droge, Arthur, and James Tabor. *A Noble Death: Suicide and Martyrdom among Christians and Jews in Antiquity.* San Francisco: Harper-Collins, 1992.

Dunkerley, James. 1988. *Power in the Isthmus.* London: Verso.

Dussel, Enrique. "The People of El Salvador." *Concilium* 169 (Sept. 1983): 61–68.

Edwards, Beatrice, and Gretta Tovar Siebentritt. *Places of Origin: The Repopulation of Rural El Salvador.* Boulder, CO: Lynne Rienner, 1991.

Ellacuría, Ignacio. "El pueblo crucificado, ensayo de soteriología histórica." *Revista Latinoamericana de Teología* (San Salvador) 6, no. 18 (September–December 1989): 305–334.

Erdozain, Plácido. *Archbishop Romero.* Maryknoll, NY: Orbis Books, 1981.

Espín, Orlando O. "Trinitarian Monotheism and the Birth of Popular Catholicism: The Case of Sixteenth Century Mexico," *Missiology: An International Review* XX, No. 2 (April 1992): 177–204.

———. "The God of the Vanquished: Foundations for a Latino Spirituality." *Listening: Journal of Religion and Culture* 27, no. 1 (Winter 1992): 70–83.

Fish, Joe and Cristina Sganga. *El Salvador: Testament of Terror.* New York: Olive Branch Press, 1988.

Fowler, William R., Jr. *The Cultural Evolution of Ancient Nahua Civilizations: The Pipil-Nicarao of Central America.* Norman and London: University of Oklahoma Press, 1989.

Freire, Paulo. *Pedagogy of the Oppressed*. New York: Continuum,1984.

Frend, W.H.C. *Martyrdom and Persecution in the Early Church*. London: Basil Blackwell, 1965.

Galdámez, Pablo [pseud.]. *Faith of a People: The Life of a Basic Christian Community in El Salvador*. Maryknoll, NY: Orbis Books, 1986.

García Ramírez, Roberto. "El Martirio en la Iglesia Latino-Americana." *Nuevo Mundo: Revista de Teología Latinoamericana* (Buenos Aires) 30 (1985): 43–70.

Gaudium et Spes. In Walter Abbott, ed. Documents of Vatican II. New York: American Press, 1966.

Geertz, Clifford. *The Interpretation of Cultures*. New York: Basic Books, 1973.

———. *Local Knowledge: Further Essays in Interpretive Anthropology*. Basic Books, 1983.

Genovese, Eugene D. *Roll, Jordan, Roll: The World the Slaves Made*. New York: Vintage Books, 1976.

Goldberg, Michael. *Theology and Narrative: A Critical Introduction*. Nashville: Abingdon Press, 1982.

Habermas, Jurgen. *Theory of Communicative Action, vol. 2: Lifeworld and System: A Critique of Functionalist Reason*. Trans. Thomas McCarthy. Boston: Beacon Press, 1987.

Hart, Janet. "Cracking the Code: Narrative and Political Mobilization in the Greek Resistance." *Social Science History* 16, no. 4 (Winter 1992): 631–668.

Hauerwas, Stanley. *Vision and Virtue*. Notre Dame: Fides Publishers, 1974.

Henríquez, Pedro. *El Salvador: Iglesia profética y cambio social*. San José, Costa Rica: Editorial DEI, 1988.

Hernández Pico, Juan. "Martyrdom Today in Latin America: Stumbling-block, Folly, and Power of God." *Concilium* 163 (1983): 37–42.

———. "The Experience of Nicaragua's Revolutionary Christians." In *The Challenge of Base Christian Communities*, eds. Sergio Torres and John Eagleson. Maryknoll, NY: Orbis Books, 1981.

Higgins, Michael James. "Martyrs and Virgins: Popular Religion in Mexico and Nicaragua." In *Class, Politics, and Popular Religion in Mexico and Central America*, eds. Lynn Stephen and James Dow. Washington, DC: American Anthropological Association, 1990.

Hobsbawm, Eric J. *Primitive Rebels: Studies in Archaic Forms of Social Movements in the 19th and 20th Centuries.* New York: W. W. Norton, 1959.

Iannaccone, Laurence. "Religious Practices: A Human Capital Approach." *Journal for the Scientific Study of Religion* 29 (1990): 297–314.

————. "Religious Markets and the Economies of Religion." *Social Compass* 39, no. 1 (1992): 124.

Ileto, Reynaldo Clemena. *Pasyon and Revolution: Popular Movements in the Philippines, 1840–1910.* Manila: Ateneo de Manila University Press, 1979.

Ingham, John M. *Mary, Michael, and Lucifer: Folk Catholicism in Central Mexico.* Austin: University of Texas Press, 1986.

Iniesta, Alberto. "Introducción" to *La sangre por el pueblo: Memoria de martirio en América Latina,* by the Instituto Histórico Centroamericano. Bilbao, Spain: Descleé de Brouwer, 1983.

Instituto Histórico Centroamericano. *La sangre por el pueblo: Memoria de martirio en América Latina.* Bilbao, Spain: Descleé de Brouwer, 1983.

Interamerican Development Bank. *Economic and Social Progress in Latin America, 1991 Report: Special Section—Social Security.* Washington, DC: Interamerican Development Bank, 1991.

Ireland, Rowan. *Kingdoms Come: Religion and Politics in Brazil.* Pittsburgh: University of Pittsburgh Press, 1991.

Jiménez, Felix. *Historia de la parroquia San Pablo Apóstol.* Managua: n.p., 1986.

Johnson, Mark. *Moral Imagination: Implications of Cognitive Science for Ethics.* Chicago: University of Chicago Press, 1993.

Justin Martyr. "First Apology of Justin." In *Early Christian Fathers*, ed. Cyril Richardson. New York: MacMillan, 1970.

Kincaid, A. Douglas. "Peasants into Rebels: Community and Class in Rural El Salvador," *Comparative Studies in Society and History* 29, no. 3 (July 1987): 466–494.

Kleist, Trina. "Villages are Fertile Ground for Rebellion." *The Gainesville Sun*, 23 January 1994, 4B.

Kselman, Thomas. "Ambivalences and Assumption in the Concept of Popular Religion." In *Religion and Political Conflict in Latin America*, ed. Daniel Levine. Chapel Hill: University of North Carolina, 1986.

———, ed., *Belief in History: Innovative Approaches to American and European Religion*. Notre Dame, IN: University of Notre Dame, 1991.

La iglesia en El Salvador. 2d ed. San Salvador: UCA Editores, 1982.

La iglesia salvadoreña lucha, reflexiona y canta. CONIP-Secretariado Cristiano de Solidaridad "Mons. Oscar Arnulfo Romero." León, Nicaragua: n.p., 1983.

Lacefield, Patrick, "Oscar Romero: Archbishop of the Poor" [interview]. In *El Salvador: Central America in the New Cold War.*, eds. Marvin Gettleman, et al. New York: Grove Press, 1981.

Laitin, David D. "Religion, Political Culture, and the Weberian Tradition." *World Politics* 30, no. 4 (July 1978): 563–592.

Lancaster, Roger. *Thanks to God and the Revolution: Popular Religion and Class Consciousness in the New Nicaragua*. New York: Columbia University Press, 1988.

———. *Life is Hard: Machismo, Danger, and the Intimacy of Power in Nicaragua*. Berkeley: University of California Press, 1993.

Lange, Martin, and Iblacker, Reinhold. *Witnesses of Hope: The Persecution of Christians in Latin America*. Maryknoll, NY: Orbis Books, 1981.

Lernoux, Penny. *Cry of the People: The Struggle for Human Rights in Latin America—The Catholic Church in Conflict with U.S. Policy*. New York: Penguin, 1984; reprint, New York: Doubleday, 1980.

Lesbaupin, Ivo. *Blessed are the Persecuted: Christian Life in the Roman Empire, A.D. 64–313.* Maryknoll, NY: Orbis Books, 1987.

Levine, Daniel. *Popular Voices in Latin American Catholicism.* Princeton: Princeton University Press, 1992.

López Vigil, María. *Muerte y vida en Morazán.* San Salvador: UCA Editores, 1987.

———. *Primero Dios: Siete años de esperanza (relatos de "Carta a las Iglesias").* San Salvador: UCA Editores, 1988.

Lumen Gentium. In Walter Abbott, ed. Documents of Vatican II. New York: American Press, 1966.

Macdonald, Mandy and Mike Gatehouse. *In the Mountains of Morazán: Portrait of a Returned Refugee Community in El Salvador.* London: Latin American Bureau, 1995.

MacIntyre, Alasdair. *After Virtue: A study in moral theory.* Notre Dame, IN: Notre Dame University Press, 1981.

Marins, José; Teolide M. Trevisan; and Carolee Charrona, eds. *Memoria peligrosa: heroés y mártires en la iglesia latinoamericana.* Mexico City: Centro de Reflexión Teológica, 1989.

Mariz, Cecília Loreto. *Coping with Poverty: Pentecostals and Christian Base Communities in Brazil.* Philadelphia: Temple University Press, 1994.

Marroquín, Alejandro Dagoberto. *Panchimalco: Investigación sociológica.* San Salvador: Editorial Universitaria, 1959.

Martín-Baró, Ignacio. "Religion as an Instrument of Psychological Warfare." In *Towards a Liberation Psychology.* Cambridge, MA: Harvard University Press, 1994.

———. "The Church and Revolution in El Salvador." Keynote speech, meeting of the Midwest Association for Latin American Studies, University of Missouri, Columbia, 1985.

Marx, Karl. "The Eighteenth Brumaire of Napoleon Bonaparte." In *The Marx-Engels Reader*, ed. Robert Tucker. New York: W. W. Norton, 1978.

———. "Contribution to the Critique of Hegel's Philosophy of Right: Introduction." In *The Marx-Engels Reader*, ed. Robert Tucker. New York: W. W. Norton, 1978.

Meléndez, Guillermo. "The Catholic Church in Central America: Into the 1990s." *Social Compass* 39, no. 4 (1992): 553–570.

Molineaux, David J. "Gustavo Gutiérrez: Historical Origins." *The Ecumenist* 25, no. 5 (July–August 1987): 65–69.

"¡Monseñor Romero vive! ¡Viva Monseñor Romero!" *Mártires de El Salvador* (Managua), no. 61 (January-February 1990): 3–5.

Montes, Segundo. *El compadrazgo: una estructura de poder en El Salvador.* San Salvador: UCA Editores, 1987.

Montgomery, Tommie Sue. "Liberation and Revolution: Christianity as a Subversive Activity in Central America." In *Trouble in Our Backyard*, ed. Martin Diskin. New York: Pantheon Books, 1984.

———. *El Salvador in Revolution.* Rev. 2d ed. Boulder, CO: Westview Press, 1995.

Morande, Pedro. *Cultura y modernización en América Latina.* Santiago: Pontificia Universidad Católica de Chile, 1984.

Moreira Alves, María Helena. "Cultures of Fear, Cultures of Resistance: The New Labor Movement in Brazil." In *Fear at the Edge: State Terror and Resistance in Latin America*, eds. J. C. Corradi, et al. Berkeley: University of California Press, 1992.

Nelson-Pallmeyer, Jack. *War Against the Poor: Low-Intensity Conflict and Christian Faith.* Maryknoll, NY: Orbis, 1989.

Niebuhr, H. Richard. *The Meaning of Revelation.* New York: Macmillan, 1941.

Niebuhr, Reinhold. *Moral Man and Immoral Society.* New York: Charles Scribner's Sons, 1960.

Opazo Bernales, Andrés. "La iglesia y el pueblo como sújeto político." *Polémica* (San Salvador) 2, no. 3 (September–December 1987): 2–14.

Parker, Cristián. *Otra lógica en América Latina: Religión popular y modernización capitalista.* Santiago, Chile: Fondo de Cultura Económica, 1993.

Paul VI. *Populorum progressio.* In *The Gospel of Peace and Justice: Catholic Social Teaching since Pope John.*, ed. Joseph Gremillion. Maryknoll, NY: Orbis Books, 1976.

Pearce, Jenny. *Promised Land: Peasant Rebellion in Chalatenango, El Salvador.* London: Latin American Bureau, 1986.

Peltz, Marxwell S. *El Salvador 1990: An Issues Brief.* Washington, DC: Commission on U.S.-Latin American Relations, 1990.

Peterson, Anna L. "Sacrifice, History, and Ritual in El Salvador." *International Journal of Comparative Religion and Philosophy* 1, no. 2 (Jan.–June 1995): 13–26.

Politzer, Patricia. *Miedo en Chile.* Santiago: CESOC/Ediciones Chile y América, 1986.

Radio Venceremos. "Homenaje de Radio Venceremos." *Christus* (Mexico City) 55, no. 632 (March 1990): 51.

Rahner, Karl. *On the Theology of Death.* Edinburgh-London and Freiburg: Nelson and Herder, 1961.

———. "Dimensions of Martyrdom: A Plea for the Broadening of a Classical Concept." *Concilium* 163 (1983): 9–11.

Ramos, Luis. "Obispo, profeta y mártir." *Signos del Reino de Dios* (Mexico City) 17, no. 49 (second trimester 1980): 12–15.

Randall, Margaret. *Christians in the Nicaraguan Revolution.* Vancouver: New Star Books, 1983.

Recinos, Harold J. "The Politics of Salvadoran Refugee Popular Religion." Ph.D. dissertation. American University, Washington, DC, 1993.

Ricoeur, Paul. *Time and Narrative,* vol. I. Chicago: University of Chicago Press, 1984.

Riding, Alan. "The Cross and the Sword in Latin America." In *El Salvador: Central America in the New Cold War,* eds. Marvin Gettleman and others. New York: Grove Press, 1981.

Romero, Oscar Arnulfo. "Fourth Pastoral Letter: The Church's Mission amid the National Crisis." Chap. in *Voice of the Voiceless: The Four Pastoral Letters and Other Statements.* Maryknoll, NY: Orbis Books, 1985.

——. *La voz de los sin voz*. With an Introduction by Ignacio Martín-Baró. San Salvador: UCA Editores, 1987.

——. *Su diario: del 31 de marzo 1978 al 20 de marzo de 1980*. San Salvador: Archdiocese of San Salvador, 1990.

Rowe, William and Vivian Schelling. *Memory and Modernity: Popular Culture in Latin America*. London: Verso, 1991.

Ruíz de la Peña, Juan Luis. *Muerte y marxismo humanista: aproximación teológica*. Salamanca, Spain: Ediciones Sígueme, 1978.

Russell, Philip L. *El Salvador in Crisis*. With a Foreword by Charles Clements, M. D. Austin, Texas: Colorado River Press, 1984.

Rutilio Grande, mártir de la evangelización rural en El Salvador. San Salvador: UCA Editores, 1978.

Samandú, Luis E., ed. *Protestantismos y procesos sociales en centroamérica*. San José, Costa Rica: EDUCA, 1991.

Samos Stibbs, Rosa Carmelita. *Sobre el magisterio de Mons. Luis Chávez y González: Estudio teológico de sus cartas pastorales*. San Salvador: Archdiocese of San Salvador, 1986.

Scott, James C. *Weapons of the Weak: Everyday Forms of Peasant Resistance*. New Haven and London: Yale University Press, 1982.

Selbin, Eric. *Modern Latin American Revolutions*. Boulder, CO: Westview Press, 1993.

——. "Revolutionary Traditions and Revolutionary Reality: People's Narratives of Revolution and Rebellion in Latin America and the Caribbean." Presented to the Latin American Studies Association, Atlanta, 1994.

Silverblatt, Irene. *Moon, Sun, and Witches: Class and Gender Ideologies in Inca and Colonial Peru*. Princeton: Princeton University Press, 1987.

Smith, Jonathan Z. *Imagining Religion: From Babylon to Jonestown*. Chicago: University of Chicago Press, 1982.

Sobrino, Jon. "Espiritualidad de la persecución y del martirio." *Diakonía* (Managua) 27 (1983): 171–187.

———. *Jesus in Latin America.* Maryknoll, NY: Orbis Books, 1987.

———. *Liberación con espíritu: apuntes para una nueva espiritualidad.* San Salvador: UCA Editores, 1987.

———. "Companions of Jesus." In *Companions of Jesus: The Jesuit Martyrs of El Salvador,* by Jon Sobrino, Ignacio Ellacuría, and others. Maryknoll, NY: Orbis Books, 1990.

Soelle, Dorothee. *Suffering.* Philadelphia: Fortress Press, 1975.

Somers, Margaret. "Narrativity, Narrative Identity, and Social Action: Rethinking English Working-Class Formation." *Social Science History* 16, no. 4 (Winter 1992): 591–630.

Stark, Robert. "Religious Ritual and Class Formation: The Story of Pilsen Saint Vitus Parish and the 1977 Via Crucis." Ph.D. dissertation, University of Chicago, 1981.

Steinmetz, George. "Reflections on the Role of Social Narratives in Working-Class Formation: Narrative Theory in the Social Sciences." *Social Science History* 16, no. 4 (Winter 1992): 489–516.

Stephen, Lynn, and James Dow. "Introduction: Popular Religion in Mexico and Central America." In *Class, Politics, and Popular Religion in Mexico and Central America,* eds. Lynn Stephen and James Dow. Washington, DC: American Anthropological Association, 1990.

Stoll, David. *Is Latin America Turning Protestant? The Politics of Evangelical Growth.* Berkeley: University of California Press, 1990.

———. "Introduction: Rethinking Protestantism in Latin America." In *Rethinking Protestantism in Latin America,* eds. David Stoll and Virginia Garrard-Burnett, Philadelphia: Temple University Press, 1993.

———. *Between Two Armies in the Ixil Towns of Guatemala.* New York: Columbia University Press, 1993.

Taussig, Michael. *The Devil and Commodity Fetishism in South America.* Chapel Hill: University of North Carolina Press, 1980.

"The Sign of Resurrection in El Salvador: A Testimony from Christians Who Accompany the People in their Struggle." In *Trouble in Our Backyard,* ed. Martin Diskin. New York: Pantheon Books, 1984.

Thompson, E. P. *The Making of the English Working Class*. New York: Vintage Books, 1963.

Tracy, David. *Blessed Rage for Order: The New Pluralism in Theology*. New York: The Seabury Press, 1978.

Tracy, Terry. "Death Squads Reemerge in El Salvador." *NACLA Report on the Americas* 39, no. 3 (Nov./Dec. 1995): 2, 43.

Universidad Centroamericana "José Simeón Cañas." "De la locura a la esperanza: La guerra de doce años en El Salvador. Informe de la Comisión de la Verdad." *Estudios Centroamericanos* XLVIII, no. 533 (March 1993): 153–326.

Useros, Manuel, and María López Vigil, eds. *La vida por el pueblo: cristianos de comunidades populares en América Latina*. Madrid: Editorial Popular, 1981.

Van Horne, Winston. "St. Augustine: Death and Political Resistance." *Journal of Religious Thought* 38, no. 2 (Fall–Winter 1981–82): 34–50.

Weber, Max. *The Protestant Ethic and the Spirit of Capitalism*. New York: Charles Scriber's Sons, 1958.

Weiner, Eugene and Anita Weiner. *The Martyr's Conviction*. Atlanta: The Scholar's Press, 1990.

Weinstein, Eugenia; Elizabeth Lira; M. Eugenia Rojas, and others. *Trauma, duelo y reparación: una experiencia psico-social en Chile*. Santiago: FASIC/Interamericana, 1987.

Welch, Sharon. *A Feminist Ethic of Risk*. Minneapolis: Fortress Press, 1990.

White, Alastair. *El Salvador*. 3d ed. San Salvador: UCA Editores, 1987.

White, Hayden. *The Content of the Form: Narrative Discourse and Historical Representation*. Baltimore: Johns Hopkins University Press, 1987.

Williams, Robert. 1986. *Export Agriculture and the Crisis in Central America*. Chapel Hill: University of North Carolina Press.

Woodward, Kenneth L. *Making Saints: How the Catholic Church Determines Who Becomes a Saint, Who Doesn't, and Why*. New York: Simon and Schuster, 1990.

Workman, Herbert B. *Persecution in the Early Church.* Oxford: Oxford University Press, 1980.

Worsley, Peter. *The Trumpet Shall Sound: A Study of "Cargo" Cults in Melanesia.* New York: Schocken Books, 1968.

Zarcos Mera, Carlos, Leonor Tellería, and Carlos Manuel Sánchez. "The Ministry of Coordinators in the Popular Christian Community. *Concilium* 176 (June 1984): 65–70.

Index

DATE DUE

OCT 16 '12			